The Growth of
Parliamentary
Parties
1689-1742

The Growth of Parliamentary Parties

1689-1742

B. W. HILL

Senior Lecturer in English History
University of East Anglia, Norwich

London
George Allen & Unwin Ltd
Ruskin House   Museum Street

ISBN 0 04 942149 2 hardback
0 04 942150 6 paperback

Printed in Great Britain
in 10 point Times Roman type
by
Biddles Ltd, Guildford, Surrey

To Judy
and William

PREFACE

Any study touching upon the early history of parties is likely to be considered in the light of the controversies initiated by Sir Lewis Namier in 1929 concerning the nature of the political structure in England in the middle decades of the eighteenth century. Namier denied that the Tory and Whig parties were important and rejected the traditional view which regarded the continuity of a two-party system since the late seventeenth century as unquestionable. At first Namier's interpretation was confined to studies of the 1750s and 1760s, but it was subsequently claimed to be almost equally applicable to the early eighteenth century. Though this extension of the Namieran thesis has been generally rejected by experts on Queen Anne's reign, it has nevertheless found its way into a number of textbooks and general studies which probably have a wider readership than specialist books and articles. Moreover, even among those who now accept the existence of two flourishing parties in Anne's reign there is still, I believe, some doubt as to the importance of the parties in the immediately preceding and following reigns of William and Mary, George I and George II. In short, it is not surprising to find Professor J. H. Plumb, in his Ford Lectures at Oxford, describing early party history as being in a 'sorry mess'.

The purpose of the present work is to trace the development of the early parties in the new situation brought about by the Revolution of 1688, through the years of their virtual monopoly of politics under Anne, and beyond this into their gradual decline under George I and George II. Party history in this period is not here treated, as in the traditional or 'Whig' interpretation, as being part of an uninterrupted emergence of the modern party system. The early parliamentary parties were separated from the successors which bore their names by a period in the mid eighteenth century when political conditions were unfavourable to party development. They also had to operate amid a different climate of opinion, more akin to that of the seventeenth century than to that of the late eighteenth or nineteenth century. Yet the difference between the early period of party history, down to 1742, and the period after 1770 can easily be overstressed, and the influence of the Namieran interpretation still results in the placing of too little emphasis on the importance of party history down to the fall of Walpole in 1742. My hope is to show how the habits of mind brought about by three generations of Whig–Tory conflict before that event became so ingrained in the practice of politics that the mid eighteenth-century lapse into multifactional strife proved partial and transient, with the result that after major issues reappeared in the 1770s and 1780s the two-party alignment was easily re-established upon a basis of past experience.

In quotations from both manuscript and printed sources the spelling, capitalisation and punctuation have been modernised whenever this is possible without loss of the original meaning. Dates are given in the Old Style unless otherwise stated, but years are assumed to begin on 1 January and not, as in contemporary usage, on 25 March (Lady Day). The place of publication of printed works is not stated if it is London.

In the course of years one receives a great deal of assistance from teachers, colleagues, students, typists, archivists, librarians and a host of others whose kindness it is difficult (and, for fear of unwitting omission, invidious) to acknowledge in detail. To all such I am grateful. I would, however, like to record my especial thanks to Professor John Kenyon, who has added to former kindness by correcting failings throughout the typescript, and to my colleague Professor James Jones, who has made many valuable suggestions for improving the Introduction and Chapters 1–4. Professor John Beattie has likewise put me much in his debt by his advice on Chapters 9–12. From the publishers and their expert readers I have received much wise and tolerant counsel. I would like to acknowledge the help of the trustees of the Bank of England's Houblon-Norman fund for their award of a grant to allow me to undertake research in the financial aspects of party history. And I warmly thank the owners of the private collections cited, for allowing me to use their manuscripts, their houses and their time, often at considerable inconvenience to themselves.

School of English and American Studies,
University of East Anglia
Norwich

ABBREVIATIONS

Add. ms(s)	Additional Manuscripts in the British Library
BIHR	*Bulletin of the Institute of Historical Research*
CHJ	*Cambridge Historical Journal* (see also *HJ*)
CJ	*Journals of the House of Commons*
CSP Dom	*Calendar of State Papers: Domestic Series*
Econ. HR	*Economic History Review*
EHR	*English Historical Review*
HJ	*Historical Journal* (continuation of the *CHJ*)
HMC	Historical Manuscripts Commission
HLB	*Huntington Library Bulletin* (see also *HLQ*)
HLQ	*Huntington Library Quarterly* (continues the *HLB*)
JBS	*Journal of British Studies*
JMH	*Journal of Modern History*
LJ	*Journals of the House of Lords*
NS	New Style
PRO	Public Records Office
TCWAAS	*Transactions of the Cumberland and Westmorland Antiquarian and Archaeological Society*
TRHS	*Transactions of the Royal Historical Society*

CONTENTS

Introduction

The practice of forming parties is as old as politics, but the beginnings of the party system of modern Britain coincided with the emergence of Parliament as a permanent institution. By changing the line of the royal succession in the Revolution of 1688–89, the legislature not only became the ultimate authority in political life but also, in so doing, underwent decisive changes in its own nature. Since 1689 Parliament has met regularly for several months each year and has been no longer subject to the sessions of a few weeks and the intermissions of up to a decade which were imposed by the Stuart monarchs.

Reasons for the annual and lengthy sessions instituted after the Revolution have been sought in such factors as a frequent need to renew the Mutiny Act, or the reluctance of the Commons to vote supplies for more than a year ahead. But behind such factors lay a more fundamental consideration: the belief of Members that only by giving themselves a permanent forum could they hope to retain control of a royal executive authority which was by its nature continuous. Arthur Onslow, one of a distinguished parliamentary family and himself a popular and influential Speaker for thirty four years, well represented post-Revolution thought when he noted that 'if parliaments sit annually, which they may always secure to themselves now, if they will, and should never depart from, it is almost impossible that any exorbitancy of power should subsist long enough to do much mischief'.

When the Prince of Orange was preparing to invade England in 1688 he was well aware of the importance to his cause of winning the legislature to his side. The declaration which he published just before setting out from Holland stated explicitly that 'this our expedition is intended for no other design, but to have a free and lawful Parliament assembled as soon as is possible'. But William did not anticipate the extent to which his new subjects would bind him to his implied promise to respect the dignity and importance of this institution. At the coronation he was compelled to swear to a new requirement to govern according to 'the statutes in Parliament agreed on, and the laws and customs of the same'. Other monarchs, it is true, had made hardly less solemn undertakings and had failed to keep them, but William soon discovered a widespread determination, not least among his own strongest supporters, that such a failure should not occur again. Within a few days of the presentation of the crown to William and Mary, the old parliamentarian Colonel John Birch made explicit what was implied in most men's attitudes, when he told the Commons that 'if King William should destroy the laws, foundations and liberties, I doubt not but you will do with him as you did with King James'.

Without the existence of such attitudes the conventions established by Parliament after 1688 would hardly have proved sufficient to prevent new incursions. Half a century after the Revolution men could still express Birch's sentiments, even if in more polished phrases. 'King William', wrote the Earl of Chesterfield in a history lesson for his son, 'would have been glad of more power than he ought to have; but his Parliaments kept him within due bounds, against his will. To this Revolution we owe our liberties.' In the opinion of Onslow at about the same time, 'a court has less power (in fact) than ever it had to pursue measures, or preserve ministers, against the sense and inclination of Parliament, or of the House of Commons alone'. The complacency of such men was to receive a jolt in the early years of George III's reign; but the shrill outcry aroused by that monarch's activity, and the strength and finality of the reaction which he ultimately aroused, were seen in the long run to justify their conviction. That the new authority of Parliament was not always exercised to the full in the eighteenth century is evidence, not of weakness, but of the overwhelming certainty which parliamentarians had in their own strength, if they cared to use it.

The transfer of executive authority from the monarchy to ministers responsible to the majority party was a slow process, taking place in the course of more than a century following the Revolution. Within the limitations imposed by the Revolution settlement, monarchs continued, in varying degrees, to play a part in government. Thus the overriding supremacy established by Parliament in 1688–89 was not, as was once supposed, of itself the beginning of full party government. But the permanent presence of a parliamentary body from that time gave the setting needed for the development of parties.[1]

After the provision of a continuous scene of operations, the most important element of the post-Revolution scene was the emergence of a relatively free electorate and press. Pre-Revolution governments interfered with electorates by altering borough franchises or suborning officials, and kept as strict a control as possible of the press through censorship. Soon after the Revolution both types of pressure were relaxed, and an era of freer elections and unmuzzled newsprints ensued. These conditions were to change for the worse again towards the middle of the eighteenth century, but in the first fifty years after the Revolution general elections often reflected strong feelings in the nation, while the newspaper press was particularly vociferous, articulate and well directed.

The main channel through which public opinion operated was the

electoral system. Despite the influence of ministerial and other patronage in many constituencies, there was adequate scope for that system to
register changes in sentiment which occurred in the country at large.
This was especially so between 1689 and 1715, a period during which
there were no less than twelve general elections. Henry St John, later
Viscount Bolingbroke, considered the weakening of the Tories by the
election of November 1701 to be due to 'the ill temper of the nation',
while James Craggs correctly forecast in 1710 that if a dissolution took
place 'as the common people are now set' the Tories would obtain a
large majority. Although the number of those entitled to vote in parliamentary elections was small by the standards of the nineteenth century,
it was not inconsiderable, and Professor Plumb has pointed out in this
connection the importance of a major increase in the size of the
electorate in the seventeenth century. By 1715 the total number of
voters was about 284,000, a proportion of one for each nine or ten
adults in the country. In some constituencies, especially the forty
English counties, the electorate ran into several thousand. But even
narrow franchises, such as existed in many boroughs, could register
local opinion effectively, though less directly. The corporate bodies
which controlled elections in 116 English boroughs, either by their
limiting the voting to their own members or by their right of appointing
the freemen voters, were themselves often elected in hotly disputed
contests. Thus Bishop Gilbert Burnet wrote, in about 1708:

'. . . the parties are now so stated and kept up, not only by the elections
of parliament-men, that return every third year, but even by the yearly
elections of mayors and corporation-men, that they know their
strength; and in every corner of the nation the two parties stand, as it
were, listed against one another'.

The widespread resistance aroused by Charles II and James II in
attempting to alter corporation charters and to purge corporation
members testifies that more than the interest of narrow local oligarchies
was at stake.[2]
    In several general elections which took place within the period of
this study, many constituencies are known to have reinforced the effect
of their voting by instructing new members to follow a particular line
of conduct in the House of Commons. But even without the use of this
device each Parliament had a definite character stamped upon it by the
election which gave it birth. Government manipulation, both in elections and by the subsequent 'management' of the Commons, might
modify but could never erase the impression left by the electorate. From
the 1690s the coming into use of poll books, a development itself indicative of the increasing importance attached to the possession of
voting rights, provides evidence to show how the voting might vary the

party composition of the House. Dr W. A. Speck's study of the voting in seven general elections from the end of William III's reign to the beginning of George I's reveals a pattern of regular Whig and Tory voters, together with a large floating vote. The latter swayed the parliamentary majority from one party to the other according to which appeared at the moment to have the better case on matters of national importance, especially the safeguarding of the Church and the Protestant succession.* Such considerations, rather than the formless interplay of numerous rival personal interests postulated in the Namieran analysis, were what interested the electorate and determined the membership of the Commons in the early eighteenth century.[3]

Reinforcing the voting minority were the unknown and much feared majority of the nation, whose best vent for self-expression was mob activity. The 'mobile' of many areas threw their weight behind that of their enfranchised betters in support of the Revolution. The overwhelming victory of the Tories in 1710, which owed much to the Whigs' recent impeachment of a High Church clergyman, was accompanied by widespread demonstrations in favour of the Church; and the 1715 election, which turned almost as decisively against the Tories, was marked by popular demonstrations against the threat they had posed to the Protestant succession. In general, the effect of the masses in political life was to strengthen, perhaps to exceed but rarely to contradict, the pattern of electoral choice. Between elections, public opinion exercised pressure upon Parliament through demonstrations, petitions and the press. The highly effective deluge of petitions in favour of war or war preparation in 1701, to which Daniel Defoe's *Legion's Memorial* asserting the people's right to instruct their representatives was a spurious but highly popular contribution, was a good example of such pressure under Whig direction. The failures of William III's army plans in 1698, of the Peerage Bill in 1719, and of Walpole's excise scheme in 1733, were all obtained by well-managed opposition campaigns in the press, based upon public revulsion at ministerial policies. Particularly strong popular responses were brought forth by foreign affairs, making it difficult for governments to avoid war in 1702 and 1739, peace in 1713, or the virtual abandonment of the French alliance after 1730. Dr G. G. Gibbs writes that when the return of Gibraltar, captured in 1704, was under consideration by Stanhope's government, 'such was the attachment cherished for the

---

*More recently, James O. Richards concludes, in his study of *Party Propaganda under Queen Anne* (Athens, Georgia, 1972), that 'there is much evidence to confirm the hypothesis that party in the ideological sense did make a difference in election results', and that 'the vast majority of Englishmen would have been offended by the proclamation of interests and connections as the basis for party distinctions or for choosing M.P.'s (significant though these connections were in coordinating election efforts)' (pp. 157–8).

fortress by parliament and public opinion by 1720 that no minister would have dared risk possible impeachment by agreeing to return Gibraltar without getting the consent of parliament.'[4]

The burgeoning of an informed public opinion in the early eighteenth century received its greatest stimulus from the decision of the Commons not to renew censorship after 1695, encouraging an unprecedented expansion in the newspaper press.* By the time Queen Anne came to the throne in 1702, manuscript newsletters were rapidly being superseded as the regular media of political information by printed newspapers, of which there were a dozen or so in London. In the week of the Queen's accession was published the first successful daily, the *Daily Courant*. The first provincial weekly was published at Norwich in 1701, and the example set by this city was soon to be followed by most county capitals and other towns of size, spreading discussion of political affairs mainly by reprinting articles from the London publications. Both the new periodical press and individual pamphlets of the more traditional pattern gave the widest possible airing to party conflict, especially in election years. It is not always realised by the modern readers of 'Augustan' literature, with its urbane social instruction and tolerant satire, how many of its writers served their apprenticeship in the fierce political infighting of Anne's reign. Swift and Arbuthnot (creator of John Bull) on the Tory side, Addison and Steele on the Whig, Defoe with his own brand of *via media*, all published political tracts and wrote for such periodicals as Defoe's *Review*, Swift's *Examiner* and Steele's *Guardian* and *Englishman*. The longer-lived publications of the early Hanoverian era, such as the *London Journal* and the *Craftsman*, were based upon these early models.

It is certain that the millions of reams of political literature which streamed off the presses every year would not have done so had they not been considered an important contribution to the moulding of public opinion. Addison, writing in the Whig *Freeholder* in 1716, noted with forgivable exaggeration that 'Whig and Tory are the first words' learned by children, and that of all the ways by which the party struggle was carried on 'I cannot single out any so prevalent or universal as the late constant application of the press to the publishing of state matters'. Censorship being impossible to reimpose upon a society ardent for its liberties, indirect attempts were made to muzzle the press by the imposition of stamp duties; but this device was largely offset by the payment of government and opposition subsidies to the editors of compliant journals. By the time of Walpole it had become clear that

*Dr W. A. Speck points out, among other interesting observations, that even before 1695 William III's censorship was not as daunting as that of pre-Revolution monarchs, 'Political Propaganda in Augustan England', *TRHS* 5th series, xxii (1972), 20.

the political press was here to stay. 'The liberty of the press', wrote one Tory peer thankfully to another in 1731, 'is the greatest security of the liberty of the subject and therefore all little inconveniences which arise from it are to be submitted to'.[5]

Closely connected with an increasingly effective public opinion was the upsurge of zeal for various reforms which began in the 1680s, reached its height in William III's reign, and began to subside in Anne's. Both Whig and Tory parties thrived on reform agitation, supporting when out of office those proposals which suited themselves. In the reign of William III the cause of preventing abuses of treason law, which had secured Whig support before the Revolution, became in the main the cause of the Tories. The Whigs' championship of the rights of electors against the decisions of the Commons was at its strongest in the time of Queen Anne's first Tory Parliament, but it did not survive into the era of Whig Ministries after 1714. Proposals for increasing the popular element in borough elections, for putting an end to the notoriously partisan decisions of the Commons' Committee of Elections and Privileges, and above all for 'place' legislation to reduce Crown influence in Parliament, attracted each party when it was in the minority, though each turned its face against such measures in the days of its triumph. Apart from a handful of measures such legislation enacted in William's reign was repealed or severely modified under his successors. The main achievement of an era of unrest was not to bring about parliamentary reform but to provide ammunition for party strife.

In the early eighteenth century it was common to trace the forerunners of both Whigs and Tories well back into the seventeenth century or even earlier.[6] The great historians of the nineteenth and early twentieth centuries followed the same tradition, eschewing extremes of causation seeking but showing a preference for beginning their story not much later than the Civil War. Thus for Leopold von Ranke 'the Long Parliament of the Restoration represented Tory principles, even before the name of Tory was heard', while 'the Whig party also existed, though its name had not yet been invented'. Macaulay considered the Whigs as 'the great party which traces its descent through the Exclusionists up to the Roundheads'. As late as 1924 Sir Keith Feiling's *History of the Tory Party* commenced unashamedly in 1640, while G. M. Trevelyan's Romanes Lecture for 1926 followed the parties 'from the days of Danby and Shaftesbury'. In extreme reaction to such views Sir Lewis Namier's Romanes Lecture for 1952 found even in eighteenth-century parliamentary politics 'no trace of a two-party system, or at all of party in the modern sense'. In 1956 Professor Robert Walcott in his *English Politics in the Early Eighteenth Century* concluded that:

'The more one studies the party structure under William and Anne, the less it resembles the two-party system described by Trevelyan in his Romanes Lecture and the more it seems to have in common with the structure of politics in the Age of Newcastle as explained to us by Namier.'[7]

Walcott's view, though treated with caution by historians specialising in his period, has been widely accepted by others.*

The names 'Whig' and 'Tory' were first used, so far as national politics were concerned, during the Exclusion Crisis. Between 1679 and 1681 three short-lived Parliaments saw the division of politicians, and then of the nation, into two camps. Those called Tories, urged on by the Anglican churchmen, espoused the cause of the throne and became committed to an ideology of passive obedience and nonresistance to lawfully-appointed monarchs, doctrines well in accord with Stuart insistence upon the divine right of kings. Those called Whigs developed the rival theories of republicanism or of contractual government revocable in the case of breach of trust on the part of the ruler, and urged the right of subjects to resist misgovernment. The ideologies, in their original forms, were to prove impermanent when the crisis had been lived through, but the heat generated at this time was sufficient for the opprobrious names 'Tory' and 'Whig' to outlive their original purposes.

Of the two sides thus created, only the Whigs may be said to have transformed themselves into a party before the Revolution, for until then the Tories were too closely associated with the monarchy to have any independent existence. The Whigs took a separate stance as early as the spring of 1679 by their adherence to the first bill to exclude James, Duke of York, from the throne. From the start they displayed considerable powers of party management in support of their aims. The Exclusion Bill was accompanied by the cleverly-engineered national scare of the Popish Plot, which brought over to the side of the exclusionists many who might otherwise have been reluctant to come out against the royal family. In the appeal to the nation which took place in 1679, before and during elections to the second Exclusion Parliament,

---

*There has been little diminution in this trend among the writers of more general historical works. Sir Ivor Jenning was one of the first to adopt Walcott's views, in *Party Politics*: ii, *The Growth of Parties* (Cambridge, 1961). Archibald S. Foord maintained that 'In 1714 and for many years thereafter, the basic political pattern was the group or connection' (Foord, 20). As recently as 1974, Dorothy Marshall, in the second edition of her *Eighteenth Century England*, while moving away from her acceptance of Walcott's views (in her first edition, 1962), can still write of the early Hanoverian era in terms of groups rather than parties and assert that whatever meaning the terms Whig and Tory had previously borne disappeared' soon after 1714 (2nd edn, 86–7).

the Whigs formed their first organisation, which included important developments in the use of the press and of political clubs. Their principal aim of exclusion was thwarted by Charles II's use of his prerogative of dissolving Parliament, but their achievement was nonetheless remarkable. By the time of the dissolution of the Oxford Parliament, the lifespan of which was one week in March 1681, they formed a clearly-identified body with a party organisation which spread through all levels of political activity. Their close approach to success was achieved in spite of the fact that, as Professor J. R. Jones's analysis shows, they were far from being homogeneous in their social and religious background. But their unity and effectiveness had no institutional stability outside the framework of Parliament and constituencies. The disparate elements of the party which the genius of its leader, Shaftesbury, had brought together were in uneasy yoke, and in particular the country gentlemen were ill at ease with the radicals who secured the leaders' control of London and other cities. When Charles II decided that he could dispense with Parliament, and found in the Rye House plot a chance to turn moderate opinion against the Whigs, their precocious unity and organisation largely disappeared, not to be revived until Parliament itself was made permanent.

If the monarchy had limited its efforts after Rye House to stamping out whiggery, the development of parties in England might have been longer delayed and very different from the form it actually took. Both Charles II and James II strove to strengthen their influence over any future legislature by campaigns to control the constituencies, instituting *quo warranto* proceedings, selecting new borough officials and corporation members, and trying to ensure the loyalty of officers in the county hierarchy. But while Charles eradicated only Whigs, James made the discovery, from the mild intransigence of the picked Parliament of 1685 and from the aversion which the Church of England showed to his catholicising policies, that the Tories too were unreliable. By 1687 James was fully engaged in repacking the constituencies, often to the detriment of his late brother's strongest supporters. His efforts came near to success in every respect but one: they alarmed landed society, Tory as well as Whig. The judgment of the aristocracy and gentry was that James wished to have a Parliament of nobodies, obscure subservient men who would place no obstacle in the way of his reducing England's legislature to the standing of most European estates. The Tories, constrained by long-standing ties of loyalty, hesitated long before deserting their King. Not until late in 1687 could they clearly be seen to be withdrawing their support from him; and even during and after the Revolution they strove, often to their own disadvantage in competition with the revived Whigs, to avoid the appearance of disloyalty. Yet the Revolution when it came was pre-eminently the work of toryism, for though the Whigs were later to claim it for their own work they could never have achieved it by their own unaided efforts.[8] But the Tories, in consenting to dethrone James, irremediably altered their own standing in politics. While loudly disclaiming any intention to form a political party independent of monarchy, they had taken a first step towards that end. The logic of their action led them to continue in the same path.

After the Revolution the distinction between Tories and Whigs was revived in very different parliamentary conditions. Every year Parliament was in session for about as many months as the total of sittings during the previous ten years, providing both parties with the opportunity for rapid development in new directions. How far, however, can the resulting bodies and their ideas be said to have amounted to a 'two-party system'? Recent historians who have restated the reality of the parties themselves, in reaction to Walcott's contentions, have been reluctant to go further and to commit themselves to the view that there was such a system—understandably so, in view of the connotations which have accreted to the term after nearly three centuries of party history. The early party alignment differed from the twentieth-century party system in many ways; yet to deny that there was any kind of system at all, on the grounds that later developments were not present, would be no more useful than to deny that cricket matches were played in the early eighteenth century because the bats looked like clubs and defended wickets consisting of only two stumps. The behaviour of the early parties displayed a reduction to the order of a political game of the conflicts which had twice in the course of the seventeenth century brought the country to revolution. The replacement of violence by stylised conflict, however immature, saw the birth of a party system. If the rules were at first few and uncertain, and if the game itself was rough by later standards, these facts are no denigration of the basic achievement.*

From the beginning the source material demonstrates that the parties had effective, if by modern standards simple, methods of ensuring unity. 'Party is little less than an inquisition, where men are under such a discipline in carrying on the common cause as leaves no liberty of private opinion', wrote the Marquess of Halifax soon after the Revolution. This was not to say that the parties possessed the sophisticated

*J. A. W. Gunn, in seeking the origin of what he calls 'the ethic of limited strife, the only scheme consistent with a functioning party system', finds its earliest statement in 1703 (Shute Barrington's *The Interest of England Considered*) and notes that it did not arise out of any earlier political theory (Gunn, 2 and 61 sqq.). The theory of the usefulness and (later) the constitutionality of an opposition party arose out of the practical experience of alternating party Ministries in the 1690s and as a consequence of their opposition activities.

organisation, stretching from Westminster through central office to constituency supporters, which marks the present British party system. Until the later part of the eighteenth century few permanent forms of party institution existed, though the party in office could use the government patronage structure for the same purpose. At Westminster the attendance of Members for important debates was mainly arranged for the government side by the Treasury officials, while the opposition relied on voluntary organisers who were responsible for particular geographical areas or groups of followers. In the constituencies the degree of organisation remained dependent for the most part upon the individual initiatives of the parliamentary candidates and their local supporters. Both in Parliament and in the provinces, *ad hoc* arrangements arose out of the exigencies of the day. 'The first Whigs', writes Professor Jones, 'had necessarily to possess, or rather develop, the organisation, cohesion, discipline, and mass appeal which made them a party, because of the intensity of the crisis through which they were living'. Expediential though the methods Shaftesbury adopted were, they displayed an inventiveness which set new standards in politics and led to new, party-oriented, patterns of behaviour. The exclusionists' techniques of organisation in the constituencies had the highest of all possible tributes paid to them, for they were often emulated, during James II's campaign against the Tories in the last year of his reign, by the agents of the court itself. If the methods which characterised the early parties were crude, by comparison with those which came into being in the last three decades of the eighteenth century, they could be remarkably effective for the parliamentary system within which they operated. Circular letters sent out by the Tory leaders in 1700, giving their followers early warning of an impending general election, supply an example of the considerable advantage which could be obtained from a minimum of organisational effort.[9]

The absence of modern party organisations and modern electoral practices, far from casting doubt upon the existence and importance of the parties, serves to illuminate more clearly the intensity of their struggle and the unity with which they acted upon most occasions. Using the surviving division lists for the House of Commons from 1702 to 1714, Professor Holmes concludes in his excellent study of *British Politics in the Age of Anne* that, of 1,064 English and Welsh Members whose names appear on these lists, 'only a small fraction, roughly one eighth, are *ever* found "cross-voting" or voting "against the party line"'. After the succession of George I the Whigs fell into successive schisms, but the voting consistency of the Tories continued and even increased. Tabulation of the fifteen divisions between 1715 and 1754 for which lists are known shows that on eleven occasions no Tory ever voted for the government, that on a further three divisions a mere seven Tory votes in all were cast astray, and that on the fifteenth occasion only a few Tories joined the government Whigs.[10] It is true that the relative absence of party discipline permitted, potentially at least, the existence of waverers and independents; but these assumed major importance only in the middle decades of the eighteenth century, when old party issues were dying and new ones had not yet come to take their place.

To take as criteria for the existence of a party system the presence of features which appeared only in the nineteenth century, rather than the obvious presence of two united and mutually antagonistic parties such as already existed at the end of the seventeenth century, is to stick upon a definition. To go further and to refuse recognition to Whigs and Tories as parties is to overlook the existence of party issues, other than the clash of patronage interests, until the Whig–Tory distinction was already obsolescent and beginning to be replaced by a Liberal–Conservative distinction in the very different conditions of the era of nineteenth-century parliamentary reform. The principal factor dividing the early parties was not any long history of ritualised two-party behaviour, but the strong consciousness on each side of shared interests and aversions concerning the issues of the day. Few politicians in 1689 could have anticipated that their actions would result eventually in the domination of Parliament by the party system; yet already in their time the burning questions which centred upon religion, the succession to the throne, and the position in society of an increasingly important monied community, all made for a cleavage as wide as any known in the nineteenth and twentieth centuries.

The characteristics of both parties were, of course, exaggerated in the public images which they bore. The Tories lived long under the imputations of crypto-catholicism and excessive veneration for kingship, while the identification of the Whigs with puritanism and republicanism was equally firmly entrenched. The very words 'Whig' and 'Tory' were themselves terms of abuse borrowed from Scottish and Irish religious strife, denoting in their original contexts the extreme Protestant and Catholic positions. In post-Revolution conditions, however, the public images of both sides increasingly became caricatures as the parties changed their stance in public affairs. The Tories—or, as they preferred to be called, the Church party—were particularly anxious to dissociate themselves from their origins, and their failure to support James II in 1688 is sufficient indication that they had by that date, in fact if not in Whig propaganda, already outlived their dalliance with legitimist theory. The Whigs showed themselves less reluctant than their opponents to adopt the name commonly assigned to them, and some like Thomas Wharton gloried in it; but experience was to show that they too were willing to abandon their early associations.

The decline of the Whigs' dabbling with republicanism was well under way soon after 1689.

But although the differences of principle were less extreme than party literature suggested, they were real enough. First among divisive issues were the causes of the Church of England and of the Protestant succession. Though not all Tories after 1689 were supporters of the Protestant succession, there were very few who could not be relied upon to rally to the Church in its need; and though not all Whigs loved the Church, all except a few republicans were for the Protestant succession. Thus each party made one of these causes peculiarly its own. Equally real were the general Whig sympathy for the financial interests of the City of London and Tory sympathy for the landed interest, though the identification was in neither case an exclusive one. On matters of taxation, foreign policy and war strategy too the parties possessed decided preferences, with Tories usually favouring the more, and Whigs the less, economical or isolationist of alternative courses of action.

If the possession of principles was a familiar theme in party claims, another contemporary theme, hardly less familiar, stated that party behaviour simply developed and systematised the struggle for office and power which was traditionally associated with court and country conflicts. It is certainly true that the Tory and Whig parties were engaged in a bitter conflict for offices in government and local administration as well as, more dangerously, in the armed services. The relationship of parties to the struggle between 'ins' and 'outs' was sufficiently damaging to those who professed party principles for Lord Cowper to deal with it in a memorandum which he drew up for George I in 1714. If the argument of self-interest alone were true, he argued:

'then the struggle would only be between individuals and not between two set bodies of men, which can only be kept up by some diversity of opinion upon fundamentals, at least points of consequence; and experience shows that many who have no designs upon preferment either for themselves or friends, but live retired on their estates, are yet as hot or hotter than any in these distinctions'.[11]

The quest for office was endemic; the parties simply absorbed it.

In 1689 the received view of the constitution saw politics as a struggle between court and country. In this view government was vested in the Crown, which was assisted in Parliament by a court party. The function of other Members was seen as the exercise of restraint upon monarchy, but not permanent opposition to it. The appearance of the first Whigs and Tories, divided on the question of the succession of James, necessitated little adjustment to the traditional picture so long as the Tories remained associated with the court and the Whigs with the country. With the Revolution, however, the Whigs were able to support, and the Tories to oppose, the court; parties, in fact, began to cut across the old pattern of politics, interchanging the court and country roles frequently and in defiance of accepted canons of political behaviour. A move by a party into continuous opposition was in theory considered to be particularly reprehensible, and was condemned as faction. Thus, as is often the case when men are found endeavouring to reconcile a new practice with the currently permissible corpus of actions, the old names were often used deliberately to obscure the new practice. On other occasions court and country terminology was used either by those who were somewhat out of touch with the realities of politics or, more generally, at times when one or both of the parties were seriously divided.

The general decline in the use of the terms 'court' and 'country' to describe situations in Parliament after the Revolution resulted from the increasing importance of party issues, though enough of the older dichotomy remained to blur the edge of partisan conflict at times, particularly where taxation and governmental patronage in Parliament were concerned. The pull of court or country on Members of Parliament often resulted in the use of terms such as 'Court Tory' or 'Country Whig', but these do not indicate the existence of permanent separate types. With rare exceptions men remained either Whig or Tory throughout their lives, but the change from court to country stance and vice versa was a common occurrence, so that the 'Court Tory' of one session might be the 'Country Tory' of the next. Such terms were principally useful in describing Members who were temporarily deviating from their party on court–country issues.* The existence of

*That there was ever a 'court party' or a 'country party', in the sense of blocs of Members voting consistently together for more than short periods and distinct from Tory and Whig parties, is difficult to maintain.

Modern analyses of division lists show the supposed members of court parties to have voted consistently either Tory or Whig, and give little or no indication of the existence of a separate 'court party' down to 1714 (see below, pp. 74n, 107n); and after that year the 'court party' consisted entirely of Whigs, representing in fact the section of that party in office.

A distinct 'country party' is even more difficult to identify. The word 'country' as used in this period is much in need of comprehensive modern analysis. Such an analysis would find several uses, often vying with each other in close juxtaposition in contemporary speeches and writings. Basically, the term 'the country' meant the nation at large, or at least the political nation; more narrowly, and as a synonym for 'country members', it referred to the amorphous mass of Members of Parliament who were representative of the nation's view at any given time. Though a Member might refer to the locality in which he was elected as his 'country', the interests of the various 'countries' were broadly similar except where specific local issues were involved, and when he spoke of 'the country' he was generally referring to the national amalgam of the localities' views on such topics of common interest as foreign affairs, taxation such cases, a few on all occasions and a substantial number on some occasions, testifies to the absence of the modern convention that no member of a party ever votes with the other side. But in a period when no rigid discipline existed, what is remarkable is not that deviant votes were cast but that they were cast, as the division lists indicate, rarely by either side before 1717 and rarely by the Tories and majority of the Whigs thereafter.

The coming of parties in Britain was neither a short nor a straight-forward process, involving as it did a complex interplay with older political practices of a very different nature. Behind these practices, moreover, lay assumptions even more foreign to the modern party. In the 1640s and again in the 1680s two successive generations failed to settle their differences in a parliamentary way and embarked upon war or revolution. As a result, there remained in the mind of every politician between 1689 and 1742 the possibility that the penalty of failure might be not simply loss of office but rather loss of life and estate. The thorough manner in which the Whigs dealt with the Tories after 1714, imprisoning and exiling their leaders and depriving their rank and file of all national and local employments, indicates a degree of animosity which was not too far removed from seventeenth-century experience.

But despite political massacres, true violence was in fact receding in the first fifty years after the Revolution. Though the leaders of both parties were impeached or attainted in their turn, Whigs in 1701 and Tories in 1715, moderation prevailed to secure their eventual safety. When Walpole lost office in 1742 the impeachment with which he had been threatened for so many years proved impossible to obtain. As violent methods of government decayed, new institutions were making for a more ordered body politic. Many of the functions of a Prime Minister emerged under Godolphin, Oxford, Stanhope and Walpole. From Anne's reign a formal Cabinet was in operation. A new govern-mental fiscal system, having its centre in the Bank of England and the national funded debt, came into existence in the 1690s and proved stable enough to survive the crisis in the bubble year of 1720. Above all, annual sessions of Parliament provided a regular scene of activity for men whose ambitions might, a generation or two earlier, have brought about recourse to the sword. A new breed of men was appear-ing, the full-time parliamentary politicians, whose energies were channelled into party conflict.

and the power of the executive. Those Members best able to represent the country's viewpoint were those who were not clients of the government, though they might be supporting it currently. The country element in Parliament was not, indeed, a fixed body of men, for those who spoke for the country were constantly changing.

CHAPTER 1

Buried Names Revived
1689-90

'How was my wonder and indignation increased', wrote Sir John Lowther of Lowther in surveying the first weeks of the Convention Parliament of 1689–90, 'when as a proper means to attain authority and power the buried names of Whig and Tory were revived in parliament, and from thence dispersed through the nation.' Lowther, one of William III's most trusted English subjects, echoed the sentiments of his master and of those who believed that the Revolution which had united the nation against James II should have made an end to the distinction between Whigs and Tories. For a few weeks after William's invasion of November 1688, indeed, this belief had seemed justified. During the elections called in January 1689, while the atmosphere of national emergency continued, parties were little in evidence, for both Whigs and Tories proved acceptable to the electorate so long as they were known to support the Revolution. But when the Convention assembled, any illusion of national unity was irrevocably shattered on the crucial problems involved in settling state and Church affairs.

At first sight the turmoil of opinion and emotion early in 1689 smacks rather of the politics of Babel than of a division on the lines of two parties. Among those whom events in the early weeks of the Convention were to classify as Tories, there was a considerable diversity of views over the royal succession. Few spoke openly for a restoration of King James, but some thought that he might be replaced by his elder daughter, Mary, William's wife, while others were convinced that the only practical solution was a regency which would allow William himself to rule, ostensibly in James's name. On the Whig side, opinion ranged from those who desired a republic to those who wanted the Prince of Orange as king, with all the powers which James had enjoyed. As to religious matters there was considerable division among the Whigs, for although the majority were adherents of the Church of England a forceful group, including over thirty known to have been of nonconformist origins, desired a radical change in Church government and ritual. The Tories were split to a lesser extent over the degree of tolerance which could safely be extended to dissenters. On both the Tory and Whig sides, however, certain clear lines of thought soon appeared which overrode all internal differences. The former were nearly all united in an objection to making William sole monarch, while the Whigs were at one in a determination to resist the return of James II under any circumstance. And in the event the Tories proved willing to unite in the face of any threat, real or imagined, to the Church, while the Whigs held together to insist on freedom of worship for dissenters. In the winnowing process of debate the extremists of both sides were to be disappointed, but the existence of fundamental sticking points and of long-standing mutual antipathy ensured the parties' survival.[1]

Of the two bodies thus arrayed, only the Whigs had any experience of party organisation outside the structure of court management and patronage, and by 1689 their once-formidable parliamentary and electoral machinery had long been in ruins. A greater lack, however, was men practised in the ways of government. Shaftesbury's associates, who had perished after the Rye House plot, had possessed administrative talent and experience; their successors were relatively untried. The most promising of them was Charles Talbot, twelfth Earl of Shrewsbury and one of the seven signatories of the invitation to William in June 1688. But though high in William's favour, Shrewsbury was only twenty-nine and had never held an important office. A more experienced leader, in opposition at least, was Thomas Wharton, son of the old Puritan stalwart Philip, fourth Baron Wharton. At forty, the younger Wharton had spent nearly half his life campaigning against the Stuarts in Buckinghamshire elections and on the national stage. But apart from Shrewsbury and Wharton new men of stature were yet to rise to national prominence among the Whigs, and the first days of the Convention demonstrated that the strength of the party lay not just in its leadership but also, as in the case of Cromwell's army, in its rank and file.

A more permanent disadvantage from which the Whigs suffered was their lack of support, compared with their rivals, among the electorally-dominant landed class. During the Exclusion Crisis they had received strong support from 'country' elements, both inside and outside Parliament, in common cause against roman catholicism and royal mismanagement. But in general the party's association with the dissenters, in a period when the latter were declining both numerically and in social standing under the impact of punitive legislation in Charles II's reign, was setting the Whigs apart from the majority of the landed interest. To some extent this situation went undiscerned during the earliest part of the Convention, when general sentiment coincided with Whig aspirations. But their weakness could not long remain concealed and, save on a few specific occasions, the alliance of Whigs and gentry was to break down for a generation after the Revolution.[2] If the party were to regain their support among the politically-dominant landed class they would have to shed the image, built up during the Exclusion Crisis, of associa-

tion with republicanism and radical social elements in the urban constituencies. The removal from the scene of the first Whig leaders, though
in the short run disastrous, would have the fortuitous effect of making
the transformation easier.

The Tories in 1689, apart from the generally conservative outlook
which they held in common, had scarcely set out on the journey towards being a self-contained political party. By their desertion of King
James their former identity as a court party was shattered, along with
their rationale of passive obedience to divinely appointed monarchy. A
court party which had deserted its king, a Church party which had
abandoned the political teachings of its spiritual leaders, the Tories
were in the utmost ideological confusion. Could they be reconstituted
as a court party under a new ruler? Some of their leading men, including
the second Earl of Clarendon, uncle of the Princesses Mary and Anne,
and Sir Edward Seymour, leader of the west country Tories, were
already voicing criticism of the Prince of Orange's known favour towards dissenters. But, fortunately for the Tories, at this point they
included leveller heads than those of Seymour and Clarendon. A
younger leader, whose influence would count for much, was Daniel
Finch, second Earl of Nottingham, son of a loyal but just Lord
Chancellor, and a man of piety and integrity who also had a large family
to feed and an eye to the practical in politics. Above all, much would
depend upon the actions of Thomas Osborne, Earl of Danby, sometime
Lord High Treasurer to Charles II, and a man of the highest ability and
political resilience. Danby had signed the invitation to William and
subsequently raised Yorkshire in support of the Prince's invasion. If
he and those who looked to him for guidance supported William's
actions in the Convention, much of the great reservoir of Tory loyalty
which was at present dammed up by doubt and vacillation would become available to a new ruler.

Crucial to the situation at the opening of the Convention was the
attitude of the Prince of Orange himself. Two points which stand out
among William's recorded views at this time are his desire to be King
of England and his dislike of English parties. From the beginning he
made no secret of his determination to be the real ruler, though to
satisfy the consciences of the Tories he was willing to share the throne
with his wife. From the end of December 1688, the invaluable notes of
his conversations with the Marquis of Halifax, the veteran 'Trimmer'
now fully committed to the Revolution, record his threats to leave the
country if James were recalled or if he were offered only a regency.
William's attitude to the party men and their leaders is also faithfully
recorded, including his 'great jealousy of being thought to be governed',
his belief that 'the Commonwealth party' wanted 'a Duke of Venice',
and his opinion that the Tory leaders who favoured a regency, especially

Clarendon and his brother, the Earl of Rochester, were 'knaves'. William's principal purpose was to curb the power of Louis XIV. If the support of England were essential to this end, the presence of divisive party strife was, he considered, inimical to it. Party opinions he viewed impartially, as they conduced to or retarded his purposes. Throughout his reign his intimate correspondence with the Grand Pensionary Heinsius in Holland was to make many references to British politics and parties, but rarely with approbation and hardly ever with sympathy for party aspirations.[3] Indeed, both parties were to be, in their different ways, frequently at odds with him; for if the Tories were monarchists at heart they could not clearly see William as their lawful monarch, and if the Whigs were completely averse from the House of Stuart they were also suspicious of royal authority *per se*. William would never obtain fully monarchist Whigs or wholly loyal Tories, but he learned to manipulate the material at hand by playing one side against the other.

The first business of the Convention, when it assembled on Tuesday 22 January 1689, was to appoint a Speaker. A moderate and un-distinguished Whig, Henry Powle, was proposed and seconded by two of his fellow partisans and elected without opposition. The Tories did not care to divide the House, but after Powle was chosen they attempted to defer consideration of affairs of state until the 28th. The proposer of the motion, Sir Thomas Clarges, had concerted his action with Nottingham, in order to allow the House of Lords time to take the initiative and forestall any 'extravagant votes' from the lower house. The scheme fell down upon the Lords' reluctance to assume the re-quired role. When Nottingham, Clarendon, Rochester and other Tories rose on the 25th to urge that their House should consider the state of the nation forthwith, they met with a decisive setback. The influential fourth Earl of Devonshire, bitter enemy of the Stuarts, rose to perform one of the many major services which his family contributed to the Whig cause by moving that the debate should not take place until their Lordships had received 'some lights from below'. Halifax, who was acting as Speaker, threw his weight on to Devonshire's side; and though, as Clarendon noted, 'the lights did not pass without animadversations', the debate was fixed without a division for the 29th, the day after the one chosen by the Commons. The decision was a momentous one. The upper house gracefully gave way to the lower on the great question of the century: the settlement of the Crown. Despite some subsequent attempts at retraction the House of Lords confirmed on this day the Commons' prior right to speak for the nation.[4]

When the lower house on the 28th resolved itself, according to order, into a Grand Committee, its mood was visible by the choice as its chairman of Richard Hampden, mover of the Exclusion Bill of 1679 and son of John Hampden, the opponent of Ship Money. The debate soon centered upon a motion stating that, as James II had 'voluntarily foresaken' government, it was thereby in demise. Some Tories opposed the motion, but wavered from complete support of Stuart government. Sir Christopher Musgrave, a prominent north country gentleman, hesitated to pronounce James's deposition, but saw clear danger in the return of the King to power. Heneage Finch, Nottingham's brother, likewise jibbed at a restoration, suggesting instead a Regency in the King's absence. Speakers in favour of the motion included many embattled heroes of the exclusion campaigns: Wharton, Sir Thomas Lee, Sir George Treby, Sir Henry Capel, and at least one veteran of Charles I's Long Parliament, Sir John Maynard, the impeacher of Strafford and one-time Solicitor-General to the Protector Richard. Alongside these spoke John Somers, another lawyer and a newcomer to Westminster whose reputation among his party preceded his election. Precedents for deposition and theories of contractual monarchy, couched frequently in the language of the Long Parliament, thundered about the ears of the uncomfortable Tories. Wharton, with the bluntness for which he was celebrated, remarked in reply to Musgrave's doubts about the legality of deposing a king that 'whether he may be deposed, or depose himself, he is not our King. 'Tis not for mine, nor the interest of most here, that he should come again'. The Whiggish resolution was reached, after long debate, that James, by breaking the original contract between king and people and by violating the fundamental laws and withdrawing from the kingdom, had abdicated the government, and that the throne was thereby vacant.

After the voting of the 28th the Commons allowed itself, for a few days, the heady illusion of disposing the monarchy as it willed. 'All men's tongues', wrote Lowther, 'were at liberty to argue and censure as they pleased, every man debated how the Government should be settled.' On the day after the throne was voted vacant the House, still in committee, ignored a hint from the Prince of Orange via Wharton that the throne might forthwith be filled by himself and Mary. Instead it preferred the lead given by the fifth Lord Falkland, whose advice was: 'before you fill the throne . . . resolve what power you will give the King, and what not'. If the Tories were divided about voting James off the throne, they were happy enough to join in circumscribing the powers of successors with supposed Whiggish predilections. Musgrave successfully moved for a committee for the better securing of religion, law and liberties. But the move was equally welcome to many Whigs, especially the country gentlemen among them, such as the old parliamentarian soldier and exclusionist Sir Edward Harley, who informed his son, Robert, the future preceptor of the Tories, of the prudence of securing existing rights from royal invasion. Among the thirty-eight Members nominated to sit on the new committee were Falkland, Musgrave, Seymour, Finch, Clarges and a number of other Tories, though the Whig names on the list, among them that of Somers, were yet more numerous. By the rejection of James the opportunity to give the law to the Crown became a supraparty matter, widely welcomed and long remembered, together with the euphoria of king making, in parliamentarians' dealing with William and his successors.[5]

Nevertheless, an incipient division between the parties became visible as a result of the committee's report of 2 February, which presented a wide-ranging list of recommendations for a Declaration of Rights limiting the powers of the Crown. Many of the items mentioned were clearly of a controversial nature, especially those which concerned treason law and the length and frequency of parliamentary sittings. In the subsequent debate on the 4th it was clear that a strong body of Whig opinion, led by old opponents of the Stuarts such as Capel and the republican John Wildman, was anxious not to include among the royal powers to be condemned such powers as would be acceptable under a Whig king. The committee was accordingly instructed to divide its list into two sections, one of which was to be 'declaratory of ancient rights' and the other 'introductory of new laws'. Thus on 7 February two lists were brought forward as required. In the first, or 'declaratory', list were condemned the instruments and exercise of high prerogative, especially James II's Court of Ecclesiastical Causes and the 'pretended' royal power of suspending or dispensing with legislation. Also condemned were the levying of taxes without parliamentary grant, the raising of a standing army in time of peace, interference by the monarch in elections, and a number of other misdemeanours attributed to the Stuarts. But many reforms which were likely to impede any future administration of the Whigs, if they took office as they expected, were placed in the committee's second list as needing new laws. These included proposals for frequent meetings of Parliament and against overlong continuance of any one Parliament, for securing corporate bodies against *quo warranto* proceedings, for securing free elections, for regulating the laws of treason, for appointing judges during good behaviour, and for preventing the buying and selling of offices.[6] The Whig majority in the committee had obtained their ends by relegating many unwelcome measures to the second list, on the excuse of getting the throne settled quickly upon noncontroversial declaratory points.* However,

*Since this paragraph was written, Robert F. Frankle has concluded that the most cogent reason for the omission of new limitations, apart from a general reluctance to delay filling the throne, was the opposition of the Prince of Orange, fearful for the royal prerogative. Dr Frankle's view is not incompatible with the above conclusions, for he points out that 'the opposition to major constitutional renovation was led by such Whig chieftains as Maynard, Pollexfen,

many of the reforms in the second list were to be obtained by the Tories in the forthcoming reign.

Before the final adoption of the Declaration of Rights a last-ditch attempt to reverse the Commons' decision on the vacancy of the throne was easily defeated. The impulse for this move came in the last two days of January from the House of Lords, which was reluctant to go as far as the Commons had gone on the 28th, resolving that James had 'deserted' rather than 'abdicated' the throne and rejecting a motion that the throne was vacant. A delegation led by Nottingham to explain this decision served only to anger the Commons, which on 5 February reasserted its former position by 282 votes to 151. The minority represented a rally of nearly all Tories and served to identify them for the future. At the outset of the debate Clarges had told the House that 'the eyes of the whole Kingdom are upon us', and the truth of his remark became clear in the next election when, as a result of their stand upon this occasion, the names of the Members who had voted against vacancy were listed and published. With the defeat of the Tories in the Commons the doubts of the Lords were also overcome. On the 6th, Danby joined the Whigs and, with other Tory peers abstaining to avoid a constitutional clash between the Houses, the Lords reversed its former decision by accepting the abdication of James and the consequent vacancy of the throne.[7] With this, and its adoption of the Declaration of Rights, matters were brought swiftly to a conclusion. The Lords itself formally proposed William and Mary as joint sovereigns. On 13 February in the Banqueting House of Whitehall Palace, where Charles I had stepped on to the scaffold and Charles II was welcomed by Parliament after his exile, the Declaration was read in the name of the assembled parliamentarians to the Prince and Princess of Orange, who then accepted the crown.

Three weeks of debate had been needed to convince doubters that no alternative solution was as generally acceptable as joint monarchy. A series of votes in the Commons had shown that the Whigs had the support of moderate Members over the vacancy of the throne and the limits of its powers, but insistence on a monarchy of William alone might have swayed the balance back in favour of the Tories. The compromise which was adopted linked a contractual monarch, in William's person, with a monarch by descent, in Mary's, a solution which harnessed Whig and Tory prejudices together in the only practical manner.

As dominant partner in the joint monarchy, William had as his first task the appointment of the royal servants. For his household he

Treby, and Somers' (R. F. Frankle, 'The Formulation of the Declaration of Rights', *HJ*, xvii (1974) 265–79).

showed a preference for Dutchmen and English Whigs. His closest friend, William Bentinck, a fellow countryman who was destined to be the founder of an important Whig dynasty, became Groom of the Stole and Earl of Portland. With Wharton as Comptroller and Devonshire as Lord Steward, William gave himself immediate access to the innermost Whig circles. More difficult was the choice of men for high ministerial offices, for the dearth of experienced Whigs made recourse to others essential, and in any case William had no desire to depend wholly on one party. Two men who possessed the qualification of experience without being associated with the extreme Tories, Halifax and Danby, were given dignified posts. The former had done much by his strong stand on the Whig side, since the Convention opened, to obtain the compliance of the House of Lords. He was rewarded with the office of Lord Privy Seal and the greater share, for the moment, of William's confidence. Danby had many long-standing claims upon William's favour, dating from his negotiation of the royal couple's marriage in 1677. On the other hand, a recent dalliance with the idea of making Mary sole monarch was sufficient for the moment to relegate him to second place in the struggle for the King's favour. After asking for the office of Lord High Treasurer, which he had enjoyed under Charles II, Danby finally accepted the position of Lord President of the Council and a step up in the peerage as Marquess of Carmarthen. Two Secretaryships of State went to younger men, one Whig and one Tory. The southern and more prestigious department was filled by Shrewsbury, whose appointment was announced the day after William and Mary's acceptance of the throne. The northern department was, after three weeks' delay, given to Nottingham, who had the advantage over other active Tories of having held no office under the last two monarchs. Although he had opposed the vacancy of the throne long enough to satisfy his conscience, Nottingham had been careful to tell William's loquacious follower Gilbert Burnet that 'he should not be sorry to see his own side outvoted'. William's choice of Nottingham was a sound one, for it did much to mollify churchmen and obtained an able minister whose career was henceforth one of unswerving loyalty to what he regarded as a *de facto* parliamentary monarchy. Since the King made clear that he had no intention of appointing either a Lord Treasurer, whether Carmarthen or anyone else, or a Lord High Admiral—an office to which the Princess Anne's husband, Prince George of Denmark, might have laid an unwelcome claim—it was clear that he intended to brook no overmighty subject. By his appointment of his most trusted ministers either to offices without a major administrative department or to the divided Secretaries' office, William inaugurated a reign in which he was in every sense his own chief minister and commander-in-chief.

In the lesser ministerial appointments William's preference for Whigs was evident. The veterans who had unswervingly acted and spoken for him in the Revolution and the early debates of the Convention now received their reward. A Treasury commission was headed by Charles Mordaunt, Earl of Monmouth, with another ardent partisan, Lord Delamere, as Chancellor of the Exchequer. With Capel and Richard Hampden also on the board for political services, the only commissioner with financial abilities was Sidney, Viscount Godolphin, who though a Tory was trusted by William. Godolphin needed both his professional and personal advantages in the months ahead, for his appointment was a source of grief to his colleagues. A notable promotion was that of Somers as Solicitor General. In the conferences between the two Houses on the settlement of the monarchy, Somers had made an impressive debating debut, arguing William's case from constitutional precedent rather than from the more fashionable Whig contract ideology which would have given as little security of tenure to any future monarch as it had allowed to James. Later tradition was to hold that Somers' reasoning did much to influence the Lords' final retraction of its objections. By his appointment within a few weeks of entering Parliament he was well set upon the route which was to take him to the leadership of his party and to the acquisition of the Great Seal.[8]

The King, by thus paying his debt to the Whigs, gave the signal for renewed party rancour. Neither side found the divided Ministry acceptable. 'The clergy and many Tories', wrote Sir Edward Harley's second son from London, 'do with all malice imaginable express their dislike of the present government.' Burnet commented in the first and franker draft of his memoirs that, though most of the chief places were filled by Whigs, 'yet they were highly displeased that they had not them all'. The Whigs' resentment was sharpened by disappointed hopes. Finding that William did not intend to accord a monopoly of office to themselves, they concluded that they had won only a battle, not the war, in their struggle against the former servants of the Stuarts.[9]

The two parties engaged in the struggle for power were in numbers fairly evenly matched. Against the 151 Tory Members listed as voting against the vacancy of the throne may be set, to anticipate the vote by which the irreconcilable Whigs came to be identified, the 174 Members who voted for the Sacheverell clause in January 1690; for only four names appear on both lists, and the remainder may fairly be taken as the hard core of their parties. There remained, however, nearly 200 Members who were either new to Westminster or otherwise uncommitted to party stands, and with these men was the key to the course of future struggles of the Convention. Later in their careers many of them would gravitate towards either the Whigs or the Tories, as party strife rendered independence more difficult, but for the moment they tended to vote with either side as the occasion demanded.[10]

In the first business after the acceptance of the crown by William and Mary, the Whigs carried the Commons easily. They swiftly passed through all its stages a bill to legalise past proceedings by declaring the Convention a Parliament, brushing aside opposition from the Tories who hoped for a new general election in which national reaction to the recent decisions might favour them. The sense of the majority was also with the Whigs when they carried bills to reverse the attainders of their martyred heroes, Russell and Sidney.

It was, however, in the settlement of the royal Revenue that the Whigs scored their greatest triumph, though in doing so they took the first step towards arousing the King's displeasure towards themselves. The question was an emotive one, dating back at least as far as the suspicions of country gentlemen under the early Stuarts that the Revenue voted by them was being used for improper purposes. With the reaction in favour of monarchy at the Restoration of Charles II in 1660 a new impulse had led to the provision of a generous Revenue for life, and this had been repeated by James II's Parliament in 1685. But in 1689 the general mood was not in favour of repeating the experiment. One Whig, William Sacheverell, expressed a widely held view when he demanded that Parliament should be able to be 'not kicked out at pleasure, which never could have been done, without such extravagant Revenue'. It was, however, the Tory Clarges who advocated triennial grants only, thus placing himself alongside old republicans like Sir William Williams and Colonel John Birch. The Whigs in office do not appear to have supported the court, leaving this task to Finch and Lowther. William viewed developments with alarm and authorised Wharton to assure the House on 1 March that he was willing to give up the unpopular hearth tax as a source of his Revenue. But though expressing gratitude, the Commons doggedly refused to be conciliated, and on the 11th the problem was postponed by its granting William the right of collection only until 24 June. William later came to the conclusion that Wharton and other Whigs with 'a design for a Commonwealth' had tricked him into giving up the best source of Revenue without commensurate return.[11]

If the King had received his first lesson in Whig intransigence over the Revenue, he was given an equally pointed setback in the settlement of the Church, and reminded that his own Calvinist sympathies were unacceptable not only to the Tories but also to many Whigs. In recognition of the resistance given by most of the dissenters to James II's blandishments in 1687 and 1688, the leading Tories had pledged themselves to some alleviation of the harsh legislation of Charles II's reign against dissenting worship. To fulfil this promise, Nottingham introduced in the Lords a bill for the toleration of public worship by dissenters, together with another bill for the comprehension within the established Church of the less radical dissenters, principally the Presbyterians. However, no offer was made to remove the political disabilities imposed by the Corporation and Test Acts, and many of the extremer Whigs, led in Parliament by the dramatist Sir Robert Howard, pressed for the removal of the sacramental tests imposed upon Protestant dissenters by these statutes. But when William intervened personally on 16 March, with a speech calling for office to be opened to all Protestants, he underestimated the loyalty of the nation—most Whigs as well as the Tories—to the Church. Carmarthen and Nottingham deserted him by voting against the raising of religious tests, and on the evening after his speech a large number of parliamentarians favouring the Church met and resolved to defend the tests. The Tories were joined in their stand not only by uncommitted Members but also by Anglican Whigs, led by Devonshire, while even Shrewsbury absented himself from the upper house to avoid voting on the question.

Such a massive display on behalf of the Church establishment gave rise to the first general Tory exultation since the Revolution. Clarges took the opportunity of the rally of Church supporters to secure on 26 March, by a majority of 188 to 149, the addition to the coronation oath of a proviso binding present and future monarchs to uphold the Church of England as established by law. These setbacks to the dissenters and to the King were decisive in determining the shape of the religious establishment. The Toleration Bill passed into law, giving a substantial measure of freedom for worship to all Protestants; but by the common consent of most Tories and many Whigs the Lords' Comprehension Bill was allowed to drop. It was a ministerial Whig, William Harbord, who administered the *coup de grace* to the latter measure; on 9 April he proposed and carried an address to the Crown to refer the matter of comprehension to Convocation, where it later met, as expected, scant sympathy. If Whigs such as Devonshire objected to the admission of Presbyterians into office, an even more potent motive influencing shrewd heads in the Commons was the desirability of keeping the dissenters politically underprivileged and dependent upon the Whig party.[12]

The net results of the religious settlement were the exclusion from benefices of some clergy who refused to take the oaths of allegiance and supremacy, and the continued existence of a substantial body of Protestant dissenters excluded from office by the tests. Politically the first result was of little importance, and the second was alleviated in the next few years by the religious apostasy or laxity of many dissenters. Among the landed gentry the already visible tendency of Puritan families to conform to the Church was accelerated. Lower down the social scale, those dissenters who were desirous of being candidates for corporation places or other local offices were affected by the general relaxation of religious sanctions, and many of them proved willing to take the sacramental test occasionally for the purpose of qualification. Such 'occasional conformists' were Whig voters or supporters, so that the political calculations of the Whigs, in allowing the Comprehension Bill to be shelved, were amply justified.

For the King, the failure of his hopes in the religious settlement was a step further towards the disillusionment which had begun when he found the Whigs unwilling to vote for his Revenue. Henceforth he tended to place his reliance for the conduct of proceedings in the Commons on two of Carmarthen's Tory associates, Lowther and Sir Henry Goodricke, who acted as the court managers. This development came as a shock to the Whigs, especially those country Members who were apt to hold the naive belief that, because they had helped William to overthrow the tyrant James, he was willing and able to abandon the traditional means of controlling Parliament. Their initial bafflement is exemplified in a letter from a Member newly returned in a by-election, Robert Harley, who wrote to his wife his first impression that 'there is a party setting up to play the old game' but added loyally, 'I am sure the King is of our side.' As it became clear, however, that the King was of no side but his own, bafflement turned to bitterness, and Whig intransigence increased.[13]

The work of the new managers was made more difficult by national military misfortunes. In March James II landed in Ireland with a French force, and the inability of Admiral Herbert, with inadequate strength, either to intercept him or to prevent subsequent reinforcement revealed a disastrous substratum of mismanagement and peculation in the naval administration. Thus, although the Commons supported a declaration of war against France in May, the search for scapegoats rendered it dilatory and obstructive about providing the means to pay for hostilities. Even the King's urgent desire for some more permanent settlement of the Revenue, after the expiry on 24 June of the period for which collection had been granted, was set aside when he received only an extension of a further six months. Nor did his mortifications end there. A Bill of Indemnity for political offences committed in the late reign, which he hoped would allay fears of a general proscription, was strongly criticised by Whigs calling for whole categories of exceptions. Such a proceeding would have largely defeated the intention of the bill and would have left many prominent Tories open to attack. It became clear, by the court managers' joining the other Tories in arguing that exceptions to the indemnity should be few and by name only, that the King was for moderation. The reaction of the Whigs, led by the fiery John Howe despite his tenure of a post of Vice Chamberlain in the

Queen's household, was to call for the removal of Carmarthen and to threaten a revival of the impeachment from which the minister had barely been saved by Charles II's pardon in 1679. The threat sufficed to get the Indemnity Bill shelved for the moment.[14]

In July, Halifax succeeded Carmarthen as the chief target for attacks by the Whigs in the Commons. In a culminating onslaught on 3 August a motion calling for Halifax's removal was rejected by only eleven votes, the leading attackers being Capel, a member of the Treasury commission, and Sir John Guise, a Whig privy councillor. It was by now clear that nothing but the removal of non-Whigs from office would satisfy those of that persuasion. William's dilemma at being thus pressed to choose his Ministry on a party basis was recorded in Halifax's notes, which faithfully portrayed his oscillation between the two parties. At the end of May the King was 'far from leaning' towards the Church party; two months later he had discovered a 'design for a Common-wealth' on the Whig side, but still feared a desire for regency on the other. On the whole, however, his fear of the Tories was subsiding. By 11 August he was considering dissolving Parliament and thought 'it was to be considered whether he might rely upon the Church party'. He hesitated, however, and still hoped 'to form a party between the two extremes'. To allow time for tempers to cool, he prorogued Parliament on the 20th.[15]

Thus ended, after seven months' sitting, the longest session of Parliament since the Restoration, with much work to its credit but even more left unfinished. Only the need to complete the latter appears to have deterred William from dissolving the Convention in the hope of obtaining a less Whiggish assembly. The ministerial Tories, especially Lowther, Goodricke and Heneage Finch, had striven hard on most occasions to implement his wishes, and if they were unwilling to permit political equality to dissenters they had at least shown themselves willing to concede the removal of purely religious disabilities. The Whigs, on the other hand, had frustrated William at almost every turn, with office holders and even junior ministers feeling at liberty to attack both his policies and his advisers. In one overriding matter, however, the Whigs could still perform for him a service which the Tories as a whole could not be relied upon to provide: the legislative settlement of the monarchy in a Bill of Rights which Whig tactics had recently with-held but could not meaningfully continue to delay. Until this bill was passed, a dissolution of Parliament was unwise.[16]

When the Convention met for its second session in October the Bill of Rights, giving statutory confirmation to the Declaration of Rights, was duly passed, but the government immediately met much criticism on the conduct of the war. Country Members of both sides pressed for inquiries into recent losses in merchant shipping and failures in the provisioning of the forces in Ireland, with a group of Herefordshire and Worcester-shire Whigs centred upon the Harley and Foley families speaking alongside Tories such as Clarges. Worse still, some Whig office holders were at best lukewarm in defence of the government, despite the notes of warning sounded by Somers and other ministerial Whigs such as Admiral Edward Russell. As a result of these attacks William drew still closer to the ministerial Tories. Nottingham was able to point out to him that the great majority of the clergy had now taken the oaths. The lead thus given by the Church was crucial, for if Tories were willing to accept the new monarchy *de facto* their capacity for loyalty was unquestionable. By the beginning of December Nottingham was telling his friends that the King 'was now convinced that he had taken wrong measures in relying so much upon the dissenters, and that he would hereafter put himself into the hands of the Church of England'.[17]

The events of December went far towards confirming William in his new approach. On the 14th, attacks on the Tory ministers and Halifax were renewed with a fury and desperation which suggest that Notting-ham's claims were now generally known. Whigs, whether in or out of office, drew together to carry a motion proposed by the country leader Paul Foley for an address to the King to 'appoint affairs to be managed by persons unsuspected, and more to the safety of His Majesty and satisfaction of his subjects'. This signal triumph they followed up four days later when the royal Revenue due to expire on the 24th was granted, not for life as William hoped, nor even for three years as the Whigs had been prepared to concede earlier, but for a single year. Extreme Whigs even urged that the words 'and no longer' should be added to the permitted period; but this was rejected by more judicious members of the party including Somers, whose behaviour throughout the session was noticeably more moderate than that of most of his fellows.[18]

The Christmas recess found the King still hesitating to take the decisive step of dissolving Parliament. He approached leading men of both sides for their advice on his next moves, including on how long Parliament should be adjourned for his best advantage. Of the Whigs consulted, the replies of Shrewsbury and Wharton survive. Shrewsbury regretted that William had not been able to establish a party of his own, based upon 'the more moderate and honest principalled men of both factions'; but since there was a need to make a choice this minister urged that the government would be 'much more safe depending upon the Whigs, whose designs if any . . . are improbable and remoter than with the Tories'. Wharton wrote forthrightly: 'with what honour can you employ those against whom you drew your sword?' Among the

Tories whose advice the King solicited was Sir John Trevor, Speaker in James's Parliament of 1685, who wrote that 'rage between opposite factions being irreconcilable the nation in general grow weary of them'. The King, he thought, should retain the present House of Commons only long enough to obtain war supplies for the coming year, and then should dissolve it with 'proclamations, removals, and other wise methods, whereby the Church party may be so encouraged'.

On the more immediate question posed by William of how long the Christmas recess should last, the advice he received was similarly divided. Nottingham argued for a period of three weeks, knowing that many Tory Members had already left Westminster for festivities in their distant homes and would not expect to be recalled in less a time. Shrewsbury countered by suggesting one week, urging a need to obtain the speedy voting of supplies. It was Shrewsbury's advice which was taken, and the House adjourned on 23 December for one week only.[19]

Nottingham's anxiety for a long recess arose from a correct assumption that if the House reassembled after one week the Whigs planned to carry a denuded chamber with ease. Four days before prorogation the Corporation Bill, designed to restore the corporation charters forfeited under the last two monarchs, had been referred to committee, where the date from which charters were to be restored was fixed at 1675, a time when Dissent had been weak on most corporations. On 2 January 1690, when the bill was reported from committee, the expected manoeuvre took place, with Sacheverell offering a lengthy clause to provide that officials who had connived in the surrender of a former charter should be incapable of holding office for seven years. In a thin House the clause was adopted by a majority of 133 to 68. Thus far the Whigs' manoeuvre had succeeded admirably, but, unfortunately for any hopes they may have had of further success, some of them followed up their triumph by an injudicious attempt to intimidate the King himself. William told Halifax that they 'had sent him word, that if he interposed or meddled' in the bill 'they would not finish the money bills'. Such a move failed to take William's measure, for to him any threat to war supplies called for drastic action. Every effort was made to bring the absent Members to Westminster in time for a renewal of the debate on the 10th, one Tory remarking that 'the King gives all the encouragement that men can desire'. In addition to the King's support, opponents of the bill could rely on the assumption that all the instincts of uncommitted Members were opposed to sweeping dismissals. Those who had surrendered the charters, the Tories argued, had been given no option but to take the course they did, and had in most cases done so unwillingly. But the most important argument against the bill was the undesirability of depriving men of their property in offices. If the clause were allowed to remain, Finch complained, men of little or no fortune, or even the mob, might swamp the corporations. In support of the clause were ranged both sections of the Whigs: the ministerialists headed by Somers and Hampden the elder, as well as the country wing. But their united powers of persuasion were no longer able to command sufficient support in the House. In a vote on amendments they lost by 174 to 179, and those who voted with the minority on this occasion were to be marked henceforth as committed party members. The bill received its third reading and went to the Lords without the addition of Sacheverell's clause.[20]

From the Corporation Bill the House turned again to the question of a general indemnity. Here the Whigs scored an initial success by introducing a bill of pains and penalties, directed against those who were to be excepted from indemnity. This bill was given its first and second readings on the 15th and 16th and referred, together with the Indemnity Bill, to be considered in committee. Before the struggle ran its course, however, William intervened. Even before the Whigs renewed their attack on his Indemnity Bill he had been annoyed by objections to his intention of personally leading an expedition to Ireland. 'The Whigs', he wrote bitterly to Portland, 'are afraid of losing me too soon before they have done what they like with me.' And if final incentive were needed, the Tories had offered a settlement of the Revenue if a new Parliament were called. Even so, William confided to Halifax his determination not to put himself fully into their grasp, for 'though he should seem to declare for one party more than for another, *if his kindness was not answered*, he could take the others by the hand'. With this reservation in mind, William prorogued Parliament on the 27th and dissolved it ten days later.[21]

The decision to end the life of the Convention after one year was taken by William only after long hesitation and extreme provocation from the Whigs. Their assumption that by their unswerving adherence to William at the Revolution they were entitled to a monopoly of office was at odds with the realities of government. Alone they could never have made the Revolution, a fact of which William was well aware, and their long period of opposition and suffering under Charles II and James II had unfitted them, both in temper and from lack of ministerial experience, for the practical tasks and compromises of government. Necessity forced William to use Tory ministers, and common sense dictated that such men, whose unswerving adherence to the Church made them representative of the greater part of the nation, should not be forced into counterrevolution by their being entirely excluded from the government in which they were accustomed to participate. The result of the Whigs' demands was that William's first Parliament, though passing much important legislation and thus earning the long-lasting respect of its successors, had degenerated into an atmosphere of party antipathy which threatened the stability of the new monarchy. Elected in the immediate aftermath of Revolution, the Convention included among its Members a number of Whigs of extremist views who would hardly have been returned in more tranquil circumstances. Moderate Members, especially in the second session, had shown a decreasing inclination to follow their lead. In the nation at large, moreover, men had cooled faster than the representatives they had returned in January 1689, and were ready for a new election. Only recourse to such a measure could force a change in the Whigs' attitude and oblige them to listen to the more responsible counsels which were beginning to be put forward by their abler leaders.

CHAPTER 2

The Whigs Attain Power
1690-95

The assembly which was to become known as the Officers' (that is, office holders') Parliament sat from March 1690 to May 1695. Down to the spring of 1693 William attempted to conduct business mainly through Tory ministers, and after that time increasingly through the Whigs; but in both cases he persisted in regarding their followers as a court party, a view which was given some colour by the presence in office at all times of at least a few members of the party not currently in favour. The King's policy, and his heavy demands for war supplies from the Commons, gave rise to a combination in opposition of several especially articulate country gentlemen of both parties. It was to be this group's criticisms of the government, given added impetus by a series of military defeats and financial crises, which helped the new generation of Whig leaders to obtain ministerial appointments and to oust their rivals after 1693; however, as the Whig-dominated Ministry espoused court policies it increasingly, in its turn, incurred the displeasure of the country coalition. But though the presence of such a coalition sometimes affected the struggle between the two main parties as they fought each other continuously and manoeuvred for or against the King according to whether his wishes favoured or displeased them, it did not diminish the struggle. The Whigs learned the language of the court, though having attained office they often continued to speak their own; and the Tories, after their exclusion from office, began to make their first faltering party sounds. With such circumstances it would be possible to describe the developments in Parliament in traditional court–country terms, but to do so would be seriously to misrepresent a situation in which court policy and country stubbornness were continually turned to party ends.*

*The present work thus takes issue with Dr Dennis Rubini who asserts 'the predominantly court–country character' of William's reign except in its 'first and last days' (Rubini, 260). Rubini's thesis favours in general the Namieran interpretation of the period, put forward by Professor Robert Walcott. Rubini's remarks quoted above were made in reply to a critique of Walcott by Professor Henry Horwitz, who concludes on the basis of a study of division lists and other material that 'future interpreters of the parliamentary history of these years [1689–1714] would do well to take considerably more seriously than

The election of 1690 has been compared, because of the strongly partisan activities which marked its course, with the elections which returned the Exclusion Parliaments rather than with the election of January 1689. The results were a considerable setback for the Whigs; for although direct royal interference in the constituencies was small and discreet, in view of the national indignation aroused by the attempts of the last two monarchs to pack their Parliaments, indications were not wanting of William's disillusionment with the extremists. A new commission of the Admiralty omitted Sacheverell. When parliamentarians dispersed throughout the country to prepare for their elections they did so, as Clarendon noted, in the knowledge that 'the King had declared himself for the Church of England, and had given public encouragement . . . to choose Church of England men'. In the ensuing brief campaign both Whigs and Tories were extremely active and both claimed confidently to emerge the stronger side. For the first time division lists played a part in the campaign, the Whigs publishing the names of those Members who had voted on 5 February 1689 against the vacancy of the throne, and the Tories producing a list of those who had supported the Sacheverell clause. It was, however, the Whigs who were on the defensive, against charges of republicanism, irreligion and political intolerance. A tract attributed to Somers was reduced to claiming that the Indemnity Bill had not been urgent because political wrongdoers were not being pursued, a palpable inaccuracy. Even more damaging to Whig aspirations were the usual criticisms of association with the dissenters and with republicanism, and the Whigs' sole aim was painted as seizure of office by any means. A squib of about this time made the typical attribution of their motives:

> For though Religion bears the name
> Its Government is all our aim.

As the election results came in the extent of the tide against the Whigs was seen. While all the leading Tories reappeared, their opponents suffered severe losses, among them the younger Hampden, Williams, Sir

[Walcott] has done the evidence for the attractive force of party ties during both William III's and Anne's reigns' (*JBS*, vi (1966) 60). A trenchant criticism of Rubini has been given by Professor Geoffrey Holmes (*History*, xiv (1969) 104–5), while the analysis of division lists carried out by Burton, Riley and Rowlands, referred to several times in Chapters 3 and 4, confirms Horwitz's assessment from 1696, there being no known division lists for the Parliament of 1690–95. For the Officers' Parliament it is surely of significance (other evidence apart) that, as Rubini admits, contemporaries made 'little if any mention of a court–country dichotomy in the 1690 general election' (Rubini, 42). William III's attempts to impose such a dichotomy on this Parliament thus took place in the context of the party struggle which had emerged earlier and which continued during and after the life of the Parliament, stimulated as much as checked by his efforts.

Edward Harley and Wildman. From distant Herefordshire, where it was reported that 'Tories talk big', to the City of London, where the four former Members representing the dissenting party were successfully challenged by four of the Church party, the story was the same, so that even the cautious William thought that in the new House of Commons 'the party of Tories will be more considerable than in the last'.[1]

Before Parliament assembled, further changes were made in the balance of the parties in office. The days of 'trimming' over, for the moment, Halifax resigned and left Carmarthen in the undisputed but not entirely enviable position of William's leading minister. A loss more felt by William was that of Godolphin, who gave up his position at the Treasury, possibly in pique against Carmarthen whom he loathed; this necessitated a caretaker commission under Lowther until Godolphin should relent. Monmouth, Delamere and Capel were all laid aside, and though Richard Hampden was brought in as Chancellor of the Exchequer, having proved more tractable than many of his fellow Whigs, the commission bore a distinctly Tory look, with Carmarthen's lieutenant, Sir Stephen Fox, another former servant of the Stuarts, taking Godolphin's place as expert member. In response to such gestures, most Tories, contrary to the wishes of their Jacobite friends, showed every willingness to take office, with a forgetfulness of former ties which the soured Clarendon characterised as 'strange blindness'. Even a Whig pamphlet noted a distinction between Jacobites and 'Tories who would bring Toryism into fashion, under a King who came to root it out'. The newly developing character of post-Revolution toryism, prepared *pro tem* to serve the new monarchy, caused an observer to refer to the parties returned to Parliament as 'Whigs and Modern Tories'.[2]

No clearer sign was visible of changed times than the nomination as Speaker, by Lowther and Goodricke on behalf of the court, of that same Sir John Trevor who had sat in the Chair on behalf of James. Although William had been predisposed to regard Trevor as 'a knave', his usefulness as a manager of the Tories in the Commons during the Convention could not be ignored; 'so well', noted one country gentleman grimly, 'hath he played his game'. By the partiality thus shown against the Whigs, William hoped to dampen strife, and in his opening speech to Parliament he called for an end to the party vendetta, assuring his hearers 'how earnestly I have endeavoured to extinguish (or at least compose) all difference among my subjects'.[3] As evidence of this intention he caused an Act of Grace to be introduced early in the session, extending indemnity for past political actions to all but a few offenders. The measure passed through both Houses without recorded opposition from the Whigs, who were not disposed to test their strength on the sort of issue which had brought about their recent downfall.

If the King expected an immediate *quid pro quo* from the Tories he was quickly disappointed. His greatest need was a final settlement of his Revenue, and the Tories were prepared to go considerably further than their rivals by voting a parliamentary excise for William's life. But to his great chagrin the customs were extended, on the suggestion of Musgrave, for only a further four years after the next expiry, which was due to take place at Christmas 1690. In view of the experiences of the last reign, even Tories were disinclined to remove all restrictions on the King's income. Moreover, although continued attacks on Carmarthen by the Whigs were deflected with comparative ease in the new House by Lowther and Goodricke, it was noticeable that the critics of 'the white marquis' included a number of his enemies among the Tories, notably Seymour and John Granville, who were not in office themselves and saw no reason for restraining their attacks on ministers. The moral which the King may well have drawn was that the Tories, though on the whole more docile than the Whigs had shown themselves to be, were by no means his ideal of a court party. His kindness was only partially answered and, unless all the recalcitrant Tories could be admitted to office, was not likely to meet with a better response in future.

If the Tories were not united, either in sentiment or in numbers, in support of the Crown, they showed themselves to be at one when facing the Whigs. The strategy of the latter, it soon became clear, was to win over the new and uncommitted Members by finding a patriotic cause for the first major division. Their challenge came on 26 April when Wharton brought in a carefully contrived bill to oblige Members of both Houses, together with office holders and suspected persons, to take an oath abjuring King James. The government speakers opposing the bill were quick to point out to the uninitiated that it was in its intention, in the words of the veteran Sir Joseph Williamson, a 'matter of party and distinction' rather than a straightforward attempt to secure the new monarchy. The Abjuration Bill was rejected by only a narrow margin, indicating how well its ground was chosen; for few parliamentarians would wish to incur, by voting against a seemingly innocuous proposal, the suspicion of being Jacobites. But the defeat lost the initiative for the Whigs, and on 2 May the Tories went on to obtain a more decisive victory, carrying by 180 votes to 156 a resolution that the lately published list of those who had voted against the vacancy of the throne in February 1689 was 'a false and scandalous libel'. Shortly after this, with the voting of supplies satisfactorily completed and William on the point of setting out for the reconquest of Ireland, the session was brought to an end after only two months.[4]

The Whigs' electoral losses and unsuccessful start in the new Parliament gave rise among them to much heart searching and ultimately to more flexible attitudes, particularly in regard to a monarch who had forcibly demonstrated his unwillingness to be the head of a party or to have his measures disrupted by the pursuit of party vengeance. But the first reaction, which came from Shrewsbury, was hardly promising. This minister had viewed the recent changes with growing alarm and barely awaited the end of the session to resign the seals of his office, giving as his reason that 'the King was engaged in measures in which he could not concur'. But though Shrewsbury could afford such gestures, since he enjoyed the unshakable regard of the King and possessed neither the need nor the desire for office, other Whigs saw no solution to either personal or political problems in abandonment of responsibility. To such as Somers and Wharton the events of the last few months indicated rather that their assumptions needed some revision. By their adherence to the often violent methods of the late Earl of Shaftesbury, the Whigs were placed totally at odds with the only ruler on whom their hopes could rest. Fortunately a fresh approach was not ruled out, for some of the party's more capable leaders still possessed the ear of the King, who, true to his promise to Halifax, had by no means left himself at the mercy of the Tories by completely breaking with the other side. Wharton and Devonshire still held their household places; and Somers, who remained Solicitor General, had contrived with his own brand of political pragmatism to rise high in the favour of the King without losing the esteem of his friends.

The process of readjustment under the guidance of such men was aided by the disappearance after the general election, or death over the next year, of several of the older generation of radicals, including Maynard, Sacheverell and Birch. The effect of new and subtler counsels was particularly noticeable in the nature of the party's relationship with the Church. By the defeat of the attempt to obtain a Comprehension Bill, early in the Convention, the dissenters were rendered more dependent on the assistance of the Whigs, who thus felt sufficiently assured of their support safely to deny the dangerous charge of associating with 'fanatics'. In the recent session signs had not been wanting that prominent Whigs were anxious to avoid further antagonising the Church. Sir Thomas Littleton, one of the leaders of the party in the Commons, had vindicated the quality of his own and his fellows' churchmanship while impugning that of the Tories as crypto-roman catholicism. He told the House:

'The misunderstanding of the nation is not from Church of England men and Dissenters, but betwixt Church-men and Church-men that would ingross the name of Church-men, to bring in tyranny and persecute all Protestant Churches abroad.'

Even Wharton, defending his Abjuration Bill, felt impelled to tell the sceptical Tories that 'this Bill is not against the Church of England'. With such words from such men the transformation of the Whigs was already under way. If their aims remained the acquisition of office in order to benefit themselves and to safeguard the Protestant succession, the new leaders were to demonstrate that for the future they were prepared to operate within the existing framework of Church and state.[5]

The emergence of the new Whig outlook was assisted by the determination of William not to give full control to either party in the Commons. His intention, it soon became clear, was to build up a court party of which the Tories, with their greater experience, would form the greater part, but from which compliant Whigs would by no means be excluded. When the King returned from Ireland in September 1690, after military success on the Boyne, his first task was to cajole Godolphin back to the Treasury, this time as First Lord. But the office of Secretary of State vacated by Shrewsbury was given to a Whig, Henry Sidney. Godolphin prepared to lend himself to the building of a court party by making Treasury resources available to sweeten Members. Sidney suggested a scheme for controlling the Commons through three managers, one each for the Whigs, High Church and 'middle party'; but this proved impracticable, and it was Lowther who remained chief manager while Trevor, from the Chair, acted as court dispenser of largesse. The Tory ministers prudently made no objections to the King's scheme. Carmarthen had already shown himself willing to obtain support for the court from any quarter, including Whigs; and even Nottingham, his concern for the Church satisfied for the moment, was willing enough to assume the language of a royal servant, disparaging to both parties.[6]

The session which began in October was at first concerned with some matters left unfinished in the short spring meeting, notably the hearing of petitions in cases of disputed elections. The procedure for dealing with petitions from unsuccessful candidates, a prominent feature of the early months of every new Parliament, was by no means so well organised in favour of the government as it was later to become, and the victory of some Whig petitioners with a good case heartened their party. The Whigs turned to an assault upon the Tory Admiral Herbert, now Earl of Torrington, whose failure to give adequate support to the allied Dutch fleet in the summer had caused its defeat off Beachy Head, with the result that Torrington was relieved of his command and lodged in the Tower. Thereafter, however, it was the factious Tories who took the lead, with a violent attack upon Carmarthen by Rochester and other peers, who accused him of violating the privileges of the upper house by imprisoning Torrington. By his willingness to espouse a court policy, Carmarthen was exposed to the jealousy of old Tory rivals still out of office, and with Seymour joining the assault in the Commons the hunted minister was hard pressed for a time. The timely discovery in January 1691 of a Jacobite plot in which Clarendon was implicated turned the tables, resulting in the latter's imprisonment and the discomfiture of Rochester.

The new year saw the further development of an important co-operation between certain Tory and Whig backbench Members which had already been visible on occasions since early in the Convention. The Whig element, led by Paul Foley since the exclusion of Sir Edward Harley, was exasperated by the King's revival of court management; and both these Whigs and the old Tories headed by Clarges and Musgrave were suspicious of government mismanagement of the war. The coming together of these two types of dissident was made easier by the obvious drift of the Harley–Foley group away from their Puritan origins, especially since the Revolution. Both the Tory and the Whig gentry concerned shared one now overriding characteristic: a dislike of ministers who appeared to be spending good public money on bad causes. The new alliance was given a measure of permanence before Parliament was prorogued by its securing the passage of an act for the appointment of salaried parliamentary commissioners 'to examine, take, and state' the public accounts for the period since William's invasion. No ministerialists sat on this body, for it was the work of men anxious to see that the huge sums being voted annually for war supplies were not being misused.[7]

The new commissioners met often during the summer of 1691, and early in November they presented a report, the first of a series throughout William's reign, condemning waste in excessive salaries, fees and perquisites. A few days later a special committee set up by the efforts of Foley, Clarges and Musgrave reported in favour of cutting the naval estimates.[8] The leading light of both the commission and the committee proved to be Robert Harley, Sir Edward's elder son; from now on he began to share with Foley the role of chief spokesman of their group of Whigs, working alongside Clarges and Musgrave in the Commons, its committees and commission of accounts.*

*The significance of this alliance, which has been noted by many historians since Feiling pointed it out in 1924, lay in its four or five vociferous speakers, its control of the commission of accounts, and its usefulness to the Harley–Foley group as a transitional stage between their disengagement from the main body of the Whigs and their adherence, after 1695, to the Tories as a whole. But the importance of the alliance in terms of votes in the Commons has been greatly exaggerated by Dr Dennis Rubini, who habitually treats the alliance as if it included all Members of the House not actually in office. Thus he includes both Seymour, who was a commissioner of the Treasury from 1692 to 1694, and John Smith (a lifelong Whig), who replaced Seymour on that commission in the party changes of 1694 and remained there until the Whigs lost control in 1699, as members of 'the country party' (Rubini, 29–30).

It was not, however, the truculence of the country alliance so much as clashes of interest between the King and the Tories which provided the main theme of politics in 1691–92, by giving the Whigs their first good opportunity to side ostentatiously with William. The opportunity came with the introduction of the Treason Bill, which was designed to amend the law of treason in order to give a fairer hearing to defendants, a measure much desired by all Tories since the Revolution. This reform was one of those which had been shelved by the committee responsible for the Declaration of Rights, by its inclusion in the list 'introductory of new laws'. The Whigs on that committee had seen no reason to deprive William of one of the monarch's traditional armaments. But the need for further protection against malicious political prosecutions exposed raw feelings even in so strong a ministerial Tory as Finch, and brushing aside the loyal Lowther's assertion that the bill would, if passed, 'encourage men to be the bolder in committing treason', the Commons gave it a third reading on 18 November and sent it to the Lords. Here the opportunity was taken to make an amendment in order to obtain a long-desired privilege: the trial of peers by the whole of that House, sitting in a judicial capacity. When the amended bill was returned to the Commons in December, ministerial Tories such as Finch and Sawyer were to be found alongside Seymour, Musgrave, Clarges and Granville in urging acceptance of the Lords' amendment for the sake of obtaining the passage of the bill. The Whigs were not slow to seize an opportunity. Conspicuous among the bill's opponents, and on their best courtly behaviour, were the leading law officers Treby and Somers, Wharton's brother Goodwin, Guise, Littleton, Capel, John Smith and Charles Montagu. The last was a distinguished newcomer who made one of the best speeches of the day with a powerful plea that a time of war was not suitable for a relaxation of the laws of treason.[9] This concerted stand by the Whigs, only a few of whom held office, was a notable demonstration of the solidarity of the party, with the exception of the Harley–Foley group, and of its desire to regain William's confidence. On the other hand, the recalcitrance of the Tories, including some ministers, was plain for all to see, as was their discomfiture when the bill was successfully blocked.

William's response to the Whigs' compliance with his wishes was not what they could have hoped. It soon became apparent that his distrust had not abated sufficiently to make him turn back to them, and he preferred on the whole to buy off his principal Tory opponents while making only a minor concession to the Whigs. Thus a remodelled Treasury commission from which Lowther was omitted by his own wish included not only Montagu, as a reward for his efforts over the Treason Bill, but also Seymour; further, the presence of Godolphin, who remained first commissioner, ensured that the Treasury would remain moderately Tory. A more serious sign of the strengthening of the Tory basis of the Ministry was that Rochester was at last sworn as a member of the Privy Council and brought to work with Carmarthen. Worst blow of all for Whig hopes, Sidney was relieved of his seals, probably to his own relief, leaving Nottingham again to perform the duties of both Secretaries of State.

The last development was not intentional but arose from a shortage of suitable men to share the Secretaryship with Nottingham, for while William was unwilling to spoil the balance of parties by appointing a second Tory he could not bring himself to admit so strong a Whig as the obvious candidate, Wharton. Serious consideration was given to Sir William Trumbull, a diplomat who, as a churchman, was acceptable to the Tories without being too closely involved in their past politics. The task of finding out whether Trumbull could be made equally acceptable to the Whigs was deputed to Portland, who wanted (recorded Trumbull) 'to know what party I was of, viz. whether of Whig or Tory, as commonly called' and who remarked that the Whigs would expect 'to have one they could confide in, and would take it ill if [they] had not such a one'. Trumbull replied that he was of no party. But Portland (continued Trumbull's narrative) 'still insisted that I would declare myself. If the Whigs would trust me, and if they were my friends etc.' Thus pressed, Trumbull finally declared that he believed not. The post remained unfilled.[10]

The reluctance to claim a party label displayed by Trumbull was shared by the ministers, but in the summer of 1692 the Ministry was finding it increasingly difficult to keep up the pretence of not being swayed by party considerations. The admission of Rochester, whose adherence to the Princess Anne made it scarcely worthwhile for him to claim to be the King's man, increased the party character of the Ministry. Nottingham might pose as being purely a courtier, impartial as between the parties, but his protest that he was 'not pleading for either' lacked conviction when he asserted to Portland:

'that though the Whigs caused the Prince of Orange to be crowned King, yet other people must keep him on the throne, for their principles, who set him up, would pull him down.'

Nottingham himself, despite his disclaimers, figured largely in accusations of party jobbery, especially in keeping out Whigs from commissions of peace.[11]

It was the war situation which brought the Tories into open conflict with their master. Every year since 1689 the King's failure to hold back French military might in the Low Countries made the Commons more difficult to handle. In the summer of 1692 the ministers' hands were forced by new military setbacks. The only major successful feat of arms was that of Torrington's successor, Russell, whose victory over the French fleet at La Hogue in May re-established the Anglo–Dutch naval dominance which had been lost at Beachy Head; and even Russell frittered away much of the acclaim he thus acquired, by failing to follow up the engagement and make projected landings at enemy naval bases. In Flanders the land war reached a low point in June after the loss of the important fortress town of Namur, despite William's spirited attempts to relieve it. When the country Members returned to Westminster they were likely to see more grounds for criticism than for praise in the military efforts which had resulted from the sums voted in the last session. Anticipating this reaction, the ministers determined to urge upon William an entirely new war strategy in Flanders, comprising a reduction of English commitment by the placing of a greater burden on the Dutch, and also a policy of primarily naval attacks on the coastline of France involving comparatively small army commitment and expense. The existing land forces in the Low Countries, they urged, were ruinously expensive and not likely to receive further support from Parliament. Present strategy, wrote Rochester forthrightly, was 'not suitable to the interest of England'; it was 'not the way to put an end to the war' urged Carmarthen more circumspectly; it was less satisfactory, wrote Nottingham, than to invade the French coastline next year and leave only a holding force in Flanders. But such concerted advice, whether or not it was the best for England, was the bankruptcy of Tory thought, from the point of view of William who had his mind set on the defence of his Dutch homeland.[12]

The Ministry's reluctance to continue the war in Flanders provided the Whigs with their cue. From the opening of Parliament on 4 November, well-organised tactics were devised by their leaders. All their strength was thrown into obtaining the necessary votes of supply, though as they were also anxious to demonstrate the weakness of the Ministry without their support they held back when the subordination of the English army in Flanders to Dutch general officers came under attack. But, after the House resolved in committee on 23 November to advise William to fill future appointments in foot regiments by English nationals, the Whigs were not slow to point out their opponents' fundamental distrust of the army which was dear to William's heart. When criticism of the government swung to naval affairs, and particularly to the well-known tendency of Nottingham to override the Admiralty in its proper functions, the Whigs were again quick to exploit the advantage, transforming the case against the Secretary into a matter of party principle. John Smith reminded the House that some members of the government 'believe you have not a rightful King but only de facto', while Wharton thundered, 'your chief men that manage matters are such as submit to this King upon wrong principles, because he has the governing power, but will be as ready to join another when he prevails'. The ministerial Tories, cornered on the loyalty issue, were forced on 30 November to submit to a resolution that William should employ 'such persons only whose principles oblige them to stand by him in his right against the late King James'. The Whig victory in the Commons was not, however, echoed in the Lords, where Nottingham was exonerated and blame for the naval mismanagement which had followed La Hogue was placed upon Russell. The Admiral was dismissed, though William softened the blow to the Whigs early in 1693 when the weight of the court was thrown on to their side in the Commons against a Tory attempt, which had the support of the Harley–Foley group, to censure the Admiralty.[13]

Concurrently with this struggle, two party measures were both rejected in closely fought debates: a new Abjuration Bill from the Whigs and a new Treason Bill supported by the Tories. Although the Treason Bill again had too much support from ministerial Tories to permit its outright rejection, the full weight of Whig opposition was able to ruin it by a wrecking amendment on 1 December. The Abjuration Bill, like its predecessor in 1690, was intended to cause maximum embarrassment to the Tories. One of their rising spokesmen, William Bromley of Baginton, was probably not far from the mark in saying that the proposed abjuration oath was 'a snare to catch good conscientious men and will not hold the bad'. Despite the able advocacy of Somers, the King's known opposition to punitive abjuration saved the Tories again.

In two other measures the Whigs showed better judgment. Their intention, as before, was to impress the King with their ability to embarrass as well as to assist him, and they thus gave their support to bills to exclude placemen from the Commons and to limit the life of Parliaments to three years. Both measures were extremely popular, appealing to long-standing resentment against executive control and the appetites of court caterpillars. The Place Bill, despite its inbuilt tendency to cut across party lines, had greater appeal to a party out of office, and observers were agreed that 'in general the Whigs were for the Bill and the Tories against'. The bill was rejected in the upper house by a combination of Tory and Whig ministerialists, an indication of strong personal pressure from the King to defeat the measure. William did not, however, care to repeat this tactic in the case of the Triennial Bill, which was introduced in the Lords by Shrewsbury. Its long-term object was to provide the electorate with frequent opportunities to refuse re-election to ministers and other placemen; but more important in the eyes of many Whigs was the immediate advantage to be obtained by setting a term to the life of the House which had already sat for three years. Only Shrewsbury subsequently proved to be committed to the bill's main object. In view of the King's disapproval, Somers and Montagu sat silent in the lower house, and their behaviour indicated the way Whig thought was subsequently to move on this charged issue.[14]

The passing of the Triennial Bill presented the King with two unpleasant dilemmas. Of these the first, that of dealing with the bill itself, was the more easily decided, and he had little hesitation in using his prerogative by vetoing the measure and proroguing Parliament on 14 March 1693. More serious and far-reaching was the question of how to deal with the Whigs, whose skilful tactics over the last two sessions had shown them capable not only of protecting his interests and of ensuring him the means of carrying on war, but also of setting his ministers at naught; for while the Whigs had been able to spoil the Treason Bill in the Commons, the Tories had conspicuously failed to do the same over the Place Bill and Triennial Bill, and had thus forced William to fall back on expedients which he preferred to use sparingly: the Lords' veto and his own. It was clear that the extent of the Whigs' future co-operation in the Commons would depend upon the measure of office they received. Their greatest truculence had coincided with the replacement of Russell in his sea command on 24 January by the joint command of three other admirals of whom two, Killigrew and Delavall, were the leaders of the Tory faction in the navy. The change was probably little more than a reflection of William's professional view of the naval misadventures of the previous summer, but it was enough to stimulate the Whigs to desperation in their campaign for advancement. That campaign had been remarkably successful. Its only failure had been the rejection of the Abjuration Bill, and this defeat was in the long run hardly of benefit to the King.

By the end of the session William had made up his mind to offer the olive branch. Immediately after the prorogation Somers was given the Great Seal as Lord Keeper, replacing the commission headed since 1690 by Speaker Trevor. At the Secretaries' office Nottingham was given John Trenchard, a long-committed Whig, as his colleague; and to add to his discomfiture he was deprived of his power in naval affairs for the forthcoming campaigning season, despite the King's private belief that he was both loyal and correct in his conduct. The 'Whig news' was reported to be that Nottingham's dismissal would follow without undue delay.[15]

Not the least factor in William's decision to move closer to the Whigs was the immense advantage they had over their rivals by the support which they demonstrably enjoyed in the City of London. In the spring of 1693, after three years of conflict with France, England was more deeply engaged in continental warfare than at any time since the Hundred Years War. Despite unprecedented taxation for war supplies, culminating in a land tax based upon a new assessment of land values, expenses were soaring above income. The solution to the problem of prolonged warfare, for a government which enjoyed the confidence of the financial community, had been shown by Dutch experience to lie in loans at an attractive rate of interest. Down to the Revolution, and especially after the stop of the Exchequer by Charles II in 1672, the City of London had been reluctant to emulate Amsterdam's willingness to lend. Even during the first years of William's reign, the continued distrust felt by the mainly dissenting City for the Tories greatly impeded the government in tapping England's vast wealth, while the Exchequer's antiquated machinery creaked even under the strain of such loans as Godolphin managed to raise. But with the appointment of Montagu to the commission in 1692, the most spectacular period of Treasury history began. Godolphin's experience was complemented by the younger man's energy and spasmodic brilliance. The first fruits of Montagu's appointment accrued to the government in December 1692, when he proposed and, with Somers' backing, ushered through a bill to raise £1 million by long-term loans; the essential feature of the Million Loan Bill's scheme was a parliamentary provision of tax 'funds' earmarked for the payment of the annuitants. The eagerness with which the loan was subscribed by the financial community was to William an irrefutable token of the Whigs' greater ability, as well as greater willingness, to finance his war against Louis XIV.

During the King's absence in Holland in the summer of 1693, further changes in office at lower levels continued with his approval. Somers in his new post instituted a searching inquiry throughout the land as to whether justices of the peace and holders of legal positions had taken the oaths and, if so, whether they were politically trustworthy. By July he reported to Portland that disaffected justices had already been dismissed in one circuit and that he was only awaiting more specific information to act in the others. His investigations, which embraced practically the whole of that section of society entitled by its standing to be considered for commissions of the peace, initiated a fierce party struggle over the next two and a half decades for control of these appointments, which were of vital importance in matters of local standing and control.

Somers and Trenchard were also engaged, by May, in building up support among Members of the Commons for the coming session, a task in which they had the co-operation of William's newest adviser, the second Earl of Sunderland. Sometime right-hand man to James II, this able politician was now, mysteriously to those who did not understand the ways of courts, much in the favour of James's successor.

Sunderland's assistance to the Whigs on Commons management, on behalf of the court, was well in line with his advice that William should rely on the Whig party alone, because of the Whigs' more wholehearted acceptance of the Revolution. In August, when Sunderland entertained the Whig leaders, together with Godolphin and Marlborough, at his Northamptonshire seat, Althorp, he probably took occasion to announce the impending disgrace of the Tory naval commanders and of Nottingham. The latter's dismissal was finally confirmed the day before Parliament assembled. With the removal of Nottingham, further changes in favour of the Whigs were widely predicted but, except for the reinstatement of Russell as Admiral of the Fleet for the coming year, these failed to follow immediately. Shrewsbury, offered Nottingham's seals, refused because of a personal commitment to the Triennial Bill, returning a firm negative to the urging of the other Whigs that he should accept the King's offer. For the moment the post was left unfilled, on the assumption that Shrewsbury would relent, for the King had little desire for a more extreme Whig.[16]

Nevertheless, William drew closer to his new ministers as a result of the session of 1693–94. Although the excluded Tories did not go into overt opposition to the Crown, their courtly instincts being as yet too strong for such a move, their discontent was visible in their sympathy for the country coalition. In November, two new Triennial Bills, one brought in each House, presented them with their best opportunity; but both bills were rejected in the Commons. Most ministerial Whigs now joined Somers and Montagu by keeping silence in the House, but speaking privately against a measure which could hardly be an advantage to their party now that the King had strengthened its place in the government. Less farsighted or more inflexible Whigs found the proposed legislation if anything too moderate, and contributed to its downfall for that reason. Soon after Christmas the Whig leaders were forced, by the passing of the Place Bill in both Houses and by William's use of his veto upon it, to take a more open stand. Wharton, Montagu and Russell combined with Lowther and Goodricke and, though unsuccessful in opposing Clarges' motion labelling the advisers of the bill's rejection as enemies to King and government, they prevented a further embittered representation to William. But a groundswell of country discontent remained, promising ill for the King if he continued to resist every attempt at the reduction of government influence. Robert Harley had told the Commons ominously that, if the King could veto bills, that House could withhold supplies.[17]

William's response in the spring of 1694 was twofold: he yielded on the least objectionable of the demands, triennial Parliaments, but again reinforced the Whig ministerialists. This process of strengthening the Whigs began before the end of the session, with changes in the

Lord Lieutenancies and in the London militia. And on William's assurance that the Triennial Bill would meet no more resistance in the next session, Shrewsbury consented on 2 March to accept the seals again. Thus there were, for the first time, two Whig Secretaries of State. At the Treasury the King's hand was forced by Montagu, who had launched a vicious attack in the Commons on his colleague Seymour and shown that in the Whig view the umbrella of the term 'court party' could not be extended to cover both Whigs and Tories at once. Obliged by this action to choose between the two irreconcilable commissioners, the King reconstituted the Treasury by promoting Montagu to be Chancellor of the Exchequer and by bringing in another vociferous Whig, John Smith, to replace Seymour. Russell was reinstated at the head of the Admiralty Board. To round off the changes, four Whig peers together with Carmarthen were raised to dukedoms, the last as Duke of Leeds. Shrewsbury and Devonshire received their new rank as reward for their active support of William during and since the Revolution. The Earl of Bedford, now created Duke, stood in a class of his own among the Whigs, not only as father of William, Lord Russell, who had been executed after the Rye House plot, but as one of the few peers who were practising Presbyterians. The fifth creation was a revival of the title of Duke of Newcastle in the person of John Holles, Earl of Clare, a Whig whose vast fortune was to descend for the most part to his nephew, the great Duke of Newcastle, and to play its part in the preservation of eighteenth-century whiggery.

These changes, and especially the dismissal of Seymour despite his impeccable service to William in the Commons for the previous two years, were the portent of a new situation in which such service was insufficient unless acceptable to the dominant party. A principal consideration which had prompted William to accede to the further advancement of the Whigs was his continued need to facilitate the raising of vast government loans. Before Parliament was prorogued, Montagu had secured the passage of a bill to provide suitable tax funds for a loan of £1·2 million and to incorporate the subscribers into a bank. The ease with which the subscriptions were raised more than justified William's support of Montagu, and the foundation of the Bank of England was to do much for the Whig cause. William was placed under obligation not only by the foundation loan which met his immediate requirement, but by the smooth manner with which the Bank was able to meet his short-term loan needs in coming years. And by the same measure which secured the King, Montagu did much to cement the alliance of the ministerial Whigs with leading dissenters in the City. It was from 1694, Robert Harley was later to think, that the dissenters acted 'against all their principles and the liberties of the nation' by adhering to the ministerial section of the party. Montagu had come far in the last year, as was testified by his ability to challenge and defeat the powerful and experienced Seymour, and his latest achievement placed him in the top rank of his party. Henceforth Montagu rather than Shrewsbury, whose insistence on the Triennial Bill disqualified him as a party tactician, joined the inner core of the Whig policy makers, along with Somers, Wharton and Russell.[18]

The changing aspect of the Whigs, more visible since they had obtained office, was a source of disquiet not only to the country Whigs, who now looked more than ever to Foley and Harley for their leadership, but also to others for whom the rapid adoption of the attributes of a court party smacked of jobbery and lack of principle. 'I doubt', Shrewsbury had written to Wharton at the time of the latest Triennial Bill, 'whether I am skilful enough to agree, even with those of whose party I am reckoned, in several notions they now seem to have of things.' Common report credited the Whigs with a desire for a monopoly of office by means of a further sweeping dismissal of Tories at all levels, from Leeds as Lord President down to the remaining Tory justices of the peace. One writer was later to compare the pre-Revolution Whigs, who were Whigs 'upon principle and by inheritance', with the post-Revolution variety, whose 'rigid and inflexible self-denying virtue could not bear the sunshine of the court, but melted away before the warm beams, like the manna of the Israelites'. This reputation was hard to deny, since it was largely justified, but the ministerial Whigs were careful to state the case for placing government in good hands, and to counteraccuse their whig critics of having republican principles. 'A Commonwealth', declared a ministerial tract in the autumn of 1693, was 'a chimera impracticable'. Such a rejection of one of the original strands of whiggery was a landmark in the development of a more practicable party outlook, which had been taking place since 1690 and which was to culminate in the eighteenth-century Whigs' habit of seeing Somers and his friends, rather than Shaftesbury's first Whigs, as the founders of their creed.[19]

The first results of Whig management began to be seen in the summer of 1694. In Flanders, where the English contingent was being assisted by more generous Commons votes, the tide of French advance was at last halted. And though a combined naval and military expedition failed to destroy the French fortifications at Brest—suffering heavy casualties including its commander, General Tollemache—this check was a setback to the strategy instituted by the Tories and served to justify William's insistence on the heavy involvement of English forces in the Low Countries. At home the Whigs continued their campaign for full political control by grasping at the greatest prize of all: the Treasury and its vast patronage. Throughout the summer they continued to press for changes in the commissions of Customs and Excise.

Though Godolphin protested long and vigorously against 'removing some men that are of one party, and gratifying some that are of another', he was finally overborne when Sunderland threw his weight on to the Whig side. Though still personally unassailable, Godolphin was henceforth severely circumscribed, outshone by the able Chancellor of the Exchequer, and deprived of the general control of patronage which his position should have given him.[20]

With military success and new marks of royal favour to assist them, the Ministry obtained the votes of supply in the autumn of 1694 more easily than at any time since 1690. Further, the Tories' four-year grant of Revenue, due to expire on 24 December, was renewed for a term of five years from the 26th of the same month with no more objection than was implied by making collection illegal on Christmas Day 1694, an expedient suggested by Seymour for the purpose of asserting the Commons' right to withhold the grant. The King, for his part, placed no further obstacles in the way of the Triennial Bill. The measure was to give to the next twenty-two years, in which there were no less than ten general elections, a particular character for political conflict, as the two sides struggled for supremacy at the polls, their mutual antipathies fertilised by almost continuous appeal to wider public opinion.

The way was opened for direct party confrontation three days after Christmas, with the unexpected death of Queen Mary at the age of thirty-two. Little regarded in politics, she had been essential to the reconciliation of many Tories with the new monarchy. Her restraining influence on William in his recent turn to the Whigs had hitherto reassured the Tories in their adversity. Her death aroused their fears and their truculence. Nottingham immediately expressed his opinion that 'some things are more expedient to be done than have formerly been thought fit or necessary'. Since his dismissal this politician appears to have done his best to avoid outright assault on the King's new ministers, but in a debate in the Lords on 25 January 1695 he joined with Rochester and other Tories in a wide-ranging attack on the government's conduct of the war, on the Bank of England and on the depreciated state of the national coinage. If Nottingham's previous restraint had served to soften party conflict, his abandonment of it sounded the tocsin for renewed strife.[21]

The Whigs' counterattack came in the Commons, where an investigation into the practices of corrupt army officials was now broadened to include political targets. An obvious one was Speaker Trevor, a well-hated Tory survivor whose activities as bribemaster-general in the Commons were resented by the country as undesirable and by Montagu as rivalling his own management of the House. Under the zealous chairmanship of Paul Foley, a committee appointed on 7 March to investigate the books of the East India Company and of the Chamberlain of London soon found sufficient material to carry against Trevor a charge of accepting a bribe from the City, and the culprit was accordingly expelled from the House. In the appointment of a successor, however, the ministerial Whigs met their first reverse. Wharton rose to nominate Littleton. But the country elements were in no mood to be overawed by a show of ministerial authority, as at the time of Trevor's election, and taking their own course they selected instead Foley. Undeterred by this setback the Whigs continued their search for Tory victims, including the highest of all, and on 27 April Wharton obtained a motion to impeach Leeds himself, for alleged bribery. At this point the King hastily prorogued Parliament, being unwilling as always to allow full rein to party prosecutions. But Leeds, whether guilty or not, was sufficiently disgraced by the investigation to prevent his ever being used again as royal adviser, though in defiance of Whig pressure William allowed him to retain his post in form. Nor was this the King's only assertion of his independence, for when Trenchard, who had been ill for some time, died in April his seals were given not to Wharton but to Sunderland's nominee, Trumbull, who had been rejected for a Secretary's place three years earlier as unlikely to satisfy the Whigs.[22]

The election of Foley by the Commons and the appointment of Trumbull by the King served as a reminder to the Whigs that, in being situated between these two forces, they were themselves by no means in possession of full security for their position. In Sunderland they had a rival for the King's ear who, though agreeing with them on the need to keep the Tories out, by no means saw government in the same terms as themselves. Sunderland viewed the problem of controlling the Commons as one for court management and, though he had no doubt that the new ministers were essential to his scheme, he was unwilling to employ them exclusively. He hoped to be able to reconcile them to working not only with his own nominees, such as Trumbull, but also with the Whig elements of the country coalition. His scheme fell down, however, upon the irreparable differences which events of the last few years had brought to the fore between the ministerial Whigs and the Harley–Foley group. To some extent these differences had been screened from view during the late session because the Ministry had been able to enlist the aid of the country sentiment against Tory management, especially in the case of the bribery and corruption employed by Trevor. But in a negotiation carried on by Sunderland, which dragged on for many weeks during the summer, both wings of the party proved unco-operative. Foley refused repeatedly to work in any way under the management of Wharton and Montagu, professing to believe that the Whig ministers could be dispensed with altogether and that 'by a little pains the Whig party will totally leave

Mr Wharton and Mr Montagu'. Wharton reciprocated this antipathy by showing round a list of Members who were to be excluded at the next election, among whom was Harley. Only Somers professed willingness to compromise; but after an interview with him in May, Sunderland's emissary, Henry Guy, had to report merely that 'he seemed much to despond because the Whig Party were divided'.

As the final flickers of hope of reuniting with the Harley–Foley Whigs died out, Somers was not the only minister who viewed the future with misgiving. A conviction was growing in the minds of Wharton and Montagu that, with Sunderland fishing for government supporters independently of the Ministry, the dissolution of Parliament in the summer, for which they had longed, would not be to their advantage. Their fears of an election in which Sunderland's influence would vie with their own were more than justified. William's decision to dissolve was taken before he left England for the campaign of 1695 and was confirmed by a conspicuous military success in the retaking of Namur, which improved the prospect of a favourable election. He was determined that the advantage thus gained should go to himself rather than to the Whigs. As elections got under way he made, during the second half of October and most of November, an extended tour of central England, including a stay of a week with Sunderland at Althorp. Though he also paid briefer visits to the Dukes of Newcastle and Shrewsbury, his public appearance at the home of the favourite, together with the earlier appointment of Trumbull, was sufficient to indicate that it was Sunderland who should now be looked to for the King's will. In exorcising Leeds the Whigs had raised up a devil yet more dangerous to their cause.[23]

CHAPTER 3

Tory Fusion and Opposition
1695-98

As the election results became available, spread as usual over several weeks, the efforts of the Ministry were seen to have resulted in a number of Tory losses in key constituencies. In the City of London the Tories lost four seats, and in Westminster two seats, while men as prominent as Seymour and Musgrave were driven to refuge in pocket boroughs. But if the Whigs as a whole improved their position the Junto, as Somers and Wharton together with Russell and Montagu were beginning to be called, could take little comfort where the gains accrued to what Burnet described as 'the sourer sort of Whigs'. Old stalwarts such as Sir Edward Harley and Sir William Williams were returned after an absence of nearly six years, swelling the ranks of the Harley–Foley group. And even where the gains were not of this sort, it was possible that the untried new men would be seduced by Sunderland to follow a court rather than a Whig line. In the event, the King's political manager did not succeed in forming a separate court party, but for some months this outcome was not clear, and the Junto found difficulty in establishing a majority until an issue arose early in 1696 which enabled them to draw together nearly all Whigs except the Harleys and Foleys.[1]

The future development of this last group lay within the Tory party, though its members long continued to be occasionally called Old Whigs, to mark their origin. Numerically few—they numbered about a dozen in the Commons[2]—they were powerful enough through the ability of their leading spokesmen to attract support from some Tory country gentlemen of their own landed standing, especially after these Tories' own leaders either died, as did Clarges in 1695, or lost much of their fire, as did Musgrave in the new Parliament. More importantly, the Harley–Foley group solidified from 1696 a growing relationship with the main Tory body, and henceforth did much to implant in its new friends the ideas and practices of party, developed in opposition to Charles II and now brought to bear on William's Ministries. The third Earl of Shaftesbury, grandson of the founding Whig, later came to think that it was Robert Harley in particular who inculcated the habit of opposition in the Tories and made them a party: ''Tis he has taught 'em their popular game', he explained, 'and made them able in a way they never understood, and were so averse to as never to have complied with, had they not found it at last the only way to distress the Government.' The era of party development which began in 1693 with the Whigs' accession to office was given its character, not simply by their easy adaptation to governmental methods, but also by the fact that the Tories showed themselves flexible enough to learn opposition tactics.

The absorption of the Old Whigs by the Tories, and the conversion of the latter to the idea of opposition, were not achieved overnight or without difficulty. The Harleys and Foleys, despite their alliance of several years' standing with Clarges and Musgrave, were long regarded with suspicion by those who had until recently been in office and had suffered from the attacks by the country coalition. Moreover, the Old Whigs' habit of keeping up some ties with old friends—for, conscious of the mutablility of fortune, they liked to keep more than one string to their bows—could cause the High Church Tories considerable disquiet in private.[3]

But these were inevitable rubs, and in the main the alliance was to hold together well for the remainder of William's lifetime. A more serious difficulty than personalities was that of the recently ministerial Tories' adjustment of their ideological presuppositions to the practical problems of exclusion from office. Their descent into open opposition was to be achieved only after much hesitation, for deeply embedded in their philosophy of government was the idea that opposition to the Crown was factious if not actually treasonable. Their way had been made easier, however, when Nottingham showed that a respected high Tory could reconcile sweeping attacks on the government with loyalty to the Revolution monarchy. Moreover, another leading, if less reputable, Tory, the adaptable Seymour, had lost little time in allying himself with the country coalition, and by the time of the general election he was concerting with Harley the opening moves of the session, in which his considerable influence would be placed behind Foley in the contest for the Speakership.[4] Nottingham and Seymour were quick to grasp political realities. For the rank and file of Tories, however, some convenient fiction was needed to ease their transition from the theory of passive obedience to the practice of opposition. Such a fiction was conveniently available in the traditional role of the country gentleman who could, by attacking the ministers on the grounds that these were leading the King into undesirable policies, both oppose and remain loyal to his government. The average Tory could not, as yet, bring himself to adopt the terminology of party, but by falling back on the permissible vocabulary of a country stance he could safely adopt the methods inculcated by his Old Whig mentors. The latter, for their part, had no objection to reviving a venerable mythology, but over the course of the next few sessions they shaped the country position into the systematic opposition standing of a 'new country party', which would in due course emerge back in office as a renovated and party-educated toryism.*

The potential strength of the ministry's opponents was obvious as soon as Parliament assembled. Foley's candidature for the Speaker's Chair went unchallenged, for his rival of the previous spring, Littleton, was ordered by William to stand down in pursuance of an understanding reached through Sunderland. Foley and his friends, for their part, honoured an undertaking to place no obstacle in the way of the smooth voting of supplies. Either the same understanding or an unwillingness on William's part to challenge his new Parliament at so early a stage accounted for the quick passage into law of a new Treason Bill. The measure brought about needed reforms in a much abused procedure, and the Tories' anxiety to get the bill was consistent with their past efforts since the Revolution. But if treason legislation was now accepted by William, the Tories' next venture, in which a lead was given by the Harley–Foley group, was not. The King's gifts of Crown property in Wales to Portland, whose services were great, had attracted attention as being too munificent. Though Robert Harley had undertaken to Sunderland in the summer of 1695 to prevent further attacks, he proved to be unable or unwilling, when the time came, to restrain his Welsh friends and neighbours from voicing their resentment at the loss of patronage which they had long enjoyed by the lease or stewardship of estates now handed over to Portland. On 14 January 1696, the House resolved to request the King to resume ownership of the lands in question. William complied with ill grace, compensating Portland by grants elsewhere.[5]

Inauspicious as were these beginnings, worse was to follow. The second half of January saw a struggle over a proposal to set up a Board of Trade, with its members to be nominated by Parliament, in place of the existing Lords of Trade. The measure took its origin from a general discontent over the heavy losses which had been suffered by commerce at sea throughout the war. Any hesitation which the Tories may have felt at such a proposal was abandoned when the ministers attempted, among other expedients for killing the Board of Trade Bill, to impose

*A study of division lists from 1696 (the first year since 1689 for which such lists are known), conducted by Burton, Riley and Rowlands, states: 'that henceforth the House of Commons was divided into Whig and Tory rather than into Court and Country, is amply supported by the evidence of the division lists' (Burton, Riley and Rowlands, 37).

an abjuration oath for members of the board. The abjuration clause was rejected after a fierce struggle by 195 votes to 188. The debates over the bill revealed a willingness of the Tories to join their Old Whig associates even to the extent of cutting down the monarchy's executive powers. 'By an odd reverse', noted Burnet, 'the Whigs, who were now most employed, argued for the prerogative, while the Tories seemed zealous for public liberty.' The reversal was, in fact, the culmination of a change of roles which had been possible at any time since 1689 and probable since the Whigs achieved power. Further, the Tories appeared, on results since the beginning of the session, to be in control; and contemporaries were not slow to grasp the constitutional implication if the situation were to continue. 'The Tories', explained the Dutch Resident carefully to his government, 'have some advantage in the House of Commons this year, it is said that various changes ought to be made in the Ministry, it being a sufficiently common practice that the dominant party should take charge.'[6]

Early in February 1696, therefore, the Tories appeared to be in a position to dictate terms. This outcome was prevented, and a sufficient ascendancy was established by the Ministry, for most of the rest of this Parliament's life, by an event which enabled the Whigs to turn the tables dramatically. This was the discovery on 14 February of a conspiracy to assassinate the King on the following day. On the 24th, William revealed the facts to Parliament. Taking advantage of Members' shock and indignation the Whigs drew up a statement of Association whose signatories were to declare William 'rightful and lawful' king and to undertake to defend or revenge him against the late King James. In the Commons the Tories decried the Association as a new form of abjuration and, when their objections were ignored, over ninety of them failed to sign the document. The scruples of the nonassociators provided the opportunity for which the Whigs had been waiting, and they quickly passed a bill incapacitating from office or seat in Parliament those who failed to subscribe. By the Tory leaders the extent of the crisis was fully appreciated, for their followers were unprepared to make a sudden choice between virtual abjuration of King James and exclusion from public life. The doubters were entreated by their less scrupulous friends and by the Old Whigs to give up their resistance, on the ground that subscriptions made under duress were not binding. After much heartsearching the instinct for self-preservation was sufficient to prevail, and the Tories were saved from the destruction planned for them. Nevertheless, scars remained, and those men who had refused the voluntary association were for the rest of their career marked out as extremists by well-publicised lists of their names.[7]

The Ministry had won an important tactical victory too, for the momentum which had carried antigovernmental measures for most of the session was at last halted. The first casualty was the Board of Trade Bill, abandoned in the aftermath of the assassination plot's discovery. Once again the parliamentary skill and resilience of the Whigs had been strikingly demonstrated in the face of initially superior numbers. And in the country at large the Ministry carried the day even more decisively than in Parliament. The Association was taken far and wide on a wave of national sympathy for William, while a new purge of justices and other officials who had refused voluntary signature completed Somers' earlier work of weeding out political opponents from local positions of importance.[8]

Nevertheless there was, in the spring and summer of 1696, a crisis for the Ministry as well as for the Tories. National finances were in unprecedented straits, with loans hard to come by and specie both in short supply and depreciated by the wide spread practice of clipping. Before the end of the session the Treasury obtained powers to replace the clipped coins with a new milled issue, defraying the cost by means of a window tax; but the milled money was hoarded as soon as minted, and little found its way into circulation. Short-term government securities changed hands at discounts of 50 per cent or more; and in the field of long-term credit the Ministry was experiencing equal difficulty, for even the Bank of England could do little to help in the eighth summer of the war. It was because William was willing to clutch at any straw of hope which seemed to offer the opportunity to keep his troops in the field that he encouraged a bill, sponsored by Foley and Harley, to enable the raising of a government loan of about £2 million by the establishment of a Land Bank, which was intended to be the country gentry's rival to the Bank of England. But when the subscription lists were opened a dismal failure was soon visible, since the Whig financial community was unwilling to lend to an institution favouring the landed interest and the Tories. The resulting recriminations of both parties did nothing to solve the great problem of supplying William's army in the Netherlands, though the Bank of England proved able to assist sufficiently to tide it over the summer. Clearly, however, even Whig financial magic could not sustain a further major campaign in 1697.[9]

Though the problem posed by the national finances was sufficiently daunting, it was not the only difficulty facing the Whigs. Since the general election, Sunderland had given continued cause for alarm by backing the Board of Trade Bill and encouraging the foundation of the Land Bank. His continued assurances to the Ministry that he was 'more than ever for the Whigs' found them deeply sceptical; 'when the fox is abroad look to your lambs' advised Russell tersely. In face of their other difficulties, however, they could not afford to break with the King's favourite, and by swallowing their resentment they remained conciliatory; early in September Sunderland reported to Portland that he had found Shrewsbury, Somers, Montagu and Russell 'tractable' or even in 'very good humour'. By their dissimulation the Whigs hoped to gain Sunderland's co-operation in the next session, especially over tactics to discredit the Tories by making further capital out of the Jacobite scare.

The general excitement aroused by the assassination plot was given a new stimulus in June by the arrest of Sir John Fenwick, one of the principals and leader of the militant English Jacobites. Before his seizure Fenwick succeeded in bribing a witness to leave the country, and the one remaining witness to overt treason produced by the Crown was insufficient, under the recently passed act, to secure conviction. Normal legal methods failing, the Ministry was determined to stage a political trial by means of a bill of attainder. Fenwick's behaviour in captivity added venom to the Ministry's political motive, for in a so-called confession he named as his collaborators several members of the government, including Shrewsbury, Russell and Godolphin. The last, much disturbed, was encouraged by Sunderland and the Junto to offer his resignation, and he did so under the impression that it would be refused as a gesture of the King's continued confidence in him. His offer was, however, accepted; the Junto's long-standing desire for his removal was thus easily accomplished. Their decision to proceed against Fenwick by attainder was not expected to have the same co-operation from Sunderland, but the Whigs were convinced that the measure gave a good opportunity for a massive show of force and party unanimity in Parliament. Somers assured Shrewsbury that 'though your Grace and Mr Russell are named, yet the charge is upon the whole body of the Whigs'. Fenwick had provided the excuse, which the Junto siezed eagerly, for making his prosecution a party rally.[10]

Accordingly, on 6 November Russell laid the subject before the Commons, which had little hesitation in resolving that Fenwick's accusations were ill founded. The bill of attainder itself, however, met vehement Tory opposition. Harley stood vigorously beside his friends, describing the bill as a contrivance to circumvent justice for political ends. But more surprising than such resistance were several important abstentions or defections among the ministerial ranks. Sunderland's lack of enthusiasm for the attainder was taken as confirmed when Trumbull absented himself from a crucial vote. Also conspicuous by absence was Attorney-General Thomas Trevor; while Sir Richard Onslow and Thomas Pelham, a member of the Treasury Board, voted for Fenwick on their consciences. But on an issue apparently affecting national safety the Ministry carried a great majority of its party, and the decisive vote on 25 November gave the bill a comfortable 189 votes to 156.[11] Such displays of conscience as those of Trevor, Onslow and Pelham were rare among the Whigs; and on the Tory side Fenwick received solid support, even from the handful of followers of Leeds who still sometimes voted with the government.

In a series of votes since the plot the Ministry had established a hold on the Commons, and it exploited that House during the remainder of the session. The King was pleased and relieved when the Commons was induced to make a grant of over £500,000 to pay arrears accrued on the Civil List since 1690. And Montagu at one stroke provided payment for some of the government's more pressing debts and secured the permanence of the Bank of England, despite some grumbling from Foley and his friends, by piloting through a bill by which the Bank grafted on to its capital a large sum of departmental securities, receiving in return for this service 8 per cent interest and statutory protection against possible future rival joint-stock banks. The failure of the Land Bank the previous summer thus provided the last occasion on which the Bank of England's hegemony was seriously challenged; Harley, despite his discontent at the suspected sabotage of his project by Whig City interests, was in later years at the Treasury to respect the unique position of the institution which Montagu had created and maintained for the furtherance of national credit and Whig domination.[12]

The clear advantage which the Ministry established in the Commons during the foregoing session was reflected in further ministerial changes between April and June 1697. Montagu became First Lord of the Treasury, formally taking the place vacated by Godolphin, whose former functions he had been exercising for several months. Somers was raised to Lord Chancellor with a barony in his family name, and Russell became Earl of Orford. Only the appointment of Sunderland as Lord Chamberlain introduced a jarring element.

With these promotions the prestige of the Junto as leaders of the Whig party was at its highest point. By the autumn of 1696 at the latest they had evolved the practice of almost daily meetings during parliamentary sessions, usually at the house of one or other minister; to these meetings other leading Whigs were invited as necessary. When tactics needed to be communicated to the Junto's followers prior to activity in Parliament, larger meetings were convened at the Rose tavern. Beyond the walls of Westminster the Junto were assiduous in social and political intercourse with their leading sympathisers, especially in financial and literary circles. The most famous of the clubs they patronised, the Kit Cat, grew out of a pre-Revolution society founded by Somers and Jacob Tonson, a bookseller, and continued to be a political and social centre for Whig politicians and literary men. The success with which the Ministry had lately established its control over a difficult House of Commons reflected the highly effective structure of command and persuasion embodied in conclaves, larger political meetings and clubs. By these means the Ministry held together a party which now monopolised all offices except those occupied by Dutch courtiers and the followers of Leeds and Sunderland. Despite the unofficial nature of their organisation, the Whigs acted in Parliament for the most part in so unified and purposeful a way as to lead nineteenth-century historians to suppose that government by party had already arrived. The judgment was superficial but nevertheless understandable. That government should consist of a party was still far from general acceptance, though the Whigs often came close to acting as though they supposed otherwise.

Yet at a time when the Whig party was about to face an entire change in the mood of Parliament, due to external circumstances, it was in some respects ill equipped to meet this change. The monopoly of policy making and of party organisation by a few men did not pass without resentment by many who, though impeccably Whig, were excluded from the inner circle. Such feelings were particularly marked among the greater landowners, who were closer in social standing to the Harleys and Foleys than to Montagu or Somers. Among such men the ministers retained the reputation of being less interested in public or party service than in self-aggrandisement. James Vernon, who as Under-Secretary and friend of Shrewsbury had much opportunity for observing his colleagues' actions, once wrote 'that the union and strength of the party appears in nothing so much as in personal respects and a care one for another'. But the extent to which the Junto were willing to push themselves and their immediate associates forward, even at the expense of other Whigs, indicated that there existed a narrower as well as a wider conception of the party membership. And when justifiable resentment was aroused by such action, the ministers' habit of dismissing such feelings as doubtful loyalty to the party did nothing to smooth ruffled feelings. Unwillingness or failure to pursue immediately and enthusiastically the measures devised by the leaders was regarded by the latter as particularly reprehensible, to be dealt with by exclusion, in fact if not in appearance, from the party's inner counsels. Shrewsbury often felt this exclusion, or at least the failure of his opinions to carry any weight. But Shrewsbury was shielded, by his status and by the King's preference for him, from the worst excesses of the Junto's intolerance. His relative immunity did not extend to his friend Vernon. On one occasion when the latter made a recommendation to the Treasury Board for an appointment which he desired, he was forced to report to Shrewsbury: 'I found a very great coldness in

Mr Montagu and Mr Smith, and I understand by Sir Thomas Littleton
. . . that it arises from a jealousy they have of me, as if I were neither
their friend nor cared for the party.' Another moderate Whig who
chafed at the Junto's control was Thomas Trevor, whose vote for
Fenwick had marked not only a distaste for the procedure of attainder
but also a disillusionment with his dictatorial colleagues which was
more strongly felt than Vernon's. Although changes of party became
rarer after 1696, Trevor was to drift into the Tory camp under the
influence of Harley.[13]

The Harley–Foley group was already irretrievably lost; it remained
to be seen whether the remainder of the Whig party would continue to
hold together despite internal and external stresses. An initial disadvantage, though one apparently unperceived or underrated by the
Junto ministers, lay in the weakening of their personal contact with
the House of Commons by the transfer of most of them to the House
of Lords. In 1696 the succession of Wharton to his father's barony
removed his robust and powerful personality from the lower house.
With the subsequent elevation of Russell, three of the Junto were now
gone, so that in future the party leadership in the Commons would not
be of the same calibre as in the past. Hardworking and loyal workers of
the second rank, such as Littleton and Smith, and even so brilliant a
debater as Montagu, did not make up for the loss of Wharton's organis-
ing ability or Russell's prestige. The new weakness, already evident to
some extent in Wharton's absence during the 1696–97 session, was to
become more pronounced after the Treaty of Ryswick was signed in
September 1697, and it brought about in the minds of English taxpayers
a strong conviction that the cost of William's army, which the Whigs
had so long persuaded them to maintain, was no longer necessary.

The Junto's response to anticipated problems in the Commons was
their usual one: to desire a further demonstration of their strength at
court. From the Junto's point of view the promotions of the spring of
1697 had two serious drawbacks: the appointment of Sunderland
despite his antiministerial gestures of the last two sessions, and the
continued failure to provide a senior post for Wharton. Sunderland's
possession of a household post was a direct challenge to party hegemony. Government was still the King's, and William was beginning to
realise that this fact needed a more explicit demonstration. The Ministry
not only had excluded all but a handful of Tories but also was coming
dangerously close to demanding the removal of court followers, of
whom the most prominent remaining in high office were Sunderland's
nominees. Already a court party in the Commons, such as William
and Sunderland had envisaged, had ceased to be a reality; for the
distinction between court and Whigs became blurred in practice, and
placemen were losing their corporate identity by merging largely into

Whig government.* The only outcome of excluding courtiers from office altogether would be that the Junto, having made themselves indispensable to William in wartime by their parliamentary and financial expertise, would continue and increase their control in peacetime. Since coming into power the Junto had in fact served William well, but the price they demanded, monopoly of government, was to prove too high. They chose to pursue their ambition to its logical conclusion: the removal of Sunderland from his newly acquired post, together with his men.

The first step in the campaign was to obtain the removal of Trumbull and thus to leave the way clear at last for the appointment of Wharton. On 1 December Trumbull resigned, alleging harassment from his colleagues, but the vacant post was given to Vernon.[14] The Junto now decided to declare open war on Sunderland, and the opportunity to strike him down occurred soon after the meeting of Parliament on 3 December, on the army issue. For many weeks both government and parliamentarians had been aware that the great question of the session would be the continuance or otherwise of the professional army which had been greatly expanded in the war. Given the King's lifetime of building up power with which to resist France, and given also the average English country gentleman's prejudices against a standing army in peacetime, there was, in Harley's words, 'very little prospect of moderate councils'. On such an issue every chance existed that the Tories could oppose the government with the assistance not only of uncommitted Members but also of even some defectors from the Whigs, for there was in that party an element which was not sufficiently emancipated from its pre-Revolution associations to follow the court line on so emotive an issue. Strenuous efforts were made by the Ministry to win over its recalcitrant supporters before the session. But despite all such exertions, and contrary to the earnest request of the King in his opening speech, a reduction of the army was successfully proposed by Harley on 10 December and confirmed by votes on succeeding days, the size of the surviving force being fixed at 10,000 men. Furthermore, the debates were accompanied by Tory attacks on Sunderland as the presumed adviser of the King's speech. The Junto seized gratefully the opportunity for an early revenge on the author of their recent humiliation. When the King personally asked Wharton to engage the Whigs to defend Sunderland he met with a cold refusal. On the 26th, despite all William's efforts, Sunderland resigned, crushed between the two parties.[15]

This usually cool politician so far allowed his resentment rein as

*Burton, Riley and Rowlands write that, so far as division lists from 1696 to 1714 are concerned, 'there seems to have been no substantial Court group independent of the parties' (Burton, Riley and Rowlands, 37).

to encourage his associates Trumbull, Guy and Charles Duncombe, a Tory banker, to launch an attack upon Montagu early in January 1698 for alleged profiteering on the newly-issued but already-depreciated exchequer bills. The intended victim was not intimidated, assuring Shrewsbury grimly that 'you will hear I have carried the war into their own country'. He soon succeeded in showing that Duncombe had himself indulged in fraud upon the bills. Duncombe was sent to the Tower on the 25th; but the matter did not stop there, for Harley and the Tories followed up the assault on Montagu. Again, however, the First Lord defended himself ably, defeating his critics by a large majority in a half-empty House which had lost interest. Notable among the majority was Sunderland's son, Lord Spencer, an ardent Whig now set firmly on the path which was to bring him finally into the Junto itself, after the death of his father.[16]

This triumphant vindication of Montagu, who in the course of the debates had been threatened with impeachment, left the Junto even less willing to reach an accommodation with the King over Sunderland. With a general election due in the summer under the provision of the Triennial Act, the acquisition of office for Wharton and a confirmation of the Junto's victory over Sunderland were essential if a repetition of the poor results of the 1695 election were to be avoided. They pressed Shrewsbury to make way for Wharton by accepting an offer from the King of the office of Lord Chamberlain, which had been left vacant by Sunderland's resignation.

'Were this settled [wrote Montagu] the agreement should be, that we would have but one common interest, the same friends and the same enemies. No measures to be kept, no friendship maintained, with those that are at defiance with the rest.'

This party ideal was countered with an equally determined stand by William, who—though he had gone so far at the beginning of February as to cut off his correspondence with Sunderland in order to avert suspicions of what a later age would call 'a minister behind the curtain'—had by no means given up his desire for his adviser's restoration to office. He confided bitterly to Portland that 'the Whigs maintain that they will not be satisfied, nor will my business be concluded to my satisfaction, if I do not please [Wharton]. Judge to what length they push matters.' He was experiencing, as several of his successors were to do, the full strength of the Whigs' determination to force themselves into every last high office. The King remained adamant, despite badgering by Somers, Orford and Montagu, but he was aware that the Whigs were too useful to be dismissed. Before the end of the session Montagu once again pulled off a financial coup by raising a loan of £2 million from the New East India Company, the Tory-favoured Old Company having managed to offer only £700,000.

William's solution to his dilemma was to retain the Whigs but to offer them no other favour. Parliament was prorogued on 5 July, dissolution following two days later, and the only sign given to the electorate before the King disappeared into Holland was the appointment of Marlborough as a privy councillor and as governor to Princess Anne's son, the Duke of Gloucester—a mild gesture favouring the Tories. Too late Somers counselled a retreat, pressing his friends to withdraw their objection to Sunderland 'though against our inclinations to serve our interests'. William left his Ministry to the decision of the electorate and waited, as Somers reflected, to see 'which faction would have the majority in the new Parliament'.[17]

CHAPTER 4

The Parties Reach Equilibrium 1698-1702

The last years of William III's reign saw two reversals of party fortunes, with the removal of the Whig Ministry complete by 1700 and that of its Tory successor by January 1702. For the first two years, Tory opposition was directed almost as much against the court as against the Whig ministers, though a small number of Tories absented themselves or even voted against their friends when the King himself was the chief object of attack. In the same years a substantial number of 'whimsical' Whigs often joined the Tories on the issues of the standing army and of land grants to royal favourites.* On both sides the deviations from party lines did not take place when attacks upon the Whig ministers as individuals were the issue. Moreover, such deviations largely ceased after 1700, as the two general elections of 1701 re-established Whig party unity.

After the elections which took place during July and August 1698 it was apparent that the Junto, bereft of the King's overt support, had probably lost their hard-won control of the Commons. From Buckinghamshire came news that the county electors and those of the boroughs of Aylesbury and Wycombe had rejected Wharton's candidates, as had those of Oxfordshire and Malmesbury. At Exeter Seymour carried the day after his exclusion in 1695. Montagu and Vernon were forced to exert themselves at Westminster against the opposition of a country Whig challenger, and Vernon noted in several other constituencies 'a strange spirit of distinguishing between the court and country party'. Somers too penned a remark, often quoted, concerning 'the most dangerous division of a court and country party', in the draft of a letter to Shrewsbury; however, after reflection he cut it out from the letter he sent. Montagu concluded that public opinion was 'not very comfortable to us', and Somers endeavoured to explain this phenomenon

*For the 1698 Parliament, I again refer to the careful conclusions of Burton, Riley and Rowlands. The authors show that of 441 Members whose party allegiances can be definitely identified, 88.7 per cent were expected in a contemporary assessment to continue to vote consistently with their known stance in 1696, and that about the same percentage of those Members whose votes are known for 1699 actually did vote consistently with that stance (Burton, Riley and Rowlands, 33–4).

to the King in terms of a nation reacting against high taxation. But to Shrewsbury he gloomily admitted that, if William chose, on another reading of the elections, to consider them a censure of the previously dominant party, there was 'nothing to support the Whigs but the difficulty of his piecing with the other party, and the almost impossibility of finding a set of Tories who will unite'.[1]

It is true that the Tory leaders were often on bad terms with each other, and by no means as reconciled to working together as they were to become after two more years of opposition; but William's decision not to attempt immediately to form a new Ministry probably arose mainly from his usual dislike of having his hand forced and from the reflection that the Junto, with all their faults, appeared to be close to his own point of view in the dominant matter of the moment: the retention of his army. However, he misjudged the ability of his ministers to implement his wishes in the new Parliament with their party divided, for the controversy over the army had caused a number of Whigs to side with the Tories and Old Whigs on this question, in what an early historian called 'an unnatural coalition'. The defectors included not only radical extremists but also much more influential elements. Of this type were the two rebels of the Fenwick issue, Pelham and Onslow, who chose to take a similarly independent stand for the disbandment of the wartime army. From early in 1698 the reinforcement of the Tories by such Whigs had presented an unusual situation, which in turn called forth a new terminology. The term 'country' being found unsuitable to describe a coalition of men divided from each other on most other issues, contemporary observers began to resort to 'opposition' or its variants.* For the next two years it was to be the Whigs rather than their Tory opponents who were internally divided, suffering, so long as the Junto clung to their offices, from the pull of the country's views upon the party.[2]

The combined opposition whose nature had been partially revealed in the last winter was to prove even more serious when reinforced by the public opinion expressed in the general election. Its leader was Robert Harley, for Foley was weakened by his exertions as Speaker and was now within a year of his death. As a former Whig himself, Harley stood in a unique position to hold together the Tories and Whig country element against the court, on nonparty issues at least, in what he liked to call a 'new country party'. Indeed, his chief political instinct was for moderation and therefore for coalition; and he would have preferred a cross-party government, formed from the moderates of both sides,

---

*Thus in January and February 1698 Vernon had 'the opposite party' and 'the opposing party' (*Vernon Corr.*, i, 463 and 466), and Bonet preferred 'those opposed to the court' to his more usual party terminology (Add. ms 30,000B, f. 41). Blathwayt (22 February) had 'the adverse party' (Add. ms 21,551, f. 7).

for he did not favour the extremists of either. But his greater hatred for the Junto, whom he often castigated for their rapacity and doctrinal laxity (real or supposed), was to force him always into the Tory camp, except for brief interludes. His closest connection with the Tories lay through the adaptable Godolphin to the circle around Princess Anne and Marlborough. Though thus no opponent of the royal family as such, Harley regretted, and meant to curb, William III's more authoritarian attitudes and actions. Over the next two sessions this politician was to be seen always in the forefront of the assaults both on the Junto and on William's court.[3]

To meet the challenge of so formidable an opponent the Junto had few remaining assets. Their lack of support from the King was re-emphasised in December 1698 when Shrewsbury at last persuaded William to accept his resignation but was not replaced. Wharton remained unacceptable. Moreover, the behaviour of Montagu was an alarming portent of the Ministry's likely weakness in the lower house. Without the prior knowledge or approval of his friends he had prepared a bolt hole in case of loss of office, by placing his brother in the lucrative office of Auditor of the Receipt until he had need of it himself. The other members of the Junto feared for a time that the action might presage immediate resignation from the Treasury, and strove to prevent this outcome.[4] In the upshot, Montagu stayed on, but he played so cautious a role in the Commons after the attacks on him during the last session that his presence hardly amounted to strength. Above all, the ministers' position was weakened by the continuance of the standing army controversy; for the King's insistence on saving as much as possible of his army had resulted in his neglect, under various pretexts, to carry out fully even the demobilisation specified by the last Parliament. With this in mind the Junto decided, in effect, that the King's wishes and their own safety from Commons attacks could not both be obtained, and they concentrated on the latter.

The opening of the new Parliament in December appeared at first to bear out Somers' forecast of the inability of the Tories to hold together. Several possible Tory contestants for Speaker were canvassed, but with none of them commanding sufficient support the Whig candidate, Littleton, was nominated without opposition. But the disposition of the Chair was, for once, far from being an indication of the subsequent behaviour of the Commons. With the lesson of the Speakership before them the Tories closed their ranks again, and within a few days the lost ground was recovered on the army issue. On Harley's motion it was decided on 17 December to reduce further the establishment to 7,000 men, little objection being offered by the Whigs. Vernon, as the

King's chief spokesman, was deeply critical of his colleagues' failure to support him; 'if after all this', he told Shrewsbury, 'the Whigs be under a disreputation as supporters of any army, they are very unfortunate, since at Court they are blamed for giving it up'.[5]

Immediately after the Christmas recess the Ministry rallied sufficiently to look for a compromise solution acceptable to both King and Commons, but in doing so it failed to please either. The ministers' suggestion was that if the figure of 10,000 men were put before the Commons as 'acceptable service to the King', this figure might be adopted. But the thunderous oratory of Harley, Musgrave and Harley's sometime schoolfellow Simon Harcourt brushed aside by 221 votes to 154 the feeble efforts of the government speakers at the third reading of the Disbandment Bill on 18 January 1699. Subsequent attempts by William to retain the brigade of Dutch Guards which had been with him in England since 1688 were similarly rebuffed. It was generally agreed that the ministers had made insufficient effort to resist the tide, and this impression was confirmed when they failed to prevent the appointment of a commission to investigate William's grants, to Portland and others, of lands which had fallen to the Crown by forfeiture after the rebellion in Ireland.

Pari passu with attacks upon the King proceeded a campaign to destroy the Whig Ministry. The first minister selected for attention was Orford, and before the end of the session the Commons had agreed to address the King complaining of Orford's tenure of two offices— First Lord of the Admiralty and Treasurer of the Navy—and of malversation in the latter department. But those whimsical Whigs who were prepared to attack the court were by no means willing to sacrifice a party leader, and the party as a whole rallied to prevent, by four votes, a direct request for Orford's removal.

The session was summed up by the poet–diplomat Matthew Prior, who thought that the country party was receiving the support of most of the new Members of Parliament, though 'most of them are and always will be Whigs'. The Tories, he observed, were well under the control of their leaders in keeping up pressure upon the court (they needed no encouragement to attack the Ministry). The army and forfeiture debates marked an important stage in the Tories' continued progress towards the regular practice of opposition as a political party.[6]

Immediately after the prorogation the Junto pressed the King in person for a strengthening of Orford's position at the Admiralty Board, by the ejection from it of his Tory rival, Admiral George Rooke. On the King's refusal to dismiss Rooke, Orford resigned. Other changes then followed which indicated William's intention to strengthen the court element in the Commons, by dismissing recently intransigent office holders and by appointing in their stead such Tories as were prepared to act with the Ministry out of loyalty to the King. The policy necessitated scraping the barrel. The vacant Secretaryship of State was filled by the Earl of Jersey, a diplomat and brother of the King's former mistress, Elizabeth Villiers. Pelham was punished for his dalliance with the opposition by the omission of his name from a new commission of the Treasury. A court tract attacked the opposition in both the present and preceding Parliaments as comprising 'Jacobites, Republicans and discontented murmurers' who 'forget their natural enmity, to satisfy their common lusts'.[7] The general drift of the King's intention was clear: another attempt at a government which would include the more moderate members of both parties.

William realised, however, that the present patched-up Ministry was at best a temporary expedient, and his summer was occupied by a complex of schemes for a more permanent arrangement. All came to nothing. The veteran Cabinet-maker, Sunderland, and his assistant, Guy, were called forth to preside over the negotiations, and even Shrewsbury consented to take part with a view to forming an administration which, it was hoped, would detach Godolphin, Marlborough and the Old Whigs from the Tories without further alienating Somers and Montagu. No enthusiasm was found in most of the persons concerned. Harley professed a polite interest but remained in the country, while Montagu, who occasionally toyed with the idea of alliance with Harley, merely nibbled warily. In the end the only major result of the negotiations was the admittance of Marlborough's brother, George Churchill, to the Admiralty Board.

In truth the ubiquitous Guy's intrigues were of little value because they left the attitude of Members of Parliament out of account. Throughout the summer the Tories were strengthened by a generally-felt indignation at the uses to which the King had put forfeited Irish lands, details of which were becoming available from the commissioners appointed to investigate the matter. With the House in such a mood, both the Junto and Harley were well aware that no Ministry could withstand the storm to come. Before the opening of the session Montagu, despairing to face another winter with as weak a basis of support as in the last, announced his resignation and took over the office of Auditor in person. He was replaced, as a stopgap, by a Whig of the second rank: the Earl of Tankerville, formerly known as Baron Grey of Werk. On the eve of Parliament, William was reported to have dined with his sometime *bête noire*, Rochester, but if this was a political gesture nothing followed from it for the moment.[8]

'Whigs and Tory are, as of old, implacable,' wrote Prior early in the session. With the removal of Montagu, the main object of the Tories' attack was Somers. Hated as the ablest member of the Junto and as the scourge of Tory magistrates, the Lord Chancellor was less open to charges of corruption than Orford or Montagu. But on 4 December the Commons witnessed a full-dress inquiry into the alleged responsibility of Somers and other public figures for the piracies of Captain William Kidd, whom they had financed to catch pirates. The case was slim, the Whigs drew together, and the attack was defeated by a handsome 189 votes to 133. But when the opposition turned their attention to a bill to resume the King's grants of land in Ireland, the ministers' reluctance of the previous year to support their master was repeated or excelled. Montagu, indeed, safeguarded himself from attacks such as that on Somers by frankly supporting the Resumption Bill. At the commitment on 18 January the loyal Vernon tried to save one-third of the resumed grants for the King's use, but he received insufficient support even to divide the House. The bill's passage was made more certain by the addition of 'place' clauses for excluding Customs and Excise officials from the Commons, and for good measure the year's land tax provision was also tacked on before it went to the Lords, to forestall expected opposition there.

Vernon now hoped that 'the Tories would be pacified, though their bill were thrown out, upon condition that the Whigs be discarded', but the matter had now gone too far for such an accommodation. When the Whig Lords, led by Wharton, made spoiling amendments, the Tories and their allies were aroused to fury. William read the danger signals and persuaded some of the bishops to allow the passage of the bill for the sake of peace. Even so, amid scenes of excitement unparalleled in this reign, the punishment of Somers and Portland as the presumed advisers of the King was called for in the Commons. Somers, as before, was sufficiently well supported to elude the attack. But Portland, left to his fate by the Whigs, was more severely handled; indeed, it was no less influential a whimsical Whig than Devonshire's son, Hartington, who successfully moved for an address calling upon the King to remove foreigners from his Councils. To prevent further attacks William prorogued Parliament on 11 April. On the same day he ordered a review of the justices of the peace on Somers' list. A fortnight later, Somers himself was dismissed.[9]

For two sessions during which both King and ministers had been constantly attacked, though for different reasons, the ordinary business of government in the Commons had been carried on only by the good offices of the opposition leaders. Discussing the matter with Shrewsbury, Vernon was of the opinion that

'. . . what your Grace observes of the behaviour of the Whigs, that even while they were discountenanced, the success of affairs in Parliament was in a great measure, owing to them, since it was in their power to obstruct them if they would; may of late, too, be said of the Tory party'.

But a government which relied on the goodwill of the opposition for supplies, and on a Ministry powerless to prevent legislation brought in by the opposition, called for drastic readjustment. Some months were to pass, however, before William reluctantly conceded the logic of a situation in which, though he remained theoretically free to appoint ministers, he was forced to choose the leaders of the opposing party after sustaining continual defeat in the Commons. A second summer of negotiation was needed to convince him that there was no alternative.

For the opening stages of this negotiation Sunderland was once more called forth to act as broker, and before the King's usual summer visit to Holland some concessions were made by the court side. To ensure the reversal of Somers' ejections of Tory justices the Great Seal was given to a Tory, Nathan Wright, who took the title of Lord Keeper; but the dissolution of Parliament for which the Tories were pressing remained a bargaining point.[10] At his departure William was probably still not decided whether to appoint a full Tory Ministry, but during his absence the death of Princess Anne's son, the Duke of Gloucester, made it imperative to pass legislation settling the further succession, after Anne, in the Protestant House of Hanover. Such a project, however, was by no means certain to be fulfilled if the House of Commons remained in the mood of its last session. Thus the King's return to England on 20 October was immediately followed by a meeting with Rochester, Godolphin and Harley. A possibly even more crucial meeting took place between William and Harley alone, in which the latter was called upon to answer for a new Commons' part in the settlement of the succession. Harley's price was a high one. Nothing short of further limitations on the power of the Crown, such as had been envisaged in the list 'introductory of new laws' drawn up by the committee which framed the limiting clauses in the Declaration of Rights, would now satisfy the Tories' fears of putting themselves under the rule of an unknown monarch; and the only consolation which Harley could offer William in regard to such limitations was that they need not take effect during his own reign. With this promise the King had to be satisfied, and the basis for passing an Act of Settlement was thus laid.

Within a few days new appointments followed. On 5 November the office of Secretary of State, which had already been made vacant by the removal of Jersey to become Lord Chamberlain, was filled by Sir Charles Hedges, a nominee of Nottingham, though the King jibbed at Nottingham himself after recent opposition. A week later Rochester became Lord Lieutenant of Ireland and Godolphin took his seat at the head of a reconstituted Treasury Board. For Harley was reserved the management of the Commons, as Speaker. To facilitate the new Ministry's control, Montagu was removed from the House by elevation to a peerage as Baron Halifax. Of the former Whig Ministry only the moderate Vernon now remained in an important office, to signify, nominally at least, that the King had succeeded in preventing the formation of an entirely Tory administration.[11]

That a dissolution of Parliament did not follow for a further six weeks may probably be attributed to news which reached London on 1 November of the long-awaited death of Carlos II of Spain, who left his vast possessions in Europe and the Americas by testament to Louis XIV's grandson, Philip of Anjou. Louis thereupon renounced a treaty concluded with William earlier in the year for partitioning the Spanish Empire between the Dauphin and the imperial candidate, a treaty which had succeeded an earlier one of 1698 assigning most of that Empire to the Prince of Bavaria, who had subsequently died. Though William was aghast, the Tories' first reaction was to welcome the new development, for they believed that the partition treaties' assignment of Naples and Sicily to the Dauphin was dangerous to English trade with the eastern Mediterranean; the Duke of Anjou, who stood at several lives' distance from the French succession, seemed unlikely to unite these strategically key territories with France. But though William lamented that his new Ministry was unaffected by French bad faith he accepted the inevitable; and on 19 December 1700 the expected dissolution was finally announced.[12]

Most accounts agree on substantial Tory electoral gains, with thirty former Whig Members failing to secure their return. This in itself did not represent a large enough swing to give control to the Tories, but the pattern of voting in the Commons was to show that a decisive majority of new Members was on the Tory side on most occasions. Among the new men returned on this occasion were one Tory and one Whig of unusual abilities who would play a major role in politics for nearly half a century to come, namely Henry St John and Robert Walpole. The Tory victory was signalised in contest for the Chair. To oppose Harley's candidature the Whigs put forward Sir Richard Onslow, a popular Member and a frequent opponent of the Junto during the last three sessions; thus they emphasised the re-establishment of unity in the party. But the Tories did not repeat the mistake of divided counsels which had given Littleton the Chair in 1698, and Harley was elected by 249 votes to 125.[13]

Members were in a sober mood in January 1701, with news coming in that the Dutch troops manning 'barrier' fortresses in the Spanish Netherlands were being disarmed by the French, nominally on behalf of Philip. There was still, however, a strong disposition among Tories to censure William for concluding treaties without recourse to Parliament. Voltaire was to remark of this time that the English, 'in whom the fury of the spirit of party sometimes extinguishes reason, were crying out at one and the same time against William, who made the treaty, and Louis XIV, who broke it'. When the King communicated an appeal from the States General for English ships and men, the Commons agreed by unanimous resolution to honour the commitment. But when the Tory Jack Howe opened the attack on the partition treaties on 15 February, William's cause was defended only by Vernon. On 29 March Portland was voted guilty of high crimes and misdemeanours for his part in negotiating and signing the second treaty. Such was the anxiety of the Junto not to involve themselves in Portland's cause that the motion passed with little objection, though a similar motion against Somers, for applying the Great Seal to the treaty, was opposed by the Whigs and narrowly rejected on the ground that the former Chancellor had acted only out of duty to the King. William, justly incensed at the behaviour of the Whigs to Portland, now ensured that the Tories were given particulars of the 1698 treaty which made it clear that not only Somers but also Orford and Halifax had been aware of the negotiation's details. On 14 April all three men were impeached.[14]

On 1 March the Commons took up the succession question. Foremost in the minds of most Tories was the opportunity to complete the programme of limitations on the Crown which had been frustrated by the Whigs in the drawing up of the Declaration of Rights, had been partially carried out by the Triennial and Treason Acts, and now stood in need of supplementation in the light of further experience of William's rule. Thus when Spencer rose on the 5th to propose the settlement of the succession on Princess Sophia of Hanover and her descendants, Harley suggested, as had Falkland on 29 January 1689, that consideration of the succession should be preceded by consideration of limitations. The House then passed resolutions stating that under the proposed settlement all Privy Council matters should be discussed in the full Council, with participants signing for their decisions, and that no foreign national might be a councillor, Member of Parliament, holder of civil or military office, or possessor of land granted by the Crown. On the 10th more points were added, including the provisions that the Hanoverian monarchs should not involve the realm in war to aid their foreign possessions without the consent of Parliament, and that royal pardon should not be pleadable by impeached persons. Three days later final clauses were added for preventing Crown officers or pensioners from sitting in the Commons, and for ensuring the appointment of judges during good behaviour, removable only by addresses from both Houses. It was the Tories and their leader, Harley, despite the latter's tenancy of the Chair, who demanded most of the limitations. But the testimony of the Prussian Resident in London, Bonet, makes it clear that, contrary to later Whig assertions, various limiting clauses received the support of a number of Whigs too. As often, on such issues, old party instincts triumphed over new party tactics.[15]

Thus far, the Whigs had been subdued. They were given their opportunity by the heel dragging of some Tories in the voting of war contingency supplies. The first rally came on 7 May, with the appearance of a petition from the Grand Jury of Kent asking the Commons to 'have regard to the voice of the people! that our religion and safety may be effectually provided for'. The petitioners present were imprisoned, but in succeeding weeks the Junto organised an extensive campaign encouraging constituents to protest against Tory lack of support for William's treaty commitments. In their attempts to discredit the Ministry the impeached men were aided not only by public opinion but also by the House of Lords, in which they were already exercising the talents for management that they had so often displayed in the lower house. Moreover the King himself, despite his recent displeasure with the Whigs, was not minded to see his best war ministers punished further. Somers and Orford were given the formality of a trial and acquitted, and the impeachments of Halifax and Portland were hurriedly dismissed by the Lords on 24 June when Parliament was prorogued. In private, some Tories promised bitterly to revive the impeachments before the voting of supplies in the next session.[16]

But it was by no means certain that the King would allow the existing House of Commons to meet again. True to his policy of letting neither party obtain complete dominance he had refused to remove leading Whigs from the Privy Council. By the end of the session he was even less inclined to accede to Rochester's request for the dismissal of some Whigs who remained in office, headed by Vernon. For meeting the essential needs of a government likely to be soon at war the Tories were in no way as helpful as the Whigs had been in the late war. To their relative lack of enthusiasm was added, in William's eyes, an element of personal insult when the Ministry proved unable to restrain its followers from reducing by nearly £200,000 the Civil List granted to him in 1698 and applying this sum instead to war supplies. Nor, despite this failure, had the new ministers proved less high-handed than the old in dealing with William. On one occasion Rochester, as reported by Jersey, 'took the liberty to tell the King that princes must not only hear good advice, but must take it'. Gone were the days when the Tories had been courtiers. If William was forced to hear the doctrines of 1680 and 1688 from any ministers, he might well wish to choose those men whom experience had shown to be capable of obtaining what was dearest to him: the means of opposing France. Though he went to Holland without making any changes, he was in no pleasant frame of mind towards the Tories.[17]

Cut short by prorogation, the quarrels of the session were revived throughout the summer in a furious war of pamphlets. To the cynical amusement of their opponents, the Tories defended their recent proceedings in the case of petitioners by a rigid interpretation of the rights and privileges of the House of Commons. In addition to this they put forward an elevated view of the ministerial role which was well in keeping with Rochester's own, criticising the king's right to appoint men unacceptable to the Commons. The most celebrated example of this genre, *A Vindication of the Rights of the Commons of England* by a Tory Member, Sir Humphrey Mackworth, denied that ministers could plead the king's command to justify their actions and firmly insisted upon ministerial responsibility to Parliament; with this popular manifesto the Tories may be said to have reached full independence of monarchy as a party. Confronted by such arguments the Whig polemicists felt constrained to reaffirm their party's priority in the holding of Whig principles and to throw doubt upon the recent conversion of their rivals: ' 'Tis urged on behalf of the Party', stated one tract, 'that they have renounced their former Tory principles . . . and that instead of submitting all things to royal will and pleasure, they are now for depressing the prerogative and exalting the power of the Commons . . . 'tis more probable that they dissemble.' As to the Tories' attitude to the Protestant succession, maintained the same writer, one point was still clear: the Jacobites looked to the Tories rather than to the Whigs.[18]

More difficult to answer than the claim to share principles which the Whigs believed to be their own was the Tories' renewed affirmation that the Whigs had themselves adopted Tory principles. The case was best stated in Charles Davenant's *The True Picture of a Modern Whig*, in which the 'Modern Whig' is made to ask:

' . . . what have we in us that resembles the Old Whigs? They hated arbitrary Government, we have been all along for a standing army, they desired Triennial Parliaments and that Trials for Treason might be better regulated, and 'tis notorious that we opposed both those bills.'

Such arguments were hard to refuse directly, and the most famous of Whig tracts at this time relied upon counterattack. Somers' *Jura Populi Anglicani* took as its nominal theme the case of the Kentish petitioners, portrayed as the representatives of the nation mistreated by a faction in Parliament. Upon the combination of Tories and Old Whigs Somers poured scorn: 'It is methinks hard to say how a faction blended with such a number of names noted for their inveteracy to the true Tory-principles can be called a Tory party.' As to the Tories' dalliance with the Commons' rights, Somers maintained that the House of Commons was for the moment in the hands of the Tories, but that the rights of the people of England were still in the keeping of the Whig party.

The Whig appeal to the people was accompanied by a brisk campaign to obtain petitions calling for a dissolution. Nor did the Junto neglect to put their arguments to the King. Somers argued that, whatever may have been the case in 1698, public opinion was now alive to the danger of war; the pull of the country would no longer split the Whigs and prune the armed services. William, however, at first professed himself unconvinced, 'the Tories giving him great hopes, and making him great promises'; and even Sunderland, who had reached an understanding with Somers on the promise of a withdrawal of Whig objections to his holding office, could only reinforce Somers' arguments and await the royal decision.[19]

In September, Marlborough signed the treaties of the Grand Alliance on behalf of Britain, and in the same month Louis XIV announced, upon the death of James II, that France would recognise his son as James III. With the last factor to influence public opinion, William came to his decision, which was to go to the country for a new House of Commons but to retain the existing Ministry for the moment. A complication arose when he barely managed, by three votes, to carry the Privy Council with him, with Godolphin, Pembroke, Wright, Jersey and Hedges arguing against dissolution; and when Godolphin resigned he was replaced by a moderate Whig, the Earl of Carlisle. The dissolution, which was proclaimed on 11 November, came as a serious shock to most Tories, even though no further changes took place at once. That the King intended to weaken them rather than to turn at once to the Whigs was little consolation. Tory opinion hardened as the shock of dissolution wore off and even Harley, though theoretically in favour of moderate government, could not afford to give sanction to the King's action and still retain his connection with his friends. When William attempted to retain him as court nominee for Speaker he refused, retiring to prepare for his re-election and to contest the Chair against a court candidate.[20]

Though hurriedly called and ill prepared, the general election served William's antiparty purposes better on the whole than might have been expected, with Tory setbacks but no excessive gain for their opponents. The Whigs found time to publish a 'black list' of 167 Members of the late Parliament. Prominent among the defeated Tories were Musgrave and Howe, who were again ousted from their respective seats at West-morland and Gloucestershire. Musgrave fell back as before on one of

Seymour's constituencies, Totnes. Howe and Davenant, also excluded, were for the moment less fortunate, notwithstanding that one observer thought that in the former case 'his party will bring him in somewhere, not to lose the effect of his voice in the House'. The conjunction between Tories and some dissident Whigs which had often been visible in the last two elections came to an end, and the reunion between ex-ministerial Whigs and their country fellows made for a clearer party division. At Westminster, John Dutton Colt, the maverick Whig, was this time backed by the Junto and was returned with Vernon against two Tories. And in the Wiltshire and Dorset constituencies, where the Junto's recent critic the Earl of Shaftesbury campaigned actively on behalf of his party, his nominees successfully contested against Tories.[21] Both sides claimed a majority, but the Whigs' estimate of a net gain of thirty seats was probably near the truth and brought them close to equality.*

The election was followed by the dismissal of the remaining Tory ministers, Hedges on the eve of Parliament's meeting, and Rochester a month later. But William hesitated to bring in any member of the Junto, preferring for the moment less important Whigs. The near-equality in the Commons was confirmed when Harley obtained the Chair by four votes, against Littleton.[22] And early in 1702 the Tories were able, by the narrowest possible margin of 188 votes to 187, to carry Hedges' bill imposing an abjuration oath on Members of Parliament, office holders and clergy, a measure now thought necessary to prevent the Whigs from making party capital out of Louis's recognition of 'James III'. The Whigs' defeat occurred on their suggested amendment to make the oath voluntary, and thus to deny to many Tories the comfort which arose from their belief that taking a compulsory oath involved no violation of conscience.[23]

The resentments of both parties came to a head on 26 February in a series of close-fought votes in which the Whigs, on the whole, came off best. From noon until eight in the evening the Commons debated a surprise motion brought by the young St John attempting to revive the last session's impeachments. In an uncomfortably full House the Whigs prevailed on the main issue by 235 votes to 221. Several further motions were thereupon discussed and decided in an angry atmosphere; the Tories succeeded in obtaining an endorsement of their imprisonment of the Kentish petitioners, but the Whigs took the edge off this success by another motion to affirm the right of subjects to petition for

*A modern attempt to settle the size of the parties is the estimate by Dr H. L. Snyder of 271 Tories and 241 Whigs, a net gain of thirty-two seats for the latter ('Party Configurations', *BIHR*, xlv (1972) 43). In practice the Tory majority was decreased by William's post-election shift towards the Whigs and by the Tories' customary inferior ability to obtain good attendance.

the calling, sitting or dissolving of Parliament. Yet another Whig motion asserted the right of impeached persons to speedy trial. In these contests the as yet uncommitted new Members in the House, on the whole, espoused the Whig side and took a stand against the revival of impeachments at a time of national peril; but the closeness of the division results held out the prospect of party deadlock in the future, to the detriment of further government business, unless the King brought himself to take a more decisive stand.[24]

Before any new parliamentary crisis could arise, however, the state of politics was drastically changed by the death of William, on 8 March, after a riding accident and a short illness. His last Parliament had been called in an attempt to temporise and thereby to quell the party strife; but the outcome scarcely justified the latter hope, and had he lived it seems likely from the steps he had already taken that he would have been forced once again to espouse a party by dismissing the remaining Tories and summoning the Junto to cope with the renewal of war. With the accession of Queen Anne the Tories' prospects revived dramatically, but it remained to be demonstrated how far they would live up to her expectation that they would be an old-style court party.

CHAPTER 5

The Tories and the Triumvirate 1702-05

In Queen Anne's reign the strife of the parties reached its height.* The dispute was fanned by the new immediacy of the succession question, now that only one frail life stood between Britain and a disputed succession; for even if the provision of the Act of Settlement were carried out—itself by no means a certain outcome—Jacobite sentiment in Scotland might provoke a civil war. The revival of war with France, which was to occupy all but the last year of the reign, again added the conflicting interests of 'landed' and 'monied' elements to the armoury of party weapons. And a party issue which had been largely dormant in William's reign, namely the active political rivalry of Church and Dissent, was early joined with the others in the conditions of the new reign. The strengthening of parties brought about equally strong reactions. From 1703 Anne rivalled her predecessor in trying to dampen party zeal. When her efforts ceased to have much effect, in 1708, the country at large acted as a check, defeating the Whigs decisively at the polls in 1710 and splitting the Tories at the zenith of their power in 1713–14.

Anne's influence was achieved not so much through a court party—which was tried and again failed—as through powerful ministers who understood Britain far better than the Dutch-born William ever had. The Queen, who ascended the throne in March 1702, had hitherto played relatively little part in the politics of her time and was almost unknown outside the small circle of her court. However, this circle included in Marlborough and Godolphin, his kinsman by marriage, the greatest soldier and one of the greatest finance ministers of the day. Apart from her husband, the genial and incompetent Prince George, Anne was closer to no-one than to the Marlboroughs, though she also retained a feeling of family solidarity with Rochester, who was now,

---

*Professor Robert Walcott's analysis of this reign on the Namieran multi-party model (in *English Politics*) was never widely accepted by others who were closely acquainted with the sources for the early eighteenth century, and has been largely rejected by Plumb (*Growth of Political Stability*), Holmes (*British Politics*) and Speck (*Tory and Whig*) as well as by a number of other books and articles.

with Clarendon, her closest blood relation apart from her half-brother 'James III'. Though she was not, in years, past the age of child bearing, it was not likely since the death of the young Gloucester that she would produce any further heir. The personality of the new monarch was by common consent a warm one, though she possessed a fair share of the Stuart wilfulness and determination to assert her rights. The result of this combination of traits was that, though she could not be driven by politicians whom she disliked, she was very willing to be led by those whom she trusted. In the course of her reign she was to trust two men more than others: Marlborough and later Harley. Neither of these two was a strong party man but both had, like herself, a preference for the Tories if forced to choose. The new Queen, like her late sister, had a genuine love of the Church of England, and was hence far more in sympathy with the party which had wholeheartedly supported the Church than she was with that which had so often been associated with Dissent. Anne, however, was by no means a proponent of party behaviour, and as Queen she had no intention of being the head, much less the slave, of either the Whigs or the Tories.

Anne's ideas on filling posts in the government were straightforward. She did not share her predecessor's reluctance to appoint a Lord Admiral and Lord Treasurer. Prince George was destined for the former place, whose business he would increasingly delegate into the hands of his nominal councillor Admiral Churchill. Marlborough was appointed Captain-General and took overall control after a short tussle with Rochester. For the next eight years he lent his authority, as far as political management was concerned, to his friend Godolphin. This able politician had already played an important part in three reigns. His testy disposition and prickly pride were well known to all who had worked with him. His better qualities included his ability to learn by his mistakes, and his conduct was to show that he had not disdained to assimilate the new techniques of government credit developed by Halifax. Godolphin remained without official appointment for two months, awaiting the outcome of Marlborough's court campaign against Rochester and the High Tories. Their beliefs received little more real attention from the new government than from the old. Marlborough intended to make a large British army in the Low Countries the most important part of the war effort, the apex of a triangle which rested on two points at home: the Commons and the Treasury. The House would be managed by Harley, who had been close to Anne's circle for several years and was ready, though in an age of party, to attempt to follow the *cursus honorum* from country to court which had been taken by such predecessors as Strafford and Danby.

The High Church leaders were almost immediately engaged in a struggle with Marlborough to decide who would occupy the second basal angle of the triangle, the Treasury. A determined and well-qualified rival to Godolphin was found in Rochester, who had been at the head of the Treasury Board when the two men had been Charles II's 'Chits'. The struggle turned, ostensibly at least, upon the conduct of war strategy. Against Marlborough's plan to support the Dutch by assisting them to recover their lost barrier fortresses, Rochester adhered to the conventional Tory view that a sea war should be fought by Britain without a major commitment of land forces on the continent of Europe. Not until 6 May, two days after war had been declared upon France, did Godolphin's appointment as Lord Treasurer signify that Marlborough's arguments had prevailed with the Queen.

Godolphin's appointment, however, was for the moment the only major setback to the aspirations of the High Tories. Rochester himself once more became Lord Lieutenant of Ireland, Nottingham took the seals as Secretary for the southern department in place of Manchester, while Hedges came in again to replace Vernon. Nottingham immediately began a sweeping change of the lesser personnel in the Secretaries' office. The appointment of Wright as Lord Keeper of the Great Seal was a guarantee that further purges of Whig justices would follow. With Jersey and Seymour as Lord Chamberlain and Comptroller the scene seemed set for a High Church renaissance in court and office. But two of the lesser appointments, at least, were to prove unsatisfactory to the Tories. Harcourt, Harley's friend who became Solicitor-General, was within three years to prove stronger in his friendship than in his loyalty to the High Church extremists. The other appointment, a more immediate cause of dissatisfaction, was that of Henry Boyle, a Whig who had no objection, as yet, to serving with Tories. Boyle was brought in and protected as Chancellor of the Exchequer by his immediate superior Godolphin, a gesture much appreciated by the City whose assistance in the coming war was essential to any ministry. During their six years together at the Treasury, Godolphin and Boyle struggled not unsuccessfully to repeat and even to exceed the feats of loan raising which had been the key to the Junto's successes during the last war. The Tories, as self-appointed representatives of a landed interest whose duty it was to bear the main burden of taxes to pay interest on war loans, often looked askance at the unholy alliance of Court Tory and Court Whig at the Treasury.[1]

For the moment the appointment of Boyle was little consolation to the Whigs. In the general election which followed the ministerial changes they lost all hope of controlling the Commons for the next three years, and were forced to intensify their already considerable efforts in the Lords. The upper chamber became their stronghold against Tory persecution as well as the platform from which they were to launch attacks upon their opponents during the greater part of the reign. The dissolution, permitted by a statute passed in the aftermath of the assassination plot to take place up to six months after William's death, was announced on 3 July. Anne's speech at the final prorogation expressed her support for the Church and her intention 'to countenance those who have the truest zeal to support it'. The preference of the Queen and the appointment of Tory ministers proved sufficient to sway many results, and the Tories were assured of a majority of well over 100 even before election petitions were considered. Howe triumphantly recaptured his Gloucestershire seat, and Musgrave his seat for Westmorland. County constituencies returned a usual majority of Tories, while in the boroughs the Whigs, especially the Junto, lost heavily. Not at any time since the Revolution had the result of a general election been less in doubt.[2]

Thus, during a summer when Marlborough was fighting his first brilliant campaign in the Low Countries, the Tories at home were preparing up and down the land to carry into statutory effect policies which had lain dormant since 1689, particularly the suppression of Dissent. Under William the dissenters had grown bold, defying the intention of restrictive legislation by taking local and national offices, packing many borough corporations and even becoming Members of Parliament. The Tories' first intention was to rectify this situation, to block legal loopholes and to reduce the strength lent to the Whigs by the political activities of Dissent. In addition the Tories were anxious to bring the Junto to account and further to extend the persecution of the last Whig Ministry by searching inquiries into alleged financial maladministration and corruption. Both aims threatened to undermine Marlborough's war plans from the start, by alienating the City of London; and Godolphin concerted with Harley plans to divert the inquiries in the Commons into fairly innocuous channels as far as possible.[3]

At the opening of Parliament there was no overt rupture between the Tories and the Marlborough faction, for the latter were as yet too insecure to risk a head-on clash. Finch accordingly proposed Harley as Speaker, and no opposition was encountered. After the delivery of the Queen's speech the two Houses stood adjourned for a week while stock was taken of the newcomers to the House of Commons. The disparity between the parties was then taken by the Dutch Resident to be represented in a division on 2 November, when the Commons carried by 189 votes to 81 the motion, which had been narrowly defeated in the last Parliament, that the House of Lords had not given the lower house justice in the matter of the impeachments of 1701. The Whigs might well have thought that such a decisive majority indicated that the matter would not end there, and that the motion heralded a revival of the impeachments; in fact the moderating influences of Godolphin and Harley were successful behind the scenes in preventing such civil disruption in time of war, but Whig activities in the Commons were subdued for much of the session in expectation of an onslaught.

On one matter the Tories could not be restrained in any degree. The great issue of the moment was a growing practice by the dissenters of occasionally taking the sacrament of the Eucharist at their parish church in order to qualify themselves for national or local office under the Test and Corporation Acts. Many churchmen, such as Bromley, felt genuine indignation at a proceeding they considered little short of blasphemous, but the main avowed intention of the Tories was in its nature political. With the recent election campaigns still fresh in their minds, they were determined to cut down the large number of Whig votes given by dissenters, especially in the boroughs. Accordingly, on 4 November the lower house gave leave for Bromley to bring in a bill to punish the offenders. Associated with him in drawing up this bill was St John, who after two years of parliamentary experience was already taking a place among the leaders of the Tories, avowing himself a follower of Harley. His party instincts, like Harley's, were not strong, but he was prepared, in his own words, to 'halloo' the Tory 'pack' to further his own career, revelling in the party political methods which had been developed by the Tories in the parliamentary infighting of the late 1690s. Only a week after the introduction of the Occasional Conformity Bill, St John was again associated with Bromley in bringing forward a report on financial malpractices alleged against the Paymaster-General, Lord Ranelagh, to which were added a few days later further reports implicating Halifax, as Auditor of the Receipt. The hunt against the surviving Whigs was on, and a new and brilliant star in the Tory galaxy was born.[4]

To counter the threatened persecution of the dissenters and of the late Whig ministers, Marlborough and Godolphin relied on Harley to build up a 'court party' in the Commons. They hoped for the assistance of the Tory and surviving Whig placemen—itself, as events were to show, by no means a fully justified hope—but for the rest they had to rely on the votes of the Whigs, where military matters were concerned, and of moderate Tories who were willing to follow the Speaker's lead in the House.[5] Such a court party, in effect a coalition of amenable Whigs and Tories, needed very careful management; for, as Professor Holmes observes, 'at all times the so-called "Court Party" included a great many politicians whose first obligation on most controversial issues was to their own party, be it Whig or Tory, and not to the Court'. The government could make a court party workable only by avoiding involvement in party issues.[6]

Disaster threatened the court ideal from the start; Parliament sat for a bare four months—long enough to provide for the coming campaign season—before the session was cut short by the ferocity of the Tory attacks. The root of the trouble lay within the Ministry itself, in the views of Rochester and, to a lesser extent, of Seymour. Early in the session Rochester withdrew himself and his followers in the Commons into truculent obstructionism. Fortunately his influence in the lower house was insufficient to obtain the rejection of financial proposals, for which the Whigs voted solidly together with the court. On one occasion, however, when Marlborough's personal income rather than the cost of war was at stake, Tory objections carried the day. The Captain-General had been raised to a dukedom after a successful campaign, but Hedges urged the Commons in vain to implement a suggestion by the Queen that her gesture should be accompanied by a permanent parliamentary grant of £5,000 a year. Even the Ministry's usual Tory supporters such as Howe and Musgrave drew off at the suggestion of so great a gift. and a motion was withdrawn on 15 December. As to the two matters on which all Tories were agreed, the Occasional Conformity Bill and the investigation into peculation, deadlock ensued between the Commons and the Junto-controlled majority in the Lords. Ranelagh was forced to resign his office and was expelled from the lower house; but the charges against Halifax were harder to prove, and after an inquiry he was acquitted by the Lords. To add to the frayed temper of the Commons, the peers returned the Occasional Conformity Bill with wrecking amendments which reduced the proposed fines. Parliament rose unusually early in the year, on 27 February 1703, with the Occasional Conformity Bill marooned and Halifax vindicated.[7]

The termination of the session so abruptly was to allow the removal of Rochester and give less intransigent High Tories time to cool off. Throughout 1702 the Lord Lieutenant had presumed too far upon the goodwill of the Queen his niece. Despite the clear warning implied by his failure to secure the Treasury, he had continued to oppose Marlborough by every means at his disposal. Not only had he encouraged his friends to attempt to thwart Hedges' efforts in the Commons, but he had pursued his favourite policy of a widely flung colonial and sea war by urging Nottingham to equip a naval expedition to the West Indies as soon as possible. Marlborough's patience was at an end, and at the conclusion of the session he persuaded the Queen to insist that Rochester should either take up his hitherto neglected duties in Ireland or resign his office. Rochester chose to resign. This gesture, however, did not signal the end of dissension. Within the Ministry the leadership of the High Church Tories now devolved upon Nottingham, who was on strained terms with Marlborough. Within a few weeks of Rochester's removal the Captain-General was assuring Godolphin that the Secretary would follow the same way if he continued to show sympathy with the intransigent Tories.[8]

For the moment, however, Queen Anne was not likely to take further action unless urgent cause could be shown; time must elapse before she made up her mind to strike down further opponents of her favourite. The chief task of the triumvirs, as Marlborough, Godolphin and Harley were beginning to be called, was to set about retaining as much Tory support as possible for the next session in the Commons by undermining the remaining High Church ministers. One way of doing this was by influencing public opinion, a task which fell mainly upon Harley. In the first months of the reign the Speaker had pointed out to Godolphin the necessity for regular publication of the government's case in the press; at that time he was thinking of Davenant and other usual writers. Soon afterwards, however, Daniel Defoe's *The Shortest Way with Dissenters*, a striking satire on the High Church campaign, revealed the possibility of securing a more powerful pen against the Tory extremists. When Nottingham tracked down Defoe and imprisoned him in Newgate, the Speaker visited him on Godolphin's behalf and struck a bargain: Defoe was to have his fine paid by the Treasury and in return was to enter secret employment to publicise the government's views and to advocate moderate nonparty policies. It was an arrangement, clandestine and highly personal, such as Harley delighted in. Defoe's embitterment by his treatment at the hands of Nottingham made a good foundation for the arrangement. Thus began the now celebrated alliance between the Treasury and Defoe, which resulted in the publication of the triweekly *Review* and in Defoe's opinion-sounding tours of England and Scotland—an alliance of importance in influencing public opinion and in making government sensitive to the forces of that opinion.[9]

A better public image was necessary for the Ministry in the summer of 1703, when opinion in Parliament seemed certain to be roused by military setbacks in Flanders and the West Indies and by the action of the Scottish Parliament in passing a bill threatening to exclude the House of Hanover from the Scottish throne, a move intended to secure a legislative union with England on favourable terms. Godolphin and Harley concerted with Bromley, who was now the Tories' most respected nonministerial Member in the Commons and a moderate in most matters not connected with religion, the government's demands for war supplies. The price of Bromley's support was doubtless the passage of a new Occasional Conformity Bill in the lower house, but the ministers could now safely permit this since they knew that the wind from the court was blowing in a new direction and that the Queen herself, persuaded by Marlborough, intended to prevent Prince George from attending the House of Lords during the debates, an overt signal of her disfavour towards the bill.[10]

Towards the end of October a more detailed scheme for preventing the obstruction expected from Nottingham was put into operation. Hedges was detached from his patron and fellow Secretary and instructed to follow the directions of Harley in the Commons; this arrangement marked Harley as successor to Nottingham as soon as the Queen could be brought to agree to the change. The Secretary's main clash with Marlborough, like Rochester's, now concerned the strategy of the war. During the summer Nottingham had obtained a treaty with Portugal which opened up a new theatre of war in the Iberian peninsula. That the Whigs welcomed the extension of England's war aims to include the conquest of Spain was no immediate recommendation of the new treaty to Marlborough and Godolphin. In later years the two men were to become more and more committed to the war in this theatre, but its immediate effect was to add to their conviction that Nottingham's continuance in the Ministry was becoming unbearable.[11]

Just as the parliamentary session of 1702–03 had made the removal of Rochester certain, so the following one brought about the final downfall of Nottingham and with him Seymour. Supplies were ushered through the Commons by Hedges, Boyle and Harley, but though Bromley honoured his bargain the Tories were otherwise difficult to control. Quickly carrying the Occasional Conformity Bill again, the Commons sent it up to the House of Lords where, despite politic support by Marlborough and Godolphin to avoid a break with the Tories, it was duly rejected outright on the second reading. Following this action, a series of sterile squabbles occupied the two houses. The Tories in the Commons threatened to re-open the quarrel with the ministers impeached in 1701, and the Junto in the Lords retaliated with attacks on Nottingham for his alleged failure to examine properly several persons suspected of being concerned in a recent Jacobite plot in Scotland. The climax of this session, however, was reached in the long-drawn-out debates of the struggle between the upper and lower chambers over the celebrated case of Ashby and White. Originating in the endeavours of Wharton to retain his control of the borough of Aylesbury in face of Tory attempts to disenfranchise Whig electors, this cause resulted after several years of litigation in a judgment by the House of Lords enabling disenfranchised electors to seek redress in the law courts—an outcome warmly opposed by the Tories in the Commons. When Parliament was prorogued on 3 April 1704, in order to break the deadlock between the two Houses, the Aylesbury case threatened to be revived in the following winter and party quarrels seemed likely to occupy all parliamentary time unless the Ministry could show a more united face.[12]

Immediately after the end of the session Marlborough was informed of some threats by Nottingham—of how the Secretary had boasted to his friends that he had the Queen's confidence and that the next Occasional Conformity Bill would be 'tacked' to a money bill to ensure its passing the Lords. At the same time Nottingham himself decided to put his case to the royal judgment and asked Anne to remove the remaining Whigs in office. To Godolphin he remarked ominously that 'the Queen could not govern but by one party or the other', and in face of his ultimatum the Queen was forced to take action. She dismissed two Tory members of the Cabinet, Seymour and Jersey; Nottingham thereupon asked to be relieved of his office and Harley became Secretary of State, with St John replacing the long-serving William Blathwayt as Secretary at War.[13]

The Queen's decision, taken on the advice of the triumvirate, to dismiss the High Tory ministers without making any concession to the Whigs was to be seen within a year to be ineffective in parliamentary terms. The Whigs were tied to ministerial policy only on the religious issue; in other matters they soon began to threaten the withdrawal of their support. And the Tories who remained in support of the government, even placemen, often fell short of ministerial expectations. The main danger for the Ministry lay in the possibility of alienating both parties at once, in which case 'court' voting would shrink to little or nothing. The shrewd Defoe, undertaking the first of his tours to assess public opinion and disseminate ministerial propaganda, wrote:

'. . . all the Whigs of King William's reign expected to have come into play again, and had fair words given them, but they see it was but wording them into a fools' paradise, and now the two ends will be reconciled and overturn the middle way'.[14]

Thus began one of the liveliest sessions of the reign. Before its end Defoe's forecast proved to have some truth, but at first there was little reason for the Whigs to make a show of independence. Compared with its predecessor the campaign of 1704 had provided few grounds for criticising the Ministry, for Marlborough's long march to Blenheim had saved Germany from French invasion, while Rooke had seized Gibraltar as a naval base for Mediterranean operations. Nor was the Occasional Conformity Bill an issue on which the Whigs could afford to try embarrassing the government. This measure went forward as planned in the hands of Bromley, whose Oxford constituents were reported to have warned him on this occasion that if he did not introduce the bill he need not expect to be re-elected. The Tory leaders now had a strong expectation of success. In support of the bill (though not, as it proved, of the tactics proposed for its support) they numbered several members of the Ministry, including Harcourt and St John. The former wrote enthusiastically that 'we shall not fail to do it unless some of our members become Trimmers, which God forbid'. At their usual meeting place, the Fountain tavern in the Strand, 150 Tories resolved early in November to hold up supplies until the bill was passed. In threatening supplies, however, they at last overreached themselves, alienating many even of their own party, so that within less than two months Harcourt himself had become a 'trimmer'.[15]

The method proposed was to 'tack' the Occasional Conformity Bill to a money bill to prevent its otherwise certain rejection by the Lords. On this issue, however, the Ministry could count upon the Court Tories and many other Tories who were not prepared to make a constitutional issue of the bill. There were excellent grounds for accusing the 'tackers' of threatening the passage of war supplies and thus endangering national safety. Against them was thrown every resource of the Ministry, and by an extensive canvass Godolphin and Harley assembled strong support. The Whigs intensified their activities of the last two sessions to bring out every last Member against the bill, gratified by the expectation that with court support they might even expect a victory. The result exceeded their most optimistic hopes. On the second reading in the Commons, on 28 November, a motion to consider the annual grant of the land tax at the same time as the Occasional Conformity Bill was introduced by Bromley and defeated by 251 votes to 134. Among those who voted against the tack were both Harcourt and St John, two white hopes of the High Tories, as well as such expected opponents as Harley and Boyle. The outcome of the debate was hailed with extravagant relief by the Whigs. To Shrewsbury, who had retired to Italy for his health, Somers wrote that 'the court exerted themselves in that matter, for the first time'. He had reason for his satisfaction. He saw, more clearly than the ministers themselves, that they had crossed a Rubicon; they had cut themselves off from the High Church-men, for a long time to come, with little or no chance of reconciliation. The Ministry was now reliant on the Whigs for war supplies. Stocks, which had tumbled in the City on the tack proposal, rose rapidly with its defeat and with the rising expectations of the Junto.[16]

With Whig assistance supplies were passed swiftly, though the ministers found it expedient in view of the mood of the Commons to put off any discussion of the subsidies owed to some of the Allies. The lower house was swiftly locked with the Lords in a further fierce dispute precipitated by Wharton over the Aylesbury electors, but the chief issue by which the Junto now sought to exert pressure on the Ministry was Scottish affairs. During the session of the northern Parliament in 1704 the Security Bill had been passed for the second time, and on this occasion Godolphin had considered that royal assent could not be safely withheld. Both Houses united in blaming him for this advice. In retaliation against the Scots they passed an Alien Act designed to coerce Scotland into accepting the English settlement of the succession, by preventing the import of Scottish staple products and by treating Scottish nationals as aliens. Godolphin, caught in a crossfire from both Tory Commons and Whig Lords, made up his mind that the Whigs must be bought off and represented in the Ministry. In the course of a debate in the upper house he was seen to consult Wharton, Halifax and Somers and, according to a Tory onlooker, he forthwith 'delivered himself entirely into their management, provided they brought him off'. Godolphin's decision to conciliate the Junto was doubtless less abrupt than this account suggests, but he was not a strong party man, and if the Whigs could be quieted on secondary issues while they supported the war effort he would work with them. Somers reflected with satisfaction that the court 'have felt, severely enough, what it is to have one party so great an overbalance for the other, (though it was their own party)'. An administrator by nature, Godolphin had no political purposes except to obtain supplies for Marlborough and to avoid public and private criticism.[17]

Parliament was prorogued on 14 March 1705, and the Triennial Act necessitated an early dissolution. The general election would give the Queen an opportunity to show her displeasure with the tacking Tories. In their wrath after the defeat they had talked of sending for the next in line to the throne, Princess Sophia, to reside in England and prepare to take over her inheritance on the Queen's death. The suggestion of a possible rival in domestic politics was the surest means of infuriating Anne; and with the Queen looking away from the Tories, as well as with Godolphin looking directly towards the Whigs, the Junto began to put out cautious feelers in other directions. Somers, for the first time since his impeachment, allowed himself to be brought to speaking terms with Harley, though the reconciliation lost its rationale when it became public, by arousing Godolphin's jealousy. In any case the Secretary had no intention of meeting the Junto's demands for office; he had another arrangement in mind. For over a year he had been trying to obtain a post of importance for the Duke of Newcastle, who was a more malleable Whig than any of the Junto, and a week after prorogation the Queen took the Privy Seal from its Tory holder, Buckinghamshire, and gave it to Newcastle. Nor did other new appointments reflect Godolphin's desire for a more substantial move towards the Junto, though the electors were left in no doubt of the Tories' disgrace. By changing a few key Lord Lieutenancies the government was able to indicate its preferences; Godolphin himself took over Cornwall from one Tory; another was replaced in Kent by a Whig, Lord Rockingham. At a lower county level there was also an effective change of sheriffs in some areas. But when Godolphin further desired the removal of the Great Seal from the custody of Wright, who was no less disliked by Whigs than Somers had been by Tories, no further action was taken, for the Queen was reluctant to make further major alterations in her Ministry.[18]

Her view was not without much sympathy from Marlborough and was entirely supported by Harley, who believed that the changes already made were sufficient to carry the elections against tackers in favour of moderate Tories and Whigs. 'I am more concerned how to deal with them when they are chosen', wrote the Secretary ominously to Marlborough, 'than under doubt of having a great majority for the Queen and public good, though some people's overzeal does not prove very advantageous.'[19] Although the Ministry presented, for the moment, an apparently solid front against the tackers, this hint of dissension within the triumvirate carried the seeds of its eventual disintegration over the question of alliance with one or other of the parties. In such a situation the Whigs, who for three sessions had been forced to support ministerial policy without reward, found their opportunity for a new drive towards office.

CHAPTER 6

The Whigs and the Triumvirate
1705-08

The elections of 1705 were conducted with extraordinary bitterness. 'Both parties', wrote a Scottish observer, 'are angry to a higher degree than ever I saw them even in the Exclusion time.' Predictably a list of the 'noble Englishmen' who voted for the tack was circulated by the Whigs. The Tory political writers responded by lashing their opponents for undermining the authority of the House of Commons, by the Aylesbury election cases, an argument which had proved useful in an earlier context in 1701. The most effective of Tory pamphlets, *The Memorial of the Church of England*, established the Whigs' alleged disruptive constitutional ends in uncharitable terms. 'The nation had a long time abounded with Sectaries', this work informed its High Church readers, 'who in the preceding century violently overturned both Church and State . . . The sons of those men yet remain, and inherit many of 'em the principles of their fathers.' Nor were the 'trimming' Tories who voted against the tack spared. 'This gracious countenance of the Tory towards the Whigs and fanatics', explained the pamphlet, was supported by a minister who might 'flatter himself that he carries so much weight in his own person, as to be able to turn the scale to which side soever he likes.' But despite such polemics the influence of the court and the reaction of moderate opinion against the tack considerably handicapped the Tories. According to the cautious calculation of Somers, 'the Parliament now chosen may probably prove very good, especially if the court see their interest, which we are told they begin to grow sensible of'. By a modern calculation, 267 Tories and 246 Whigs were returned, but only ninety of the 134 tackers found seats, while the net overall result for the Whigs was a gain of sixty seats. Among the new Whig Members was young William Pulteney, who soon attached himself to the rising group among the younger Whigs, the associates of Robert Walpole.[1]

With such results, the Queen could no longer refuse to make a concesion to the Whigs by further appointments. The former Lord Spencer, who had married Marlborough's younger daughter in 1701 and succeeded his father as third Earl of Sunderland the following year, was the newest adherent of the Junto and was at once given a projected mission to Vienna. With this first appointment of an erratic political genius was linked that of Walpole, who came into the Admiralty Board. However, the Queen believed that these two concessions to younger Whigs were enough; her recent displeasure with the Tories was no match for her rooted aversion for the leading Whigs. When the Junto pressed for the Great Seal to be given to William Cowper, the Whigs' best lawyer after Somers, she would concede only the need for a moderate Tory to replace Wright. Godolphin, under pressure from the Junto lords, backed Cowper's nomination, but the Queen was supported unequivocally by Harley. She had, the Secretary wrote to Marlborough, 'wisely and happily delivered herself from a party, and I believe she will not easily put herself again into the power of any party whatsoever'. Anne's view accorded well enough with Marlborough's own, and he hesitated to press upon her the need to appoint a Whig who, though not one of the Junto, was usually inclined to work closely with them. Thus the Captain-General had to defend himself against the reproaches of the Whigs through their strong advocates, his son-in-law and his wife. For the moment, until Marlborough's support could be enlisted for Cowper, the matter languished.[2]

Meanwhile, intermingled with the question of the Great Seal was that of the Chair of the Commons. Godolphin agreed to adopt the Whigs' candidate Smith in the belief—a correct one as it transpired—that this politician was less extremist than in former years. The Treasurer accordingly assembled and harangued some thirty office holders on the need to vote for Smith. He told them

'. . . that it might be objected that he was of the Whig party, but assured them he found those under that character, though under no obligation to this government, yet to have been hearty friends to it and for supporting Her Majesty's administration'.

The Ministry's support for the Whig candidate arose from the belief of both Godolphin and Harley that, given the near-equality of the parties and the intransigent mood of the Tories, it would be difficult to carry the House against Whig opposition. Nevertheless there remained an uncomfortable gap between the ideas of the two men. Harley feared that the further appointments which the Whigs would inevitably insist upon as the price of their support would be unacceptable, and considered that the government could continue to derive enough support in all reasonable measures from the more moderate men of both parties. It was the policy with which both men had begun, and Harley was to do his best to implement it several years later when he was in Godolphin's place. But Godolphin believed that the Secretary under-estimated both the violence of the Tories and the party discipline of the Whigs, and that any attempt to ignore both parties might leave the

Queen's servants with too little independent support to obtain majorities. Restated from Godolphin's point of view, Harley's intention was to lean on the Whigs in Parliament while the Tories remained recalcitrant, but at the same time to refuse any Whig demand for a share in government.

It was to the Treasurer's view that Marlborough, prompted by his wife, finally acceded in September. The Queen, unable to withstand her favourite's urgent requests, gave way. Before the opening of Parliament her sanction was given to the Treasurer's policy, and as a sign of this the Great Seal was at last delivered to Cowper as Lord Keeper. The Whigs had inserted the thin end of the wedge; the coming session would decide whether the Ministry would continue to follow the line Godolphin had laid down, or would draw back with Harley.[3]

The first session of the new Parliament proved lively, with average attendance higher than at any time since the Convention. The Tories assembled early to show their strength, but Bromley was easily defeated in the contest for the Chair on 25 November, obtaining 205 votes to Smith's 248. A second important vote gave the key chair of the Committee of Elections to Spencer Compton, another of the young men who flocked around Walpole. With Boyle and Smith these men formed the nucleus of a group of court or 'Lord Treasurer's' Whigs. Some Tory office holders who had failed to support the successful Whigs began to be weeded out by Godolphin, and others continued to fall away from him.[4]

The Tories' reaction to the general election and to the government's new approach was an all-out attack, with the particular intention of embarrassing the Ministry by distressing the Queen on the succession question. Their first attempt was made in the House of Lords. On 15 November, Rochester, Nottingham and Buckinghamshire brought forward a series of complaints about the lack of military success in the Low Countries, the dangers of Dissent to the Church of England, and the danger from Jacobites if the Queen were to die suddenly; they concluded with a motion calling for an address to the Queen asking her to invite the Princess Sophia to England. The attempt failed miserably, receiving only fifteen votes in that cautious assembly. But as a bid for the favour of the electoral house the motion showed a good chance of success, for its defeat threw the Princess and her son, the Elector of Hanover, into considerable alarm for the safety of their eventual succession. The Ministry, torn between offending the Queen and offending her successor, did little to allay this alarm.[5]

Very different was the reaction of the Junto, who shortly after this time set up a close correspondence with the court at Herrenhausen, a precaution which stood them in good stead in the following years. Not content with explanations of the impracticability of opposing the Queen's wishes, Somers and Wharton also brought in a bill designed to rival the Tories' bid and to quieten the suspicions of the House of Hanover. The Whigs proposed to designate a Council of Regency, the majority of whose members would be named by the Princess Sophia, or by her successor in case of her death. The Council would act between the death of Anne and the arrival in England of the new monarch. The bill neatly turned the tables upon the Tories, offering a solution to an obvious weakness in the Act of Settlement without offending the Queen, and Hanover never henceforth wavered in its preference for the Whigs.

In the Commons, where the Regency Bill was received on 4 December, the Tories could think of no better expedient than to follow the example of their noble friends by bringing a motion for the invitation of Sophia to England. Bromley, who raised the matter, may have hoped to embarrass the Whigs, many of whom were likely to be reluctant to oppose on purely tactical grounds a motion which their instinct led them to approve; if so, his method proved to be a boomerang, and the well-prepared Whigs outmanoeuvred him completely. He found himself supported not only by potential dissidents, such as Onslow, but also by Smith—for the moment out of the Chair— and by Somers' brother-in-law, Sir Joseph Jekyll. Observers drew the conclusion that the Junto were using the occasion to threaten a juncture of Tories and Whigs in support of the invitation unless the Regency Bill were adopted as an official measure. Four days later the Tories, seemingly bent upon self-destruction, again played into their opponents' hands with a motion intended to deny that the Church of England was safe under the existing administration, thus allowing the Whigs the opportunity of saving the Ministry by a majority of fifty-one votes. The Whigs also supported the repeal of the major provisions of the Alien Act passed during the previous winter. The gesture was made possible by the Scottish Parliament's repeal of its Act of Security, in the summer of 1705, and by the appointment of commissioners to negotiate a Union.[6]

The chief business of the second half of the session was the Regency Bill. Its main purpose of establishing a council of regency was not, despite Tory opposition, in serious danger. The debates turned upon the question whether the clauses in the Act of Settlement limiting the prerogatives of future monarchs should be changed. The limitations included the provision that no holder of government office should sit in the Commons after the House of Hanover came to the throne. This clause the Junto were determined to modify in order to allow ministers, expected to be Whigs, to sit in the Commons in that event; and the triumvirs, even Harley, agreed on the unreasonable nature of the clause. The difficulty remained that the back benches were still of the same mind as in 1701, so that those who proposed revision found themselves opposed not only by the Tories but also by some Whigs who were, in Burnet's words, 'possessed with the notion of a self-denying bill'. In committee on 12 January 1706, a Tory motion to enforce the provision of 1701 was only narrowly rejected, and a compromise proposal by some 'whimsical' Whigs, of whom the most prominent were Onslow and the soldier–politician James Stanhope, could not be resisted. The 'whimsical clause' passed on with the bill to the House of Lords, where the Junto ensured that it was duly wrecked. In the bill as passed, ministers and the holders of the more important minor offices were to remain in the Commons after Anne's death, subject to the new requirement that they should seek re-election if appointed while Members of Parliament. To the Junto also was owed the laying aside of that clause in the Act of Settlement which had enjoined that the Privy Council should be the advisers to the future monarch, by the signatures of its members to the advice they gave. By this means a developing Cabinet was given quasi-official recognition.[7]

These debates greatly increased the doubts in Godolphin's mind about the feasibility of Harley's desire to manage the Commons without giving further office to leading Whigs. Though the Secretary himself had continued to follow the line laid down by the Treasurer, his associates had been by no means so helpful, and there is no sign that his fellow Secretary, Hedges, bore a share in forwarding government policy in the Commons. Immediately after prorogation on 19 March Godolphin communicated to Harley an assessment of the party situation. Claiming that, except on the whimsical clause, the Whigs had voted throughout the session with the court, he posed the question whether it would be easier to keep the support of the Whigs or to try to detach some Tories.* Concerning the latter, he thought that their

*Godolphin's computation in this letter that in the vote for the Speaker there had been 190 Tories, 160 Whigs and 100 'Queen's servants' gives suspiciously round numbers, especially in the last case, which must be treated with caution. The term 'Queen's servants' mean office holders, and the great majority of these were either Whigs or Tories. Thus, immediately after his calculation Godolphin had to add, by way of qualification, that about fifteen of the 100 had voted Tory on this and almost every other issue of the session. More serious doubt is thrown upon the viability of the Queen's servants as a supposed court party by W. A. Speck's calculations, on the basis of known division lists, that the voters for Smith included twenty-seven men not known to have voted on the Whig side on any other occasion in this or the former reign (these were, in fact, the Tories who followed Harley's lead), that forty-seven of Godolphin's Queen's servants are not known ever to have voted other than Whig in Anne's reign, and that only seventeen at most of the said servants could be regarded as having no party ties ('The choice of a Speaker in 1705', *BIHR*, xxxvii (1964) 20–46).

recent behaviour had shown them to be inveterate extremists; nor did he see much prospect of amendment. What clinched the matter for the Treasurer, however, was his certainty that the winning over of Tories would alienate the Whigs completely. His uncompromising conclusion was that future policy should include the detachment of Tories to the Ministry only if this could be done without the loss of a single Whig. Of the three men who had guided England's policies since 1702, at least one was now irrevocably committed to alliance with the Whigs.[8]

Godolphin's determination was enhanced by the prospect that the Union with Scotland, which was necessary to secure the Hanoverian succession, would be supported wholeheartedly by the Whigs. As a first step in his programme, his nominations for English commissioners to negotiate the Union included all five members of the Junto, but no Tories other than ministers and Archbishop Sharp of York. In the commission's meetings in coming months the Junto took the lead in discussion with an eye to future alliance with the Scots even to the extent, as Newcastle believed, of enlarging the Scottish representation in the Commons from a proposed thirty-six to forty-five Members. If his assessment were correct, the Whig party derived rich benefit, in terms of parliamentary votes, in the half-century after the Union.[9]

The rift which was slowly widening in the triumvirate over parliamentary management was increased in the summer of 1706 by new developments in foreign affairs. Marlborough's victory at Ramillies made the States General anxious to improve their barrier of fortresses in any peace negotiation, causing Halifax to remark to Somers that 'if they insist upon too much, it will be the greater tie upon them, not to make peace till it is procured for them'. But Whig anxiety to continue the war despite success in the Low Countries could not be shared by most Tories. And while differing attitudes on the conduct of future peace policy were beginning to take shape, the Junto were also making a major attempt to return one of their number to high office. They chose Sunderland, as the most likely to be acceptable to his father-in-law, Marlborough. The post they demanded was Hedges' Secretary-ship of State, and though Marlborough would have preferred to satisfy them with some lesser office or honour he was obliged, on Godolphin's insistence, to give his concurrence at the end of July. But, contrary to former practice, the views of Marlborough were far from immediately persuading the Queen, who responded to the proposition with a refusal which reflected her emotional abhorrence for the Junto. She again found a potent ally in Harley. In a memorandum drawn up for her towards the end of August the Secretary urged that if a minister were ejected at the wish of an opposition party then 'that party is the government and none else'. His views were faithfully reflected a few days later in the Queen's response to an assertion by Godolphin that the Whigs would not support the government if their terms were not met. 'Making a party man Secretary of State', she wrote, 'when there are so many of their friends in employment of all kinds already, is throwing myself into the hands of a party.'[10]

Faced by the Queen's stubborn refusal, the Junto stepped up the pressure. Somers and Halifax were deputed to see Godolphin and let him know, in Sunderland's words, their resolution

'. . . that this and what other things have been promised must be done, or we and the Lord Treasurer must have nothing more to do about business; and that we must let all our friends know just how the matter stands between us and the Lord Treasurer, whatever is the consequence of it'.

The threat could not be ignored. In tearful scenes the Queen resisted the pressure. Godolphin wavered, and asked Harley's view of how the Commons could be managed without the support of the Whigs. But less than ever did the Secretary's vision of 'the gentlemen of England' rallying to the Queen seem practical politics. The Tories did not conceal their hostility to the Treaty of Union, and if the Whigs too were rendered intransigent its ratification in Parliament might be as disruptive of ordinary business as the Regency Bill had been in the last winter. In the end it was Marlborough's authority which turned the balance with the Queen. 'I take leave to assure you, in the presence of God,' he told Anne, 'that I am not for your putting yourself into the hands of either party.' But with the Tories in their present mood, he contended, Godolphin could not 'be supported but by the Whigs, for the others seek his destruction, which in effect is yours'. For almost the last time the Queen allowed herself to be overborne by her old friend. Sunderland's appointment to the southern department in place of Hedges was announced on the eve of the opening of Parliament on 3 December.[11]

After four and a half years of relative quiescence, during which the Queen's chosen ministers had been given time to fall out with the Tories, the Junto were beginning to put forward their challenge to royal authority, such as William had been made to feel in 1689 and again in 1698. Though they were not to dominate the Ministry for a further two years, they found Marlborough and Godolphin, for the moment, closely in accord with their own views, especially as regards foreign policy. Despite the occasional tendency of some Whigs to show independence of judgment, especially on the question of place legislation, the Whig leaders had largely recovered control over the rank and file. As in William's war, it was the determination to dominate Louis

XIV, whatever the length of the struggle, which drew all Whigs into a united body. To this motive was added, from about the time of the Regency Act, another one less often openly avowed: that of keeping on good terms with the Elector of Hanover. The Elector's policy was to continue the war not only until the House of Habsburg was established in Spain but also, if possible, until his own family was established in Britain. The chance of a successful attempt by the Pretender to obtain sufficient support in England or Scotland at Anne's death would be distinctly less if his protector, Louis XIV, were still at war with Britain when such an attempt was made. Anne's bad health, despite her relative youth, henceforth gave the Whigs every motive to conciliate only the future royal house. The chief obstacle to their ambitions, apart from Anne herself, was her new friend Harley, whose dislike for the Junto had never diminished. Somers, Halifax, Orford, Wharton and Sunderland were among the ablest Englishmen of their generation and their patriotism was unquestionable, but to the Queen and the Secretary their virtues were outweighed by their moral and political defects.

When the session began, however, there was no immediate sign of dissension and supplies were voted smoothly. Moreover, the delicate business of the Union appeared at first to go almost equally well. The terms agreed upon by the commissioners of the two countries allowed Scotland to be represented by forty-five seats in the Commons and sixteen representative peers in the House of Lords. The Scottish Parliament considered the matter first, and on 28 January 1707 the Queen was able to announce to the English Parliament that the treaty had been accepted there. A bill to ratify the treaty passed through all its stages in the Commons, and an attempt by Nottingham in the upper house to extend some of the provisions of the Test Act to Presbyterian Scotland after the Union, a wrecking motion, was defeated without difficulty. The Act of Union became law on 8 March and the date of Union was fixed for 1 May.[12]

With the main question settled, however, a new difficulty was raised by Harley, who encouraged and even tried to strengthen a Tory bill designed to protect English traders against advantages derived by Scotland from the combination of the two countries' customs arrangements. This attempt to prevent the kind of economic benefit for which the Scots had surrendered their political autonomy aroused all Scotland, and infuriated Godolphin. While the Junto held up the bill in the Lords, the Queen was persuaded that the Union would be in danger if she gave it her consent. One week before Union day she agreed to prorogue Parliament to ensure that the bill would be abortive. It had, however, served the purpose of making Harley more popular in England.[13]

On the other hand, the Treasurer strengthened his own position by making closer his ties with the Bank of England. With government credit gradually declining under the burdens of war expenses, and with a parliamentary provision which rarely matched up with the Ministry's real needs, the Treasurer was able with Whig assistance to improve the currency of exchequer bills by an arrangement whereby the Bank undertook to circulate the bills in return for the prolongation of its charter so long as the bills should remain at large. The advantage to the Bank was a virtual guarantee of its permanence.[14] To the Tories the transaction was later to seem a sell-out to the monied men. The continuing balance in the Ministry was again reflected in a reshuffle of legal offices which took place at the end of the session. Cowper was raised to be Lord Chancellor, but Harley's friend Harcourt was promoted to Attorney-General, with Halifax's brother James Montagu taking Harcourt's place as Solicitor. Marlborough and Godolphin could do little to offset the political effect of Harcourt's advancement; but on such matters as peace feelers from a war-weary France, in which Harley had shown himself likely to take a view similar to that of many Tories, business was quietly removed from his hands and given to Sunderland.[15]

The major ministerial crisis before the next session centered not on foreign affairs, however, but on the Church. In April the Whigs got wind that the Queen had promised two vacant sees, Exeter and Chester, to two Tory divines. The filling of the vacancies was of considerable potential importance for the Whig majority in the House of Lords. Godolphin was soon given to understand that the Queen's action gave great offence to his new allies, and that their riposte in the next session would be an attack upon George Churchill, Marlborough's brother, who controlled the Admiralty in the name of Prince George. The Junto then suggested a compromise arrangement: they would not object to Blackall at Exeter if the Queen would give up the idea of appointing Dawes to Chester and would accept a candidate of their own for a third see which had fallen vacant at Norwich. The Queen indignantly refused to sacrifice either Dawes or Blackall and denied that the appointment had been advised by Harley. The Junto disbelieved her and, at a meeting called in August at Althorp, decided on an all-out attempt to remove the Secretary and his associates from office.[16]

Whig prospects for the forthcoming winter were generally improved by the coming of the forty-five new Scottish Members to the Commons, even though these were divided into cliques which were almost an unknown quantity in England. But further than this the status of Parliament itself, as a result of the Union, might be altered to the Whigs' advantage. In Scotland it had been assumed that the new arrangements would bring about a new, rather than simply an enlarged, Parliament.

This belief had some bearing on the sitting English Members, since the provisions of the Regency Act would exclude a number of lesser placemen, mostly Tories appointed in the early years of the reign, from any new House of Commons. The Junto determined to press for a decision that Parliament was 'new', a view with which Godolphin agreed. The Tories and Harley demurred, and in an exchange of letters the Secretary and the Treasurer once again recapitulated their old arguments upon party management. But neither would concede an inch to the views of the other; Godolphin's letters became more curt, Harley's longer and more metaphorical. Parliament, Harley maintained, could not be 'transubstantiated, the elements and accidents the same but the substance altered'; party government rendered the administration 'like a door which turns both ways upon its hinges'. In September their correspondence petered out into angry silence.[17]

Before the first Parliament of Great Britain assembled in the autumn of 1707 the European situation had altered many political calculations. The Emperor Joseph, by deciding upon the conquest of Naples, had contributed to the failure of a plan agreed between his general, Prince Eugene, and Marlborough for a joint attack by land and sea upon the French homeland at Toulon. After the Italian campaign Joseph concluded with the French the Treaty of Milan; by this treaty French garrisons in northern Italy were allowed a safe conduct to France, whence they, or other troops released by their arrival, reached Spain in time to turn the scale against the Allies at the battle of Almanza. Intricate and covert peace negotiations with France appeared to indicate that Louis XIV would now be willing to concede recognition of Queen Anne and to allow the Netherlands to the Dutch, providing Philip of Anjou were allowed to obtain the Spanish possessions in Italy. But though rumours of a good peace to be obtained were afoot in England, Godolphin and Marlborough were now wholly committed to obtaining the Spanish inheritance entire for the Archduke Charles. Thus Parliament assembled with the names of Toulon and Almanza drumming up dissatisfaction, while Tory backbenchers were beginning to grumble at the continuance of war conducted apparently for the benefit of the House of Habsburg. To meet these criticisms the Ministry had no plan and little prospect of a united front.[18]

The session of 1707–08 demonstrated the parties at their most factious, introduced the complicating element of Scottish affairs at Westminster, and resulted in the final destruction of the triumvirate. The Whigs prepared to attack the Admiralty, and to join with the Tories in criticising the army administration in Spain and opposing the government's desire to retain a separate Privy Council for Scotland.

The Junto's main purpose was to demonstrate to Godolphin that he could not control Parliament while most of their members remained out of office and Harley remained in. Of the Ministry's usual Whig supporters only the band of 'Lord Treasurer's' Whigs were prepared to rally to Godolphin. The ministerial nightmare of a dual opposition from the main bodies of both parties became for a period a grim reality.

On the preliminary issue the Whigs carried the day; Parliament was resolved on 10 November to be 'new', with the aid of almost all the Scottish Members present in the Commons, and several Tory officials due for exclusion under the Regency Act were immediately disqualified from sitting. In both houses the Whigs then turned determinedly to their promised attack on the administration of the Admiralty. The debates were concentrated nominally on the loss of convoys in the previous summer, an oblique approach which engaged the support of the Tories, so that for several weeks the ministerial leaders were hard pressed by the two-pronged assault. But in threatening Prince George and Admiral Churchill the Junto overreached themselves and forced Marlborough and Godolphin into a temporary reconciliation with Harley in rallying the court's forces. Moreover, the attack on the Admiralty allowed the Ministry to obtain the co-operation of several Whig grandees, including Newcastle, Somerset and the second Duke of Devonshire, which Hartington had become, in defence of the Queen's husband. These were joined early in December by Smith, Boyle, Walpole and Compton in a conference suggested by Harley and convened by Godolphin; the outcome of the conference was a declaration by those present that they were withholding themselves from the Junto's pressure for unreasonable measures.[19]

This gesture was followed by the collapse of joint Tory and Whig attacks. The Tories, believing that the government was about to abandon its connection with the Junto, saved the Admiralty in the Commons on 13 December by withdrawing their opposition in a decisive censure pressed on by Montagu, Onslow and the rising Whig lawyer Peter King. The Junto, for their part, abandoned their attacks in the Lords on the army but carried there on the 19th a resolution that no peace could be honourable or safe which left Spain and its American possessions in the hands of the House of Bourbon. With this sudden return to normal party hostilities the Queen gave public assurances that she would not come to terms with either party; but in private she assured the Tory Archbishop of York that she meant to give no more countenance to the Junto, though all Tories would be welcome in the new scheme of administration. Some Whigs too, she added, would have her favour if they acted in her interest. For a few days it was thought that the Junto's intransigence had resulted in the government's being set on the basis preferred by Anne and Harley:

Tory-orientated but with some Whig support. As a first indication of moderate policies the Whig leaders in the Commons were informed of a compromise proposal on outstanding ecclesiastical appointments, for though the Tory clerics were to have Exeter and Chester, as promised, compensation would be given elsewhere. Consequently, early in January 1708 the appointments were announced of the Whigs Trimnell at Norwich and Potter as Regius Professor of Divinity at Oxford.[20]

At the Christmas recess the triumvirs seemed again united and in command of the Commons. The appearance was illusory, and the situation changed in favour of the Junto almost overnight. On the last day of December one of the clerks of Harley's office, named Gregg, was found to be in treasonable correspondence with the French minister of war, Chamillard, and in the subsequent inquiry the Whigs made every effort to implicate the Secretary himself.[21] Though not successful in this, they weakened his position and hastened his fall. The period of six weeks which followed the discovery of Gregg's treachery was one of confused ministerial negotiations, of plots and counterplots. None of the participants were scrupulous about the means they used. Harley was negotiating, by the second half of January 1708, with some of the Tory leaders for the formation of a new Ministry, with or without Godolphin. The Treasurer was equally ready to sacrifice the Secretary, and Marlborough proved willing to dispense with either colleague, though he preferred to keep Godolphin.[22]

The fight, when it came, ostensibly concerned a parliamentary crisis which the Tories precipitated by an attack on the management of the land war. Though they had held back on the naval inquiry they were not disposed, in the afterlight of the Lords' resolution of 19 December, to overlook the defeat at Almanza and the general weakness of the Allied armies in Spain. Harley and St John, in their clandestine attempts to negotiate a Tory alliance, were placed in an awkward position, for both had some responsibility for officering and reinforcing the army. Their solution to the dilemma was the compromise of defending themselves on the score of Almanza while remaining silent when the general principle of waging war in Spain was criticised. The Secretary at War had to admit in the Commons on 29 January a fact which had become clear in previous debates: that of the 29,000 men provided by parliamentary votes for service in Spain only 8,600 had actually been present at the battle, though he pleaded several extenuating circumstances. When, however, a powerful younger Tory orator, Sir Thomas Hanmer, went beyond specific criticism and stated that the government 'had neglected making peace last year', these ministers attempted no defence. While not succeeding in pleasing the Tories the compromise added fresh evidence for Godolphin and Marlborough, who were already well aware of Harley's intrigues, of the Harleyites' desire to conciliate the Tories.*

While Harley, St John and Harcourt continued to canvass the Tories without success, the Junto resumed their pressure in Parliament. A Tory motion in the Commons on 3 February for an address censuring the conduct of the war in Spain was supported by sufficient Whigs led by Jekyll to pass without division. Two days later the Junto opposed Godolphin in the upper chamber by joining with Tory peers to defeat a government attempt to extend the life of the Scottish Privy Council. Thus harassed, and unable to dislodge Harley from the Queen's favour, Marlborough and Godolphin sent in their resignations and absented themselves from the usual Sunday Cabinet meeting on 8 February. Newcastle, Somerset and Devonshire threw their weight against the Secretary at or just after this meeting. Even so, and despite Harley's failure in the time available to obtain sufficient promises of Tory support, Anne would have formed a Ministry under him. But on the following day the Lords, on Wharton's motion, appointed a committee of seven Whigs to interrogate the condemned Gregg in the hope of obtaining evidence for impeaching Harley. The Secretary resigned on the 11th, followed by St John, Harcourt and Thomas Mansell. The triumvirate had ended and, with the exit of the Harleyites, Godolphin and Marlborough had no recourse for support but to the Whigs.[23]

*Godfrey Davies wrote, on the authority of a report in the Algemeen Rijksarchief at the Hague by a Dutch agent: 'The Tory ministers had not replied to the attack on war aims, but only to the assault on conditions in Spain' (see 'The Fall of Harley in 1708', *EHR*, lxvi (1951) 252). G. Holmes and W. A. Speck give convincing evidence for supposing that Marlborough and Godolphin were already much alarmed at Harley's manoeuvres before 29 January (*EHR*, lxxx (1965) 673–98).

CHAPTER 7

Whig Advance and Tory Recovery 1708-10

Even during its period of decline between 1705 and 1708 the triumvirate had done much to keep the parties in check. The removal of Harley and the consequent weakening of Marlborough and Godolphin ushered in a situation whereby party-dominated government could not much longer be averted. During the remainder of Queen Anne's reign a struggle was carried on to see whether the Whigs or the Tories would triumph. Each group was bent upon extirpating the other as a political entity. Bishop Burnet was aware of this situation when he noted in his journal, probably in 1708, that the conflict of the parties in every sphere of public life might come, 'in some critical time or other, at the death of a prince, or on an invasion, to have terrible effects'. That the nation did not in the end come to blows does not diminish the reality of the threat which thinking men feared. It was, perhaps, because contemporaries were fully alive to the dangers attendant upon a disputed succession that the last years of Anne's reign exhibited, not another civil war, but only the sharpest nonviolent conflict in the history of British parties since the Revolution.

The two parties were at this time, despite the earlier start enjoyed by the Whigs, in many ways remarkably similar. Both had developed, in the struggles of William's reign and after, a close cameraderie in Parliament which held good not only in the obvious party issues but also in many other matters where, in the words of Swift, Whig and Tory differences were no more at stake 'than the length or colour of your periwigs'. Both had an effective *ad hoc* organisation in the two Houses, and that of the Whigs was unusually excellent by the standards of any age before the late nineteenth century. Standing party funds for electoral and other purposes hardly existed, but on both sides the richer party members contributed heavily whenever necessary— Wharton is an outstanding example. In nothing, however, did the parties resemble each other more than in their determined and sustained pursuit of office and power. For those, both Tory and Whig, on whom the issues of the day weighed relatively lightly, office getting was often all-important. But even the zealots of the two sides, those men whose actions were decided primarily by party principles, were willing to flex those principles in the pursuit of power. Despite reiterated Tory assertions that it was the Whigs who wished to control the monarchy, the experiences of William's reign had shown that the Tories themselves, if faced by a hostile monarch, were capable of taking a party position almost indistinguishable from that of their opponents. And in the coming years the Whigs, despite their frequent attacks on religious intolerance, were themselves to abandon the dissenters when it suited them to do so.[1]

Nevertheless the differences between the parties remained real enough. In 1708, as in the early years after the Revolution, certain fixed rallying points stood out for both sides: no Tory would stand by while the Church was under attack, and no Whig would countenance any succession to the Crown except that of the House of Hanover. And as the health of the childless Queen declined gradually these older issues became strengthened by the problem of peace which had been adumbrated in the session of 1707–08.

The prospects of the government on the morrow of Harley's removal were not bright. The ministers' calculations in forcing out their colleague had not, in Marlborough's case at least, included the resignation of his friends. This action, causing greater dislocation and weakness than expected, foreshadowed further troubles. For the Whigs, however, the future held no fears. During November and December 1707 there had been a division in their ranks, but even this was by no means incapable of exploitation by the Junto's well-tried system of alternately attacking and stroking the government. The removal of Harley, with his awkward tendency to draw moderate Whigs off from their party in the name of the Queen and in the cause of national interests, was reported by Halifax to have 'once more united all the Whigs in the House of Commons'. Both Halifax and Somers, in writing their accounts of the events of January to Portland, confessed themselves surprised by the ease of their victory, though they modestly admitted that their tactics in Parliament had something to do with it.[2]

As for the Tories, they too might well have thought that their greatest obstacle was removed. The Harleyites were no longer in office to frustrate them at every point, by drawing off their own moderate men on every important issue. Now Harley and his friends might rejoin the party or remain in political isolation for ever. Their decision was not long delayed, and when an opportunity to show Tory sympathies was presented they seized it. In the last three years, since Godolphin had first turned to the Whigs, the safety of the Church as a privileged establishment had been increasingly doubted by most Tories; and a consequent increase of literary political activity, especially among the clergy, was bringing about a revival of the extreme pre-Revolution doctrines of passive obedience and nonresistance to lawful monarchy. An occasion for a Harleyite show of sympathy with the extremists, if not with their extremer doctrines, was a dispute between the Jacobite Dean of Carlisle, Francis Atterbury, and his Whig bishop, concerning the dean's discovery of a loophole in the episcopal right of visitation. If Atterbury's case went unchallenged the result might be the embarrassment of many Whig bishops by the overwhelmingly Tory lower clergy. Somers accordingly introduced in the Lords a bill to rectify the situation, but it did not pass the lower house in February without strong criticism from the Harleyites. The mending of Tory ties was under way.[3]

As soon as Parliament was prorogued on 1 April the Junto turned to the task of forcing their way into the Ministry. As yet they had benefited little from the fall of Harley and his friends. Boyle's promotion to the northern Secretaryship, though in no way a counterweight against the Junto, could hardly be considered as a success for them; and both Walpole, who replaced St John as Secretary at War, and Smith, who took Boyle's place as Chancellor of the Exchequer, had in December participated with Boyle in the ministerial Whigs' gesture against extremism. Few observers doubted that the Junto would press on with their campaign for office for themselves; indeed the Imperial Envoy wrote of Godolphin as 'checkmated' by them as early as February. This opinion reckoned without the Queen. She refused to appoint Somers in any capacity or to advance James Montagu in Harcourt's place as Attorney-General. Her tenacity throughout the summer of 1708 in seeing the question as 'whether I shall submit to the five tyrannising lords or they to me' compels admiration. Godolphin himself saw the need for further concessions and made every effort to conciliate the Whig leaders. He employed his usual method of threatened resignation against the Queen but found that it made no impression; she refused to give way. Before she could be brought to compliance a general election was needed to change the parliamentary situation.[4]

In the first elections for the Parliament of Great Britain, which took place in May, the weight of the Treasury and the energy of Sunderland were thrown strongly against the Tories and Harleyites. All accounts agreed that the Whigs gained on balance thirty seats or more in the English and Welsh constituencies, which made them stronger in Parliament by over sixty. Their victory was confirmed when it was seen that, of the forty-five Scottish Members returned, all but a handful were Whigs at Westminster, whatever were their affiliations in terms of politics north of the border; this was demonstrated in the voting on election petitions, which were decided almost uniformly in favour of ministerial or Whig candidates. The Whig leaders professed themselves satisfied, and Sunderland went so far as to rejoice at 'the most Whig Parliament [there] has been since the Revolution'. Among the losers the Harleyites suffered particularly severely in proportion to their numbers, for St John did not venture to contest his former seat and was unable to find another in this Parliament, while Harcourt was subsequently unseated upon a petition.[5]

If comradeship flourishes in adversity, the Tories and the Harleyites had a good motive for drawing together. Both were increasingly becoming convinced that the war in Spain was, like John Bull's lawsuit in the wittiest of peace tracts,* a 'bottomless pit' into which British money was being poured without result. The reconciliation accordingly went on steadily throughout the summer. Marlborough heard of an attempt to bring Rochester closer to Harley, though nothing seems to have come of this for the moment, and Bromley's attempts to soften the attitude of Nottingham against the man who had supplanted him as Secretary in 1704 met little encouragement. But approaches in the Commons were more fruitful, for Bromley himself was not unwilling to have Harley's support in his candidature for the Chair. On this question, as on that of the war, the Tories and Harleyites could face the next session with some unity.[6]

The Junto too were engaged in mending their fences, preparatory to a new lunge for power. They had long wished to loosen the hold of the Churchill family on the control of war, beginning with Admiral George Churchill. In the previous session this desire had done much to split the Whig forces, for ministerial Whigs had been unwilling to join in an attack while Marlborough and Godolphin might yet turn back to Harley and the Tories. This danger was now diminished, but the Junto were determined not to repeat any errors which might have been responsible for past discord between themselves and the new generation of younger Whigs who were seeking a real role in the party's counsels; in the past the Junto had often been accused within the party of exclusiveness in their decision making. As a first step in widening the basis of the responsible leadership the important Walpole and his brother-in-law Townshend were won over, together with Walpole's friend Devonshire; thus Godolphin was left without some of his best supporters from among the Lord Treasurer's Whigs of the last session.

The Whigs chose to make their attack on Churchill and the Prince at the Admiralty the first demonstration of party solidarity. In mid October the lords of the Junto were joined by Devonshire and Townshend as well as by several other peers in delivering their ultimatum to Godolphin: Prince George must be replaced at the Admiralty by the adaptable Pembroke, whose two posts of Lord President and Lord Lieutenant of Ireland would then be freed for Somers and Wharton.

*John Arbuthnot, *The Law is a Bottomless Pit*.

Sunderland, describing the confrontation, wrote that the Whigs had 'in a body declared to Lord Treasurer, that if this is not immediately done they must let the world and their friends see they have nothing more to do with the court'. In view of the election results the threat was a potent one. As a first step, they threatened to oppose the Ministry's choice for the Chair, even though this was the Whig Onslow. The Treasurer prevaricated, offering the immediate appointment of Montagu as Attorney and of Robert Eyre as Solicitor-General. As it happened, the Whigs might have spared themselves the implacable resentment they raised in the Queen by their open requirement of the removal of Prince George, for the Prince, long a semi-invalid, now lay dying. For the moment Anne had no strength to argue further. Almost carelessly, for nothing mattered after her husband's death which took place on 28 October, she agreed to the appointment of Pembroke, Somers and Wharton in the posts desired. In return, the Junto ordered their candidate for the Chair, King, to stand down in favour of Onslow.[7]

The new Ministry, shared now by Marlborough and Godolphin with the Junto, was to last for two years and be marked by many internal tensions. The Whig leaders had not lost their abilities after nearly a decade out of office, but their well-established colleagues were more formidable as rivals than the second Earl of Sunderland had been in William's reign. A number of 'Lord Treasurer's' Whigs still could not be relied upon to follow the Junto if a contentious policy failed to find the agreement of the Treasurer. The same was true of the Scottish Whigs, many of whom responded more to government patronage than to the wishes of the English Whigs. The Junto's response to the problems which faced them was to move warily in the first session and to continue to delegate more responsibility to the younger Whigs, especially in the lower house. The latter process did not come about overnight; it was a continuous trend which went on for the rest of the reign as Walpole, Stanhope, King and such other lawyer–orators as Jekyll, Montagu, Eyre and Nicholas Lechmere became increasingly prominent. Nor was the process at first an unquestionable advantage, for it was to lead to an irresolution of counsels in 1709–10 such as had rarely been visible in William's reign. But though the Junto continued to dominate the party, and to show their old brilliance on occasion in managing the House of Lords, the influence of the new men was to be increasingly felt.

Despite election success, reinforced by the hearing of petitions in the Commons and abandonment of the decent formality of a committee of elections, the Whigs' first session in the new Parliament was not entirely satisfactory. The Tories found opportunity for worrying the

Ministry over the cost of the war in Spain, and Harley's knowledgeable attacks in January 1709 gave particular disquiet. The Whigs carried a long-desired statute for naturalising foreign Protestant refugees from Louis XIV's Europe, and, by permitting the new citizens to take the sacramental tests at any Protestant church, increased Whig voting strength in immigrant constituencies. But Wharton's desire to remove the tests for English dissenters found no more support from his party now than it had in 1689. The Whigs were further divided when the Junto supported a bill for bringing Scottish treason law into line with the stiffer English practice. This measure should, by English logic, have appealed to the Scottish Whigs as making Jacobite invasion more dangerous to rebels; but it ran up against united Scottish opposition— including that of the Junto's closest allies, the 'Squadrone', led by Roxburgh—based on national pride in Scottish law. The measure was barely carried; and with Halifax opposed to the Treason Bill, the Whigs and even the Junto ended the session in disarray.[8]

In the pursuit of foreign policy, however, the Whig party was united. By way of preparation it carried an address to the Queen asking her to continue friendship among the Allies after the war, an end which could hardly be achieved unless the Emperor's claims in Spain were satisfied. Peace negotiations with France broke down in May after Louis XIV had yielded to most of the Whigs' demands, including the removal of Philip from the Spanish throne, but had refused articles 4 and 37 of the proposed preliminary terms, which called upon him to obtain his grandson's ejection within two months on pain of a resumption of hostilities. Both in this negotiation and in a consequent and successful second attempt to conclude a Barrier Treaty, in which the Dutch were given almost all they wanted in the Netherlands and equal trading rights with Britain in South America, the Junto were bent rather upon keeping the Dutch in the war than upon the ostensible objects of the negotiation. Marlborough and Godolphin were, at best, uneasy partners in this policy, and Marlborough left the Barrier Treaty to be signed in October by Townshend. Godolphin reported to the Captain-General that pressure to continue the war was being put upon him by the Governor and Deputy Governor of the Bank of England:

'Sir Gilbert Heathcote, who is Governor, said to me, [he wrote,] Pray my Lord, don't let us have a rotten peace . . . I call anything, he said, a rotten peace unless we have Spain, for without it we can have no safety.'

Godolphin added by way of comment: 'you will see that as all the malicious people will rail, if there be no peace, so those who wish best will be very uneasy at any peace under which they do not think themselves safe'. Marlborough consoled himself, as he had every season since 1704, with the belief that the next major battle would be the last and decisive stroke which would batter France to its knees. The result was the battle, a technical victory, fought at Malplaquet. In all the annals of war, contemporaries could find no precedent for this crimson page. The carnage provided ready material for Tory propaganda for several years to come, intensifying the argument which could be made out on the lines of a selfish Whig 'financial interest' perpetuating the war for the Whigs' own profit.[9]

It was the need to meet such propaganda and to rally all Whigs, after the limited successes of the last session and the unpopular diplomatic activities of the recess, which determined the leaders' thinking for the session of 1709–10. For a start they required, as often, some new mark of royal 'confidence' with which to face Parliament. At or soon after the appointment of Pembroke to the Admiralty, Marlborough and Godolphin had promised that he should be replaced in due course by Orford. The time had now come to claim fulfilment of this promise. Unless the appointment were made, Sunderland urged Somers, the only course was 'just before the meeting of Parliament, to take our leave of them, by quitting, and have nothing more to do with them'. Sunderland was the youngest member of the Junto, but he was well apprised of their technique. Somers himself was reported to be threatening resignation. In the upshot, however, Marlborough and Godolphin yielded and added their arguments to those of the Junto with the Queen. Orford was restored to his old office of First Commissioner of the Admiralty in November.[10]

The new session proved to be decisive in settling the future of the Ministry, not as the Junto hoped by confirming Whig control, but by arousing national reaction against themselves and against Marlborough and Godolphin for the rest of Anne's reign. The Whigs sought a major publicity counter to opposition attacks on their war policy, and found it in presumed Tory loyalty to the exiled House of Stuart as evidenced in the revival of the pre-Revolution doctrines of passive obedience and nonresistance. For years, divines had been preaching ideas perilously close to these doctrines, and in 1708 Atterbury aroused Whig indignation by bringing them up on the occasion of the election of a Lord Mayor of London. On 5 November 1709 a lesser but equally vociferous clergyman, Dr Henry Sacheverell, chose the anniversary of the Guy Fawkes plot and of the landing of William in Torbay in 1688 to preach at St Pauls a sermon, subsequently published, which carefully blended pre-Revolution political theory with personal innuendo directed at Godolphin's churchmanship; this gave the Junto the excuse they wanted and at the same time removed any scruples which the Lord Treasurer might have had about using it. The main business of the 1709–10 session became, therefore, the national spectacle of the impeachment of Sacheverell, *faute de mieux*, in an attempt to expose the extremes of Tory ideology and to justify the exclusion of the direct line of the House of Stuart in and after the Revolution. All that the Whigs succeeded in doing, however, was in exposing an unresolved conflict in their own thought: that between their pre-Revolution theories of contractual government and their present consciousness of the need for a stable and hereditary Protestant monarchy under the House of Hanover. And in the process of impeaching a clergyman they were to convince the nation that whiggery was indeed, as the Tories maintained, a continuing menace to the established Church.[11]

The impeachment of Sacheverell was carried without difficulty by the Whig majority in the Commons, and throughout the remainder of the session attention accordingly centred on the Lords, where the drama of the case was played out. The main efforts of the Whig speakers, who appeared before the Lords as managers of the impeachment on behalf of the Commons, were concentrated upon the first article of the charge, which reasserted the right of resistance as demonstrated in 1688. Lechmere unequivocally stated the philosophy of political contract, going on to maintain 'that the rights of the crown of England are legal rights, and its power stated and bounded by the laws of the kingdom; that the executive power and administration itself is under the strictest guard for the security of the people'. All the managers condemned the doctrine of nonresistance, though most were careful to qualify this by explaining that they referred to 'unlimited' nonresistance.* Walpole posed the distinction in a question to their Lordships:

'Because any man, or party of men, may not out of folly or wantonness commit treason, or make their own discontents, ill principles or disguised affections to another interest a pretence to resist the supreme power, will it follow from thence that the utmost necessity ought not to engage a nation in its own defence for the preservation of the whole?'

Another future first minister, Stanhope, roundly pronounced absolute nonresistance to be 'inconsistent with the law of reason, with the law of nature, and with the practice of all ages and countries'.

*The difficulties facing the Whigs on the subjects of contract and resistance are described by J. P. Kenyon, who justly characterises the impeachment as 'a gamble, intended to re-establish Whig political ideology when all else had failed' (see his 'The Revolution of 1688: Resistance and Contract', in Neil McKendrick (ed.), *Historical Perspectives . . . in Honour of J. H. Plumb* (1974) 43–69).

The vestigial element of contract theory in the thought of some Whigs, played down in practice by a generation of their leaders since 1689 and wisely eschewed by such farsighted speakers as Walpole, thus received a new airing. However, more important for the immediate future was that more recent element of Whig theory which was prepared to condemn nonresistance only if this were carried to extremes. The Whig managers' reason for confining their condemnation to *unlimited* nonresistance is not far to seek; Halifax and Sunderland are found only a few months later explaining to an alarmed court at Hanover 'that the Whigs are by no means for a republic, nor for rendering the crown elective'. Although the possibility of resistance to the Crown remained implicit in much Whig thought after the accession of George I, it was no longer overtly stated. And near the end of the eighteenth century Edmund Burke was even to contend that the qualified defence of resistance displayed by the Whigs at the trial amounted to his own belief that the Revolution was a nonrepeatable episode.

If the post-Revolution theory of whiggery was thus modified, so too was that of post-Revolution toryism. Harcourt, as Sacheverell's leading counsel, could not deny his client's printed assertions but tried to define nonresistance as applying only to the Crown-in-Parliament rather than, as had palpably been originally assumed, to the monarchy itself. Such an interpretation allowed Tories to justify their own resistance to James II in 1688, and to accept the subsequent parliamentary settlement of the Crown. Though Harcourt was not primarily concerned to redefine Tory doctrine, his arguments usefully accommodated Tories who accepted that settlement. For immediate purposes, however, it was Sacheverell himself who did most for the party cause. His unrepentant defence of the views with which he was charged in the first article, as also of those with which he was accused in the second and third articles concerning the unreasonableness of religious toleration and the danger to the Church under the present administration, rallied together both extreme and moderate Tories and welded them into as nearly united a body as they were capable of being.[12]

Such a development had been foreseen by the Harleyites, who swiftly saw that the impeachment was a chance to 'break the Whigs', though they feared that it might also 'raise the Tories to their old madness'. Both the hope and the fear were realised. The wave of fury among churchmen, together with the House of Lords' sense of responsibility as a judicial body, carried Sacheverell through a comfortable trial and the easy punishment of suspension from preaching for three years. In the course of the proceedings two members of the Whig patriciate, Somerset and Argyll, contributed to the softening of his sentence. Their action was the result of the Queen's personal involvement and intriguing, and was followed swiftly by promises of reward; Argyll was given the prospect of the Garter, while Somerset was fed by the Queen with the belief that he would be the head of a new Ministry. Finally, the Sacheverell episode completed Newcastle's drift back to the Queen after his desertion at the time of Harley's fall in 1708.[13]

The widening of rifts among the Whigs by the desertion of such grandees as these was the opportunity for which Anne had waited two years. The first and most important convert to the court had been Shrewsbury, after his return to England in 1706. The triumph of the Junto in 1708 appears to have decided him that a needed peace would be long in coming if their influence were not removed. As doyen of the surviving Revolution Whigs, Shrewsbury was a key acquisition for Harley in preparation for the next attempt to form a mixed Ministry independent of the Junto. But if the moderate Whig nobility was thus wavering by 1710, the solid face of the Junto itself was showing larger cracks. Somers, the reported chief opponent of Wharton's extremism in 1708–09, continued to be estranged from him. Halifax was discontented with most of his friends; they were now in office, but there seemed little hope of Halifax's return to his old place at the Treasury while his friends needed Marlborough's military ability and Marlborough insisted upon retaining Godolphin there. To heighten Halifax's dissatisfaction, he had been passed over in favour of the younger Townshend for conducting the peace negotiations with France. In the Commons there were signs that such dissensions were being repeated further down the Whig hierarchy, even though the Barrier Treaty was ratified and supplies were carried for a further campaign. A Place Bill drawn up upon the lines of the 'whimsical clause' of 1706, intended to exclude all but about sixty office holders from the House, was introduced by Edward Wortley Montagu, a Country Whig, and supported by many of his fellows as well as by the Tories; as a result it passed the Commons despite ministerial opposition and had to be destroyed in the House of Lords. This new sign of backbench independence was additionally demoralising for the Whig leadership because of its appearance at the time of the failure over Sacheverell.[14]

The ending of the session on 5 April 1710 began the last phase of the Ministry's existence. Until recently the Queen had not been forthcoming as to her intentions, but with the prorogation she felt strong enough to take the first steps by dismissing some Whigs. On the 6th Godolphin went off to his favourite recreation at Newmarket without any apparent premonition of disaster. Anne's first step was to dismiss the Duchess of Marlborough from her presence; since 1707 she had openly preferred Mrs Abigail Masham, who acted as intermediary with Harley, as her new favourite. On the 14th Anne went on to remove her Chamberlain, the Marquis of Kent, and without consulting her minister appointed Shrewsbury instead. This last move came as a surprise to observers and as a severe shock to most Whigs; Harley's complicity in any plot to change the Ministry could be taken for granted, but the involvement of Shrewsbury made the attempt altogether more formidable.[15]

At the end of May Shrewsbury and Harley informed Godolphin that the Queen was now determined to dismiss Sunderland. At this point the ministers might possibly have saved themselves by a show of solidarity, and the Junto had actually planned joint resignation if any of their number were dismissed. Instead, they were persuaded to negotiate with Harley and, to Godolphin's indignation, even entertained some hope of participating in a new Ministry from which the Treasurer would be excluded. Thus when Sunderland was dismissed on 14 June hardly a politican stirred to save him or to prevent his replacement by a fairly colourless Tory, the Earl of Dartmouth. But though the new ministerial arrangement which the Queen and her advisers had in mind envisaged appointments from among those Whigs who had shown in the past a willingness to work in harness with moderate Tories, any promises made to the Junto were spurious. Thus the Whig lords who had pioneered the technique of threatening mass resignation failed to use it to save the man whose appointment in 1706 had been the signal for their rise and whose dismissal was intended to presage their fall from office. Deprived of the usual crisp counsels of Wharton, who was at his post in Ireland, they hesitated, tried to compromise, failed to use it to save the man whose appointment in 1706 had been the signal for their rise and whose dismissal was intended to presage their fall from office. Deprived of the usual crisp counsels of Wharton, who was at his post in Ireland, they hesitated, tried to compromise then surrendered. The only resistance to the Queen came not from politicians but from the directors of the Bank of England, four of whom gained an audience to insist that she should retain Godolphin and keep the existing Commons. They were dissuaded from withholding government loans less by her assurances than by Godolphin himself, who was alarmed on behalf of Marlborough's already financially-handicapped forces. At the end of June the election of two Whig sheriffs in the City was also taken to indicate the attitude of the 'financial interest'. Godolphin plucked up courage to remonstrate with the Queen for seeing Harley. The charge was only too true, but it came months too late.[16]

The future now lay with Shrewsbury and Harley, the old allies of the Triennial Act, who in spirit had often stood closer to each other than to their party colleagues. On their present juncture depended the possibility of a 'mixed Ministry'. The more energetic Harley was the leader of the two men, though Shrewsbury's moment was to come briefly but decisively on the other's eclipse four years later. For the moment the Duke was offered the post of Lord Treasurer, which he prudently declined; the man of the moment was clearly Harley. The latter, however, preferred to control a Treasury commission, for the higher post would have involved him in leaving the Commons. Godolphin's fall was hastened by news of the failure of a peace negotiation renewed at Gertruydenberg in the spring, in which Louis XIV had rejected an even stricter interpretation of the terms offered in 1709. But this event was not unexpected, and the ultimate stimulus was provided from another quarter. For six weeks the Bank of England had been threatening to cut off short-term loans to the Treasury, and on 3 August the directors refused to make further advances unless the Queen would give another personal assurance that there was to be no change of government and no dissolution of Parliament. This time Anne refused to give any promise, and five days later Godolphin was dismissed.[17]

The new Treasury Board contained Harley and two of his close associates, Poulet and Mansell. Harley himself became Chancellor of the Exchequer. No further changes could be made for the moment, until the new commissioners proved their ability to surmount the credit famine; but they proved capable of dealing with the problem by persuading a syndicate of Tory financiers to make the immediately necessary loans, a move which obliged the Bank to resume its usual flow of credit for fear of having its monopoly usurped. By early in September, therefore, the new government appeared to be in a position to carry out its intentions. But the hope of a mixed Ministry was soon to be disappointed by the solidarity of both parties. The Tories were in no mood to join in any arrangement which did not include the dissolution of the existing House of Commons, as Bromley had made clear as soon as Harley was appointed. Nor, as Rochester made equally clear, would their leading figures tolerate being kept from office. This still-important party patriarch could hardly be left out of any credible scheme which was to include Tories, especially as the Queen was adamant against employing the only other Tory of equal eminence and ability, Nottingham. Rochester replaced Godolphin as Lord Lieutenant of Cornwall, a powerful sop to his pride, and the dissolution of Parliament was soon afterwards announced.[18]

With this event the last hopes of the Queen and her new advisers for a moderate Ministry were destroyed, for the Whigs determined to resign. This time they showed no hesitation or lack of unanimity such as had occurred earlier in the year; they had had many weeks in which to make up their minds. Harley's efforts to retain Boyle and Cowper were defeated by the determination of the men in question; the tides of party instinct were running too strongly for him. Boyle's departure left the northern department of the Secretaries' office open for

St John, whose loyalty in 1708 and great abilities made it difficult to avoid his pressing demand for promotion beyond his former status of Secretary at War, though his burning ambition made him feared by the Harleys. Harcourt, after a short interval, took the seals as Lord Keeper. Rochester and another Tory, Sir John Leake, replaced Somers and Orford as Lord President and First Lord of the Admiralty respectively. Walpole yielded up his post of Secretary at War but chose, for the moment, to retain the lucrative office of Treasurer of the Navy. By allowing him this place the government doubtless hoped that the most formidable Whig in the Commons would be muzzled, but events were to prove otherwise.

Among others who retained their positions as token of the Queen's desire to offset the new appointments were Marlborough, the Whig privy councillors including the Junto, and most of the minor office holders. At the same time Shrewsbury and Harley refused to allow sweeping government electoral pressure to be used on behalf of the Tories. But if they hoped thereby to avoid too great a Tory victory in elections the hope was vain, for it was clear before half the results were available that the outcome was a landslide for the Tories. Contemporary reports agreed upon a majority of at least two Tories for each Whig who secured his election. Even in the most easily controlled constituencies the massive swing in public opinion resulted in losses for Whig patrons. Sacheverell and the national desire for peace had brought about a result which exceeded the wildest hopes of the Tories and the worst fears of the Whigs.[19]

With these results much in mind, commentators posed the question: who was likely to be in control of the government, Harley or Rochester and the extremists? The former was, as all acknowledged, the Queen's first adviser and the man who above all others had wrought the recent changes. But as the renegade of 1704 he was not, and never again would be, entirely trusted by the Tories; they boasted that he was a 'necessary ladder' for their own climb to power, and that when they were ready they would 'throw away that part of the scaffolding'. The new Chancellor, however, wrote confidently to Newcastle that 'as soon as the Queen has shown strength and ability to give the law to both sides, then will moderation be truly shown in the exercise of power without regard to parties only'. This ominous miscalculation ushered in four years of strife which outdid every party excess since 1689.[20]

CHAPTER 8

Tory Dominance and Whig Recovery 1710-14

The last four years of Annes' reign were to see the continuance of a two-to-one Tory majority in the Commons, but the course of the struggle in these years nevertheless showed that the two parties were not as unevenly matched as the numbers suggest. The Tories could not rely upon the support of the Queen but the Whigs, at least from the autumn of 1711, could count on the unequivocal support of the House of Hanover in most matters. The Junto's control of the House of Lords continued down to the beginning of 1712, and even after the creation of twelve new Tory peers at that time the reassertion of the Whig dominance there remained a distinct possibility in every debate in which the conclusion of peace or the nature of the royal succession was the issue. In the press the Whig pamphleteers grappled on terms of at least equality with their Tory rivals, powerful though the latter were after being joined regularly by Jonathan Swift in the autumn of 1710. And even in the lower house the remaining Whigs were not to be without a source of strength denied to their opponents, for henceforth they were a united body while the Tories were splintered by personal and public disputes. It was to be these disputes, polarised from 1713 on the issue of the succession, which allowed the Whigs to carry their policies to victory, to bring about the Hanoverian accession without military incident, and to condemn the Tories to the wilderness.

The key division among the Tories centred upon the personalities and policies of Harley and St John, for Rochester proved to be less active than expected and died in May 1711. St John, returned to the Commons after two years of enforced residence among the Tory squires of Berkshire, had moved far from the moderate Harleyite position he had still professed in 1708. Back in office only as a result of Harley's failure to retain Boyle and other Whigs, St John burned to remove the remaining Whigs from government service, to place himself once more at the head of the Tory extremists on religious issues, and to secure his hold on the party by concluding a quick peace even if this meant abandoning the Allies. Harley, aided by Shrewsbury, preferred to retain the surviving Whigs in office and to continue the war until he had time either to persuade the Allies to come into a peace treaty or, if necessary, to force them to accede to realistic terms. The full implications of the two men's positions were not yet clear in 1710, but the difference between Harley's middle position and St John's reborn party extremism was spelled out early. The former's views were explained in Defoe's significantly named *Faults on Both Sides,* and in the same author's warnings of the dangers of party strife to government credit in *An Essay upon Public Credit* and *An Essay upon Loans*; the Secretary's policies with regard to peace were explicitly explained in the newly founded *Examiner,* in which with the assistance of Swift he launched an attack on the Whigs, Marlborough and the Allies with venomous expertise. From 25 November, when Parliament assembled, Harley's more moderate aims were already under challenge.[1]

From the Whigs too the first challenge to moderation came before the commencement of the session. Though they were virtually helpless in the Commons for the moment, they still had powerful allies in the City. In October and early November the Bank was again making difficulties for the Treasury, blaming the change of government for credit problems, though the root trouble lay in the existence of a large quantity of government scrip which was passing at high discounts because it was without parliamentary security. Thus the first months of the new Parliament were complicated not only by the credit crisis but also by Tory indignation at the actions of the 'monied men', an attitude which threatened in its turn to alienate those same men still further from the Ministry. Calling for the impeachment of Godolphin and other members of the former government, and criticising Harley's policy of retaining the armed forces at full strength until good peace terms were secured, the Tories began to obstruct the long procedure of voting the apportionment of taxes. Greatly encouraged by the mass of new and mostly young Members elected to revenge the martyred Sacheverell and put a stop to the war, the extremists formed themselves in February 1711 into the October Club, about 150 strong, for planning the coercion of the Ministry while consuming the heady October ale.[2]

Second only to the Tories' desire to extract blood from the former ministers, for financial or other mismanagement, was their determination to force the hand of the new Ministry in the matter of retaining minor Whig personnel, especially in departments controlled by the Treasury. Within the Ministry itself the weight of Rochester, St John and Harcourt was added to the pressure, making some concessions essential. George Clarke, who had been dismissed by Godolphin for voting against the election of Smith as Speaker in 1705, was accordingly restored to the Admiralty Board. Even so, Harcourt commented bitterly in private: 'I wish all other offices was filled with as good men. Good God, what a glorious government this we have.' Walpole, who had continued to oppose the Ministry, was dismissed from his remaining post. But the effect of such changes was not so much to sate as to excite the appetite of the Tories. Their aim remained, in the words of Swift, 'to call the old ministry to account and get off five or six heads.'[3]

To divert the Tories the government provided a programme of legislation calculated to meet the approval of both the Church of England and the landed interest. A bill to provide funds for establishing fifty new churches in the London area was introduced and passed into law in the course of the session. The Ministry also supported a long-desired Tory measure, the Property Qualification Act, which made the possession of land of £300 annual value a necessary qualification for a borough representative, or £600 in the case of a knight of the shire. However, these measures did not prevent many Tories from supporting Wortley Montagu's Place Bill, which again passed through the Commons, supported this time by the united Whigs, a rare victory for the vigorous but numerically handicapped opposition there. Whig support of the measure did not, however, stretch so far as forcing it through the Lords; for the Junto, place legislation was still a useful tactic in opposition rather than a desired end in itself.

The unruly activities of the Tories led the government to some desperate actions. On one occasion Harley was able to force the Commons to resume its routine but necessary business only by threatening that Parliament would have to be dissolved; and in a division on 20 February, over a Tory attempt to unseat James Montagu for alleged electoral malpractices, the Chancellor actually voted with the Whigs. The impasse at which Harley's administration had arrived by the first week of March was such that the service departments were unable to stave off creditors by further promises, while the Tories were far from appearing ready to tackle the complex problems of the floating debt.[4]

The Gordian knot was severed in an unexpected and dramatic fashion. On 8 March a French spy attacked and wounded Harley, whose popularity rose overnight on a wave of indignation and sympathy throughout the land. From his sickbed he continued to put the finishing touches to a scheme making provision for permanent parliamentary interest-payments on the unsecured debts. It was during Harley's illness, too, that his first open quarrel with St John came to a head. During the dispute with the October Club the Secretary's position had been ambiguous. He became the victim of the club's spoiling tactics, but on the other hand he had not always backed up his leader's tactics. Among the handful of 'Harlekins' reported as following the Chancellor in his defence of Montagu, the name of Henry St John is conspicuously absent.[5]

The Secretary's bid to control the Tories was beginning but it was unfortunately timed, both by reason of Harley's accident and because of other developments which strengthened the Chancellor in the

Cabinet. With St John's strong backing a naval and military expedition was being prepared for the capture of Quebec. Harley could not view so great an expense with enthusiasm while the Treasury was struggling to honour existing commitments, and in this view he had the support of Shrewsbury and Rochester. The latter was finally detached from St John after news arrived of the death of the Emperor Joseph and the consequent succession of the Archduke Charles to the Habsburg dominions. The prospect of Charles's controlling both the Empire and the territories of the Spanish Crown was distasteful to both the British and the Dutch, and made any peace which left Philip V in Spain seem more desirable. But at an emergency Cabinet meeting convened to prevent the expedition, on the grounds of the imminent cessation of hostilities, it was St John's view which prevailed, possibly because the Queen wished to favour Mrs Masham whose brother was the force's military commander. The Secretary's victory was achieved, however, at the expense of alienating the more responsible Tories. Harley was to spend several years untangling the web of misappropriation which St John's friends spun out of the Quebec expedition's expenses.[6]

The Chancellor's control of the Tory party was established, *pro tem*, by his funding scheme. As a preliminary his brother, 'Auditor' Edward Harley, reported to the Commons on 4 April that £35 million voted by Parliament down to 1710 had not yet been accounted for. The 'lost' millions constituted a technical deficit resulting from cumbrous auditing procedure. In view of the little real evidence of misappropriation by Godolphin's administration produced in the Auditor's report, and of the necessity for preventing a witch hunt which would have further alarmed the City, there can be little doubt that the report was drafted to allow the Tories to let off steam fairly harmlessly until the new scheme provided a solution to credit difficulties. On 2 May the long-awaited proposal was unveiled. A commercial company was to be set up to exploit the fabled wealth of the trade to South and Central America and at the same time to incorporate in its capital the nation's miscellaneous unfunded debts. The commercial aspect of the scheme encouraged the government's creditors to buy South Sea stock with their depreciated scrip, and an annual parliamentary grant to the company of 6 per cent of the capital so subscribed provided the necessary element of funding, enabling the company to pay its stockholders even if no commercial profit ensued. The proposed South Sea Company was presented to the Tories as a financial rival to the Bank, and there was thus no difficulty in persuading them to provide the necessary funds. But whatever the Chancellor encouraged the Tories to believe, he himself realised that the financial services of the Bank could not be superseded, and he took care in the bill to protect its joint-stock banking monopoly in all essentials. This largely satisfied the Bank, though the

Whigs attacked the scheme with their usual determination, if without success, as it passed through Parliament. At the prorogation on 12 June the government's debts were secured by regular funds. This achievement, together with Harley's pleasuring of the Tories, constituted a remarkable conclusion to a career in the Commons already famed for 'trickery' and political dexterity of a high order, for as soon as parliamentary business was concluded the gratified Queen bestowed upon Harley the post of Lord Treasurer and the title of Earl of Oxford.[7]

Like the Junto after their accession to the House of Lords in the last reign, the new Lord Treasurer was to forego, by his elevation, a good deal of his parliamentary influence. The removal of his presence in the Commons, moreover, could hardly fail to result in the increased power of St John in that House. Oxford's associates had recently been given to understand that the Secretary might be dismissed if he did not mend his ways, but his great energy and abilities, suitably channelled, were needed in the difficult peace negotiation which lay ahead. In this negotiation, however, the Treasurer meant to keep close personal control and to exclude his ambitious colleague from real authority. The solution to the problem of Commons management which Oxford seems to have considered was to set up a rival there to the Secretary, in the form of a strong Chancellor of the Exchequer. Political rumour, ever active, had it that he was planning to bring Boyle back. Oxford certainly approached Hanmer, a politician whose role from the Tory back benches was in some ways similar to the position which Harley had occupied there in William's reign. Hanmer had at first been prominent in the October Club, but he was now disillusioned by their irresponsibility. For the moment, however, Hanmer refused to be tempted though expressing himself cautiously, in the words of the intermediary Bromley, as 'satisfied with the measures taken.' Bromley, as Speaker, was not considered to be available for the post. The general support of both men, however, was to be useful to the Treasurer when he had to fall back upon Robert Benson, who was no match for St John.[8]

The summer of 1711 was occupied by a secret negotiation between Britain and France, mainly on the basis of leaving Philip in Spain if he would provide privileges for the South Sea Company in trade with the Spanish colonies. The Dutch were to be given a satisfactory barrier, but less than that promised in the Townshend Barrier Treaty. St John was not informed of the negotiation by Oxford and Shrewsbury until April, but he then expedited its progress. Preliminary articles conceding the British requirements were signed at the end of September. Shrewsbury developed belated scruples concerning the lack of regard for the Allies and withheld approval, but his was the only dissenting voice.

The open move for peace gave the Whigs their opportunity. Some Tories, including Nottingham and Hanmer, were known to share Whig fears that peace would lead to an opportunity for a Jacobite restoration as soon as the Pretender's chief protectors ceased to be enemy powers. An active literary campaign appealed to such Tories to desert their fellows and save the Hanoverian succession. In October a meeting of Whig lords, together with Walpole, was held at Orford's Cambridgeshire home to draw up a plan for defeating the peace preliminaries. The main attack would perforce be in the House of Lords, though Walpole would carry the flag for the depleted body of Whigs in the lower house. To attract Tory support, however, the Whig leaders needed a clear gesture from Hanover. This was duly given, supporting the unmistakable hostility of the Emperor for the British government's peace proposals. On 13 October the preliminary articles, communicated by the Imperial Envoy, were published in the Whig *Daily Courant* for all readers to form their own conclusions; and early in December, in time for Parliament's meeting, the Elector's representative, Baron Bothmer, handed St John a memorandum declaring that his master's policy was that Spain must be won for the imperial candidate.[9]

The Hanoverian *démarche* found the Ministry in some respects unprepared. Rochester's mediatory influence had been removed in the summer by his death, and St John was in a bitter and unco-operative mood towards Oxford; the failure of his Quebec expedition in the summer left him much mortified, though the Treasurer was reported to have been 'just as merry as usual' when the news arrived. The Secretary was kept busy arresting the publishers of a flood of antipeace tracts, which Swift countered by putting the ministerial case in *The Conduct of the Allies*. But as the main danger lay in the upper house it was Oxford who would bear the brunt of the opening of session. He approached some leading Whigs, including Somers and Halifax, though the sum of his efforts was probably no more than an attempt to persuade some peers not to oppose the peace measures, by promising a future coalition. His offers were scornfully rejected. More hopeful was the Treasurer's approach to known Tory supporters of the Hanoverian succession. They at least could hardly doubt his determination to have a Protestant succession. In addition he had a concession to offer churchmen in return for their loyalty to the government. Summoning a meeting of Tory leaders in the Commons, including Bromley and Hanmer, he intimated that he was now prepared to countenance a measure against the practice of occasional conformity if this would buy the support of the small group of Tory peers around Nottingham who had hitherto been opposed to the abandonment of Spain to the Bourbon. The concession came too late. Nottingham made known that he would vote with the Whigs on the preliminaries.[10]

With great craft the Whigs, while parleying with Oxford, had come to terms with 'Dismal', who was now reported by Poulet to be 'as sour and fiercely wild as you can imagine anything to be that has lived long in the desert'. As the price of Nottingham's support they were prepared to outbid Oxford and abandon the dissenters. Although the Whigs assured the dissenting leaders that an Occasional Conformity Bill was to be conceded only as a temporary expedient, and were eventually to keep their promise of repeal, the step was one which they could only justify in terms of the end's justifying the means and by pointing out that they could obtain a milder bill than the Ministry might propose. They followed Nottingham's announcement with an even more telling stroke. On 6 December, the eve of Parliament's meeting, they published in the *Daily Courant* the Elector's protest to St John against peace without Spain. Any parliamentarian who placed more hopes in future than in present royal favour now knew exactly where his interest lay. The Queen in her opening speech asked the support of both Houses in the making of peace. So far as the Commons was concerned she did not ask in vain, and the Whig amendment was defeated by 232 votes to 106. Eleven Tories responded to the Elector, including Lord Finch, John Aislabie and Thomas Pitt; their gesture was not forgotten after Anne's death. But the Tories as a whole, even most of those who usually adhered to Nottingham, were more concerned at this point with the need for peace than with its remoter consequences. In the Lords, Nottingham was given the honour of moving the amendment; and by a majority of one vote, which was increased to larger figures in subsequent divisions, the House decided that no peace could be safe or honorable which allotted Spain or the Spanish Indies to any Bourbon. In the course of the debates Wharton threatened that any minister who attempted to conclude such a peace 'might answer for it to the House with his head'.[11]

The success of Nottingham's amendment made it clear that the Lords could not be relied upon to ratify any treaty concluded on the basis of ignoring the claims of the Habsburg. The Tories were despondent, and even the Queen wavered for a moment, but a little reflection brought about a clearer view of the situation. Within a few days Anne decided to adopt Oxford's expedient of creating twelve new Tory peers to redress the balance in the Lords. While this step was being prepared Nottingham's Occasional Conformity Bill passed swiftly through all its stages in his House and was sent down to the Commons on 19 December. The following day it passed its second and third readings there and was returned to the upper chamber with only minor amendments. In the words of one amazed Member, the bill 'passed in both houses, and not one word said against it'. The measure which had disrupted parliamentary business for three successive sessions between 1702 and

1705 was thus lightly adopted. But the sacrifice of the dissenters seemed in vain. On 31 December twelve prominent or influential Tory commoners were gazetted as new barons.

The unexpected outcome of the Whig attack in the Lords met with much bitter criticism; the strident opposition to the younger Pitt's creation of eleven peers in his first year of office in 1784 is a measure of the reception accorded to Oxford's dozen in a day. But the Whigs were for the moment helpless, and this was emphasised by the dismissals and other punitive measures which took place among office holders who had voted against the Ministry in either House. The greatest to fall was Marlborough, whose services were in any case no longer needed. The Commons had been investigating army accounts since the last session, and before Parliament rose on 22 December every Member was in possession of a document which accused the Captain-General of peculation. With him was accused Walpole, as the late Secretary at War. The charges were largely trumpery, but they were difficult to answer in the recess. Before Parliament reassembled Marlborough had been deprived of his post; a few months later the renewed threat of prosecution obtained his withdrawal from England. Walpole was expelled from the Commons by a highly partisan vote, when the House met, and was sent to the Tower vowing 'I heartily despise what I shall one day revenge.' His removal and the continued absence of Stanhope, a prisoner of war since 1710, left the Whig party in the Commons still further denuded.[12]

The creation of the new peerages gave the Ministry only a precarious majority in the Lords, though in the event it was to prove sufficient. Even in a renewed struggle over the Place Bill, which passed the Commons as in the previous session, the Whigs were not able to carry the day in the Lords on 29 February 1712, when the Junto were defeated by five votes over a Tory amendment which would have postponed the measure's operation until after the end of the reign. The bill was then allowed to drop, being of no further use as an embarrassment to the Ministry. In the Commons the vote which secured Walpole's expulsion on 17 January heralded a series of new disasters for the Whigs. On the 24th another vote confirmed Marlborough's disgrace for the world—and especially the Allies—to see. As the preliminary to forcing the Dutch to give up their rights under Townshend's Barrier Treaty, several resolutions and votes condemning that treaty were obtained in February, sweeping Whig resistance aside. In these matters the energies of the October Club were given full rein, since the Club's main outstanding aims now largely merged into the Ministry's campaign for the peace. Even the appearance in late March, when the October Club's independence of the Ministry seemed to be on the wane, of a 'March Club' soon amounting to about fifty antiministerial Tories, did little to hamper the peace campaign, though the March men gave some indications of the way in which they might develop, by their generally Hanoverian sympathies and by marked aversion from Secretary St John. One of their earliest and most spectacular initiatives was in fact the assistance they gave the Whigs in defeating one of the Secretary's henchmen, a commissioner of trade named Arthur Moore, when the latter attempted to plead parliamentary privilege against his creditors. The incident presaged a far more important attack on the same Member and upon the Secretary himself, by the same combination, two years later.[13] For the moment, however, no distant prospect of a major Tory revolt could deter the Ministry in its parliamentary preparations for the reception of the peace terms, when these should be decided in the congress which had begun in January at Utrecht.

The peace negotiations proved to be, after the manner of their kind, more difficult and more protracted than had been hoped, so that the governments' intention of getting the treaties ratified before the end of the session was far from being fulfilled. But on 9 May St John, urged on by the Queens' impatience for peace, dispatched to the new Captain-General, Ormonde, the soon-to-be famous 'restraining orders', instructing him to avoid contact with the enemy. With peace unconcluded, however, the Allies preferred to fight on for a further campaign. When Ormonde's inactivity became obvious the matter was raised in the Commons by Walpole's lieutenant, Pulteney. Unfortunately for any Whig hopes which were raised by this gift of the gods, the matter appears to have been badly mismanaged in Walpole's absence. St John had no difficulty on 28 May in obtaining the rejection of a motion calling for a more active campaign in Flanders. The unusually low number of 73 voters brought out by the Whig motion against the government's 203 reflected a lack of careful preparation; the members of the Scottish Squadrone were not even notified of Pulteney's intended motion. In the Lords Halifax dropped a proposed similar motion, rather than test the Ministry's narrow majority, on Oxford's assurance that the terms of an advantageous peace were to be communicated within a few days. And on 6 June the Queen announced to both Houses the news that Philip V had agreed to renounce his title to the French succession; she spoke confidently of a peace to follow. In the Commons, where the Whigs were still demoralised from the vote of 28 May, no formal attempt was made to oppose when an address of thanks was proposed and carried, protests being shouted down.[14] The last hope of preventing the peace by parliamentary means was dead. Nevertheless, when Parliament was prorogued a fortnight later serious problems remained, and the struggle was transferred to the court and the Cabinet.

The crushing of criticism in Parliament did little to avert a growing tension which was arising in the Ministry. An outward sign of the differences was St John's outspoken chagrin early in July when he was given at his own insistence the title of Bolingbroke—but with the rank, below Oxford's, of Viscount. More dangerous were quarrels over the peace policy now to be pursued. As Oxford and Shrewsbury became more anxious to avoid giving the Dutch a real grievance, Bolingbroke became even more ready to abandon their interests in the peace terms. It had already been decided that the Secretary should himself go to Paris in order to expedite the slow process of the negotiation at Utrecht, but he set off instructed only to prolong the Anglo–French ceasefire and to conclude the formalities of Philip's renunciation.[15]

During his absence the fears of Oxford and Shrewsbury mounted. Such fears were justified, for if Bolingbroke did not actually exceed his instructions he was certainly more than indiscreet in urging the French to insist that the States General should give up the key fortress of Tournai. Oxford was privately informed that the Dutch were beginning to show themselves willing to abandon their attempt to fight on, so long as this strongpoint was secured to them. Bolingbroke returned to England to press for a general election, being certain that a war-weary electorate would strengthen his hand by returning the Tories in even greater numbers. In a violent Cabinet dispute at the end of September all the outstanding issues came to a head, but the views of Oxford prevailed: Parliament was not dissolved, nor was peace signed at once as Bolingbroke wished, nor was Tournai abandoned to the French. But in the Ministry disunity resigned; the Queen wept, Dartmouth talked wistfully of resignation, Bolingbroke left London for some hard hunting, and Oxford retired to his chamber to nurse the rheumatism of which he was a victim.[16]

Five more months were to pass while the plenipotentiaries—with the exception of those of the Emperor and the Elector of Hanover who still preferred to fight on—continued to put the peace terms into proper form, and until the treaties were concluded, Parliament was repeatedly prorogued. But in March 1713 the main treaties between Britain, Holland, France and Spain were at last concluded. A separate commercial treaty between Britain and France, the work of Bolingbroke who saw it as a move towards closer political relations in the future, undertook to establish a reduced scale of tariffs on many commodities between the two countries.[17]

The church bells of London rang out for the peace on 3 April and Parliament assembled on the 9th. The Whigs returned with a spirit of determination to save what they could by opposing the ratification of the treaties. The Tories were less single-minded. Despite the achievement of their aims they were reported by Bromley to be discontented by their long wait through the winter; subsequent events were to show that, for some of them at least, the dissatisfaction extended to aspects of the peace itself. For the first month, while the political treaties were under consideration, Whig opposition made little headway and the Tories held together. But a growing element of Tory unease was noted in the case of the commercial treaty, in which Bolingbroke had allowed woollen goods to be excepted from the reduced tariffs, a matter of great concern to Britain's manufacturers.

In this situation the Whigs saw their long-sought opportunity for splitting their opponents. Like many Tories, some of their Members had gone into the country during the long delay before Parliament's meeting. But while the Commons was hearing numerous petitions against the commercial treaty the Whigs' usual good organisation was restored, truants were brought up to London again, and fences were mended with the Squadrone and other Scots. This reconciliation was made possible by an unwise ministerial decision to extend the malt tax to Scotland. On 1 June the Whig lords sprang a bomb in the House of Lords when a motion for leave to bring in a bill to repeal the Union, pressed on by angry Scottish peers, was supported by solid Whig voting and only narrowly defeated. As in the case of their support of the Occasional Conformity Act in 1711, the Whig leaders showed themselves apparently willing to sacrifice long-held policies, in this instance the parliamentary Union, for temporary advantage. It is by no means certain, however, that they would have pushed the repeal bill through; and in any event they kept in mind, as in the former case, the point that any sacrifice made now might be rectified later provided that the overall end of the Hanoverian succession were obtained. Towards this end they had now taken a considerable stride, for they had the solid support of the Scots in both Houses for their next move. In the Commons they turned to the ratifying bill for the commercial treaty. Until the last minute the attitude which would be taken by many of the discontented Tories remained in doubt. Then Tory discipline, never as strong as that of the Whigs, broke spectacularly. On the third reading on 18 June the bill was lost by nine votes. The pressure of public opinion through petitions, a *volte-face* by Hanmer who represented the wool county of Suffolk, and the removal from the Commons of Bolingbroke's restraining hand, all had led to a desertion by about eighty Tories.[18]

By this victory the Whigs in the Commons secured an initiative which they were to retain until the end of the reign, with the help of the dissident Tories and others who joined them later, for with the conclusion of peace a new issue had come to the fore: the succession. Of the Tories who had followed Hanmer only a minority were concerned principally with the wool issue, but many were worried by

Bolingbroke's pro-French policy and the advantages for the Pretender which were assumed to follow from this. Furthermore, rumours were rife that behind Hanmer's action lay the secret authority of Oxford himself and that Bolingbroke suspected some such devious dealing. Oxford was not, however, ready to break openly with his colleagues, and the Tories who had voted against the commercial treaty needed to be pushed further towards a definite commitment to Hanover. Before the end of the session the Whig leaders made every effort to provide that push. The outcome was Wharton's successful motion in the Lords on 30 June for an address to the Queen, asking her to press for the removal of the Pretender from Lorraine or any other friendly country. In the Commons the same motion was entrusted to Stanhope, who was attending his first Parliament since his release from Spain. Here, as in the Lords, there was little outright objection; and no-one doubted that the until-recently cowed Whigs had wrested a considerable tactical advantage for facing the electorate in the general election which was due in the autumn, and for the subsequent parliamentary struggle in which they would ensure that the succession was the chief issue.[19]

The disaster for the Tories brought by the session of 1713 further exacerbated the relations of the two leading ministers. As soon as Parliament was prorogued another crisis broke out, Bolingbroke leading a strident chorus of dissatisfied Tories against the Lord Treasurer. Bolingbroke demanded a purge of the Whigs remaining in office and aimed, as the Jacobite Member George Lockhart thought, 'at nothing less than being Prime Minister of State'. He was encouraged when Hanmer, again approached by Oxford to take some office, refused and went off into the country; the Secretary was also heartened by a slight coolness of the Queen towards Oxford since the Cabinet controversy of the previous September. But Bolingbroke miscalculated his strength in the Closet. He was planning to capture the support of Mrs Masham, by a bribe whose nature was much to occupy the next Parliament, but the transaction was not yet sufficiently advanced. At first, however, circumstances appeared to favour his bid, for throughout July Oxford was unwell and in his absence the administration of the Treasury and much other business came to a standstill. The Lord Treasurer's unwillingness to delegate responsibility had become more marked as his fear of his ambitious, weak or trimming colleagues grew. As a first step in the scheme for reconstituting the Ministry, Benson was raised to a peerage on Bolingbroke's recommendation and was replaced as Chancellor of the Exchequer by the Jacobite Sir William Wyndham, an able young knight of the shire returned by Somerset in 1710 and now much under the Secretary's wing. Oxford, however, countered this move swiftly, obtaining the relief of Secretary Dartmouth, at the latter's long-standing request, in favour of Bromley. For a moment, indeed, this appointment seemed to Oxford's followers to hang in the balance, but the Queen acceded to his suggestion; if Bolingbroke had succeeded in impressing her with the inefficient nature of the existing administration she was not prepared to turn aside Oxford's reasonable suggestion for its improvement or to place herself in the hands of a less trustworthy, if more energetic, adviser. The Treasurer was also successful in persuading Hanmer to accept the government's nomination as Speaker in the next Parliament. Like Harley in the last years of William's reign, Hanmer did not feel that acceptance of the dignity of the Chair brought the same total commitment to a government as was entailed by ministerial office. The Treasurer thus ensured that a Tory of Hanoverian sympathies would hold the key post in the Commons. On the whole, Oxford's friends thought that he had exerted himself successfully.[20]

The quarrels of the ministers gave but little immediate help to the Whigs in the general election which took place in August and September. Conscious that the influence of the Queen and the weight of public opinion were still heavily against them, as in 1710, the Junto again sought a counterweight in the influence of Hanover. But in spite of their pleas for financial assistance or, failing that, for the presence in Britain of the Electoral Prince George, the Hanoverian court preferred the path of caution and avoided giving what would have been unforgivable offence to Anne. Furthermore, the Whigs faced a new disadvantage in many of the borough seats, where the effects of the Occasional Conformity Act were beginning to be felt. The result was an overwhelming Tory victory of about 360 seats to 190, the majority including all but fifteen of the eighty English county seats.* The Whigs' first reaction to these results was understandably gloomy. Reporting Stanhope's assessment, the Hanoverian Envoy wrote to his court: 'He does not think there will be fewer Whigs in the next Parliament, but he has a very bad opinion of it'. But further reflection brought more hope. The election campaign had brought into widespread use, as a result of the events of the last session, the term 'Hanoverian Tories'; and though there was, until the Commons assembled, no means of determining how many of the Tory majority were of this type, there were no grounds for thinking that their number was diminished as a result of the electorate's choice. Henceforth a full campaign of Whig press propaganda was directed towards increasing the doubts held by sympathetic Tories about the intentions of the Ministry in regard to the succession. Tactics

*The unusual accuracy with which the party numbers in this and the succeeding Parliament are known is due to the existence of the contemporary Worsley List. See Sedgwick, i, 162–87 and Eveline G. Cruickshanks, 'The Tories and the Succession', *BIHR*, xlvi (1973), 176–85.

for the forthcoming session were under discussion at a conclave at
Althorp before the last election results were in, and there can be little
doubt that much attention was devoted to the means by which the
Hanoverian Tories might be split from their fellows.[21]

Between the election and the meeting of Parliament, however, almost
six months were to elapse. Initially the Ministry decided to postpone
assembling the Members until after Christmas. The main reasons were
continuing internal quarrels and the Cabinet's inability to compromise
between Bolingbroke's advocacy of satisfying the Tory extremists and
Oxford's preference for a more pragmatic parliamentary programme.
In the course of these quarrels the Secretary succeeded in obtaining
the support of Mrs Masham and the sympathy of the Queen. By a
commercial contract signed in Madrid in March 1713, Britain had
obtained from Philip V the Asiento or monopoly of slaving to Central
and South America. This privilege had been obtained for the benefit
of the South Sea Company; but the contract was formally assigned to
the Queen as the head of government and she, with Bolingbroke's
connivance, chose to reserve a small percentage of the profits of the
trade nominally to herself, actually to her bedchamber woman, while
reassigning the remainder to the company. The directors of the company, encouraged covertly by Oxford, protested vigorously and made
their discontent at the arrangement widely known; if the stockholders
who were former government creditors were expected to share their
profits with another who had no such title to them, the whole rationale
of the setting up of the company would be flouted. To add to the Lord
Treasurer's unease, he discovered that Bolingbroke had involved the
Queen in chicanery concerning a separate treaty of commerce dealing
with British trade to the Spanish homeland; this treaty, signed in the
autumn, involved the receipt by the Secretary's friend, Moore, of a
bribe from the court of Madrid to adopt 'explanatory articles' deleterious to British merchants.[22]

While ministerial differences deferred the calling of Parliament, the
problems of the succession were revived in a dramatic manner. On
Christmas Eve, 1713, the Queen suffered an almost fatal illness. For
over a month Bolingbroke and Mrs Masham were constantly with her.
By 17 January she was sufficiently recovered to attend a Cabinet meeting, but she suffered a serious relapse in the last week of the month,
and until her condition improved a panic ensued in the City.[23] On the
19th a widely sold tract, *The Crisis*, by the Whig essayist and newly
elected Member for Stockbridge, Richard Steele, declared the Protestant succession to be in danger. Parliament's meeting could not be
deferred beyond 16 February, the date to which it was currently
assigned, and on that day the Commons duly assembled and chose
Hanmer as Speaker. But then, after some preliminary business, both

Houses were adjourned for a fortnight until Anne was able to deliver her speech.

Thus it was not until 2 March that the speech was delivered and the main dealings of the session began. After announcing the conclusion of the treaties with Spain, Anne complained that 'there are some who are arrived to that height of malice as to insinuate that the Protestant Succession in the House of Hanover is in danger under my government'. But her indignation had a ring of falsity to many ears, for numerous rumours were abroad of royal favour to the Bourbon kingdoms, as shown in the recent commercial treaties, and perhaps of plans to restore the Pretender in the event of her death. At first, however, the Whig leaders were content to let the leaven of national alarm do its work, and to establish ties with those Tories who shared their views on the succession. A new Place Bill sponsored in the Commons by the Hanoverian Tory country gentlemen was again given the full support of the Whigs in that House, and the Ministry did not care to oppose it. The bill was later to be rejected as usual in the upper house, though only by the narrowest possible margin of an equality of votes.* And on 18 March, the eve of the Easter break, the Hanoverian Tories showed a cautious move towards the Whigs over a Tory motion for the expulsion of Steele; for though the motion was successful, with only about twenty Tories actually opposing it, a larger number significantly abstained by their absence.[24]

Soon after Easter there was a hardening in the public attitudes of both Bolingbroke and the Hanoverian court, forcing first the Tories who looked to Hanmer and then the Harleyites into the arms of the Whigs. In the aftermath of the Queen's illness, which left her clearly weakened, the Treasurer along with Bolingbroke and Anne herself had secretly inquired whether the Pretender was willing to embrace the Church of England. By late March all three were aware of James's indignant refusal to change his religion. But whereas Oxford was thereby finally driven to cleave to the House of Hanover, despite the attitude of that family to himself, it was otherwise with Bolingbroke. The Secretary had even less to hope for from Hanover. His aim became to strengthen the Tory party, with himself as its leader, so that he could sit as arbiter between Stuart and Hanoverian when Anne's death should come and could thus be able to dictate terms to either, with a preference for the Pretender if the latter's rule could, by compliance if not by conversion, be made compatible with the preservation of the Church of England; for Bolingbroke was not so foolish as to suppose that the Church party would ever accept a monarch on any other terms. The attitude of Anne remained enigmatic, but she began to permit Bolingbroke and Ormonde

*In the Lords a tied vote counted as a loss for the motion before the House.

to purge the government and armed forces of remaining Whigs.* On 4 April the speeding of this process was foreshadowed by Bolingbroke, when he announced to a large meeting of Tory Members that the Queen 'would not leave a Whig in employ'.[25]

The reciprocal hardening of the Hanoverian attitude came on the 12th of the same month, when in response to strong pressure from the Whig leaders the Hanoverian Envoy, Schutz, applied to Lord Chancellor Harcourt for a writ to be sent to the Electoral Prince to take his seat in the House of Lords as Duke of Cambridge. Those who knew of the jealousy with which the Elector regarded his son, and of the violent reaction which any such proposal had always elicited from Anne, possessed a measure of the danger in which the Hanoverian court now feared their claims to be. The Whigs were convinced that this stroke was what was needed to bring the wavering Tories over, and in committee on the 15th they put the matter to the test in a vote on whether the succession was in danger. With 467 Members present the Commons heard Hanmer, who was out of the Chair, state that 'he hoped the House would never descend so low as by this vote to screen a ministry' and that 'he knew many honest and sensible men who were afraid the succession was in danger, and he was sure the authority of the House of Commons would not convince them otherwise'. There followed the amazing spectacle of the Speaker, followed by fifty or more other Tories, voting with the Whigs against the Ministry. In such circumstances the ministerial victory by forty-eight votes was a pyrrhic one.[26]

But Bolingbroke and his friends thought otherwise. The Secretary had his own plans for rallying the Hanoverian Tories to the party on a Church issue, and in the course of May a Schism Bill was introduced by Wyndham and passed through all its stages in the lower house. Proposing that from 1 August all schoolmasters should be required to declare their conformity to the Church liturgy and to be licensed by a bishop, the bill was intended to tear out Dissent at the roots, by destroying its educational system. In the Lords the Whigs were equally unable to prevent the Hanoverian Tories from rallying to the Church. The bill thus narrowly passed into law, but as an attempt to solder the divided Tory party it was a failure. Tories who feared the Pretender remained full of suspicion for Bolingbroke. Such men, moreover, were considerably more numerous than even the vote of 15 April had indicated. Men willing to commit themselves against their party on that occasion ranked as Hanoverian Tories and were subsequently regarded as being the hard core of the Pretender's Tory opponents; but many

*It has been argued that Queen Anne herself was not in any sense in favour of her half-brother's restoration (Edward Gregg, 'Was Queen Anne a Jacobite', *History*, lvii (1972) 358–75); but if positive evidence is lacking, her actions at this time throw doubt upon the argument.

others who would not openly admit, on the evidence then available, that the Protestant succession was in danger from the Ministry wanted no part in a Stuart restoration. On 24 June, after the indefatigable Wharton had produced solid evidence that James's agents were recruiting in London, the Jacobites in the Commons dared not oppose when Somerset's son, Lord Hertford, proposed that the House should offer the enormous sum of £100,000 for apprehending the Pretender if he should land in the British Isles.[27]

The Whigs' main counter to Bolingbroke's attempt to rally the Tories came, however, in exposing the Secretary's chicanery over the Spanish treaties. Assisted by the Harleys a resolution was carried in the Commons on 9 June for an address asking Anne to dispose of her share of the Asiento 'for the use of the public'; while on the 30th the Lords took up the Spanish commercial treaty, appointing a committee composed of Oxford and Whig peers to draw up an address stating the 'insuperable difficulties' caused by that treaty. In both Houses searching debates and interrogations exposed Bolingbroke's methods, and his commercial-cum-political plans stood ruined.[28] Early in July an electric atmosphere in Parliament and in the country, comparable with that at the end of the session of 1699–1700 when William was under attack, needed only a spark to cause an explosion. Even before the last stages of the parliamentary investigation, Bolingbroke despondently informed the French ambassador that he was only awaiting the end of the session for an opportunity to resign. Then at the eleventh hour, Anne intervened to prevent further inquiry into matters which concerned her so closely. On 9 July, when the Commons had just given its consent to an unusual request by the Lords to examine several of its sitting Members in connection with the affairs of the South Sea Company, Black Rod knocked upon the door with the Queen's message of prorogation. To the Whigs it seemed that royal favour to the Pretender had robbed them of the chance to bring down his ministerial supporters.[29]

Fate, and the strain of the last six months, had decreed otherwise; within three weeks of Parliament's dismissal Queen Anne was dead. Under the influence of Bolingbroke and Mrs Masham she had toyed for months with Jacobitism and peculation. Her last days were tortured by the need to decide between irreconcilable ministers. Oxford had recently drawn up an aide-memoire to tell her that 'all the Whigs and much the greater part of the Church are united in a jealousy of some foul play and design for the Pretender'. But it was the perpetual 'teasing' of Mrs Masham and Bolingbroke which finally drove her to action, and on 27 July Oxford was himself dismissed. After fierce Cabinet quarrels in her presence the Queen, her spirit almost broken, retired to her bed of sickness. But she had enough will left to refuse to call upon the tainted Bolingbroke to form a new Ministry, and by this belated restraint she possibly spared her country civil strife at her death. On the 30th her condition was sufficiently serious for Lord Chancellor Harcourt to constitute a Privy Council, which was attended by a number of the Whigs who remained members, including Shrewsbury, Somerset and Argyll. On the suggestion of Harcourt the Council advised the Queen to appoint Shrewsbury as Lord Treasurer, and she complied. For the second time, a quarter of a century after the first, this shy statesman proved essential to the nation. The appointment of so undoubted a supporter of the Hanoverian succession was a measure for which Harcourt, his subsequent deliberations on the possibility of a Jacobite coup unknown or forgotten, was later well rewarded by the House of Hanover. On the morning of 1 August the Queen died. The new royal family, and with them the Whigs, entered into the inheritance for which all had fought so desperately.[30]

CHAPTER 9

Tory Defeat and Whig Schism
1714-17

Owing to the survival for at least a generation after 1714 of the issues which had hitherto sustained the parties, the decline of their importance was slow and far from complete by 1742. The succession question received fresh impetus from the Old Pretender's invasion in 1715, and remained a matter for serious concern to Ministries until at least the failure of the Young Pretender's descent in 1745. And though Walpole usually attempted, like the Junto, to avert national suspicion of a Whig menace to the Church of England, a substantial element of the party ensured that the religious issue remained active and was dramatically revived in 1736 by anti-Church legislation and other attempted measures. For the rest, the parties' mutual antagonism, on small issues as well as great ones, was sufficient in itself to stoke the old fires down to Walpole's fall and beyond. Research on division lists carried out by Romney Sedgwick and his collaborators for the official *History of Parliament: the House of Commons, 1715–1754*, whose tabulated findings are often cited for the remaining chapters of this book, indicated a remarkable degree of consistency in Tory voting throughout the period. Whig voting, it is true, was often divided after 1716 by successive party schisms; but to assume that opposition Whigs always voted with the Tories to form a stable 'country party' would be to misrepresent the case. Indeed, a consistent pattern is observable of the refusal of Tories and dissident Whigs to work together except for brief periods. Down to the end of 1741 the Tories remained reluctant to bring down one Whig government in order to elevate another, and when they agreed to bring down Walpole they did so under the impression that a 'broad-bottom' war coalition was to be formed. They soon learned better. The opposition Whigs returned their antagonism with interest, making little secret of their dislike of the necessity which forced them to seek the assistance of the Tory party, and ensuring that the Tories should not share their triumph when they forced their way into office.

Despite the periodic threats by George I and George II to turn to the Tory party, as being more complaisant towards monarchy than were the Whigs, no Hanoverian in fact seriously contemplated an alliance with the Tories as a party while the Jacobite menace remained real.

The possibility of admitting the Hanoverian Tories to office was prevented both by the refusal of nearly all of them to desert their friends and by the determination of all Whigs to keep them out. Contrary to later mythology, Whig Ministries, even Walpole's at the height of its power, could rely upon fewer than a third of the House of Commons as placemen, and many of these were not reliable upon all issues. To remain in office the ministers had to satisfy the Whigs, who objected to Tories promoted over their heads. In such conditions the possibility of a return to the preparty pattern of court–country politics, such as Bolingbroke proclaimed from 1716 onward, was strictly limited. The term 'court party' could be useful for describing ministerial supporters in situations when not all Whigs were on the government side, but the court party could include only Whigs. Similarly, the description of 'country party' could be useful, alongside 'minority' and 'opposition', in referring to the Tories and opposition Whigs collectively; but such terms provided only a verbal blanket to cover a variety of men with few ideas or aims in common. When Walpole's active career ended in 1742 the two parties were still very much in evidence.

Although few Tories were so unrealistic in August 1714 as to suppose that the new monarch would favour them against their rivals, some hoped for a mixed Ministry under Shrewsbury or even Oxford which would include the more moderate members of both parties. Not many can have anticipated the swiftness of the Tory party's decline during the first eighteen months of the new reign; by the beginning of 1716 the Tories were almost helpless. From this situation the party recovered somewhat in the following year, to occupy the subsidiary, but still important, place in politics which they were to retain for nearly half a century. That they recovered at all from Whig attempts finally to destroy them may be ascribed to the demonstration, in the 1715 and subsequent general elections, of the majority which they continued to hold in most of the large-franchise constituencies; it may also be ascribed to the ferocity of an attack which overreached itself even in the eyes of moderate Whigs, fanned the suspicions of the royal family and its German advisers, and encouraged the development of quarrels among the Whigs themselves.

Such initial Tory hope as existed was not entirely dashed by the composition of the Council of Regency appointed under the terms of the Regency Act. The Council took over the functions of monarchy on behalf of the King until he should arrive in Britain. The Regents nominated by George, in addition to the officers of state who were members *ex officio*, were found to include four Hanoverian Tory peers headed by Nottingham to reinforce three who were official members. Thus although there were eighteen Whig members the Tories might, if united, have constituted a sufficiently formidable minority to deter their colleagues from extreme measures. This appeared especially so in view of the absence from George's list of most of the Junto. The latterly moderate Halifax and the now somewhat inactive Orford were present, but the names of Somers, Wharton and Sunderland were glaringly missing. Somers had been known for some time to be ailing, but no such reason was available in the case of the other two men. A shrewd observer, the moderate Whig Sir John Perceval, was doubtless correct in attributing their exclusion to the King's belief that they were 'too violent and unacceptable to the body of the nation'. But though George studiedly avoided extremes his Regents gave, in practice, no concession to Tory aspirations, and acted in unity to discourage the Jacobites. The only prominent person to dare suggest proclaiming the Pretender proved to be Bishop Atterbury, and the coolness with which his suggestion was met by Bolingbroke and Harcourt served to convince the bishop of the hopelessness of his cause, for the moment at least. But if the bulk of the Tory party avoided real commitment to James, as it was to do on all occasions, the Tories' prospects of office were not thereby improved. The Earl of Mar, more realistic than most of his colleagues, wrote that he saw little prospect of good either for the divided Tories or his own continuance in office as Secretary for Scotland. But even he did not foresee the extreme of desperation which caused him, with a small band of followers, to set up the Pretender's standard at Braemar little more than a year later.[1]

After a new swearing-in of Members, which had commenced on the first day of the reign, Parliament met for business on 5 August 1714. Despite the ardent wish of most Members to remain in the country at this season, there was a full attendance. The Tories made the first move. In response to a reminder from the Council of Regency that the royal Revenue had expired with the Queen's death, Wyndham and Bromley rose to propose a Civil List of £1 million, which was £300,000 more than Anne had enjoyed, brushing aside on grounds of tactical expediency the doubts of their followers about the wisdom of such an action. This blatant attempt to curry favour with the King was easily parried. The Whigs, with commendable restraint, held back from supporting the Tory proposal, hinting disingenuously to Bothmer of even better terms to be obtainable on another occasion. Their superior discipline gained them their point, as it often had. Without the expected votes of the Whigs the ministers found insufficient support among their own rank and file, and the proposal was shelved without having brought its sponsors much credit. No more than in 1689 or 1690, in fact, could the Revenue be governed simply by party considerations. The granting of a generous Revenue was stopped in August 1714, as the Whig journalist Boyer announced, by a single transcending motive:

'the wisest of both parties being of opinion that the only way to preserve our excellent constitution is to keep the Crown still dependent for
extraordinary subsidies on the House of Commons.'

As in the case of William III, the House began the way it meant to
go on.

Nevertheless the Whigs did not let the short session pass without
some indication of their superior concern for the King. On 13 August
Horatio Walpole, younger brother of Robert, took the initiative with a
proposal for paying war subsidy arrears which were owed to Hanover
for the payment of Electoral troops. The Tories could not openly
oppose this, but some of their number obligingly raised objections
which threw doubt on their willingness to please. Altogether the Whigs
had managed a not unsuccessful parliamentary commencement to the
new reign, and since little further was possible against the Tory majority
in the present Parliament, it was prorogued on the 25th. Apart from
formal meetings for further prorogation it never met again.[2]

The time for shadow boxing was over. At the end of August the
Regents dismissed Bolingbroke on orders from the King. Since the
death of Anne, both he and Bromley had been virtually suspended
from independent action by a requirement that their official correspondence should pass through the hands of the Regents' secretary,
Joseph Addison. Bolingbroke's office was solemnly sealed up upon his
dismissal to prevent the removal of possibly incriminating documents,
and the southern department remained vacant for the moment. Bromley retained his seals only until 17 September, when he was replaced
by Townshend. Further changes, however, awaited the arrival of the
monarch, who set out on a stately progress from his Electoral capital
on the day of Bolingbroke's dismissal, travelling by the usual route
through Holland. Resting for several days at The Hague, he gave an
ostensibly favourable reception to the Earl of Strafford, the British
Ambassador and lately one of the plenipotentiaries at Utrecht, who
duly sent optimistic reports home. The leaders of both parties meanwhile put finishing touches to their proposed speeches of self-justifica-
tion to the portly German who represented Nemesis. But there was a
difference between their expectations: while the most for which the
Tories expressed a hope was a government drawn from both parties,
this represented an outcome which the Whigs dreaded. The astute
former Chancellor Cowper was particularly anxious lest George
should be induced to prefer a balanced or nonparty Ministry such as
William had always desired. In a written dissertation which purported
to consider judiciously the merits and disadvantages of both parties
from the point of view of the monarchy, Cowper was careful to call

the King's attention to the need for such 'moderate counsels as will render you King of all your divided people'. But, he submitted, if an equality of favour were shown to the parties 'an equal degree of power, tending at the same time different ways, would render the operations of the government slow and heavy, if not altogether impracticable'. And since there was a necessity to favour one side or the other, Cowper confidently left it to George to choose the Whigs.[3]

The King's choice, when he arrived at Greenwich on 19 September, had already long been made, in consultation with his Hanoverian ministers. His reasoning, to judge by his actions, had not differed greatly from Cowper's. Bothmer, who as the man on the spot was the principal among the King's Electoral advisers at this point, had indeed recently suggested appointment by merit 'without regard to whether a man is a Whig or a Tory'; but since he immediately qualified this by excluding from consideration anyone who had served in the Queen's last Ministry, almost the only Tory of the necessary quality and experience to fulfil this criterion was Nottingham, who duly became Lord President as the reward for his unswerving support of the Protestant succession. The rest of the appointments in the first weeks after the King's arrival made a clean sweep of the old Ministry. Shrewsbury, who was combining the posts of Lord Treasurer, Lord Lieutenant of Ireland and Lord Chamberlain, asked to be relieved of all but one of them; he was taken literally at his word and left with only the last position. The Treasury was put into commission under Halifax, who became an earl, and the Lord Lieutenancy went to Sunderland. The southern Secretaryship was occupied by Stanhope, to many people's surprise. Wharton, in recognition of his career of undeviating whiggery, was given the Privy Seal, which was supplemented the next year by English and Irish marquisates. To Orford, Marlborough and Cowper were restored their old posts of First Lord of the Admiralty, Captain-General and Lord Chancellor respectively. Further down the scale Walpole became Paymaster, which helped to lay the foundation of his financial fortune. His old post of Secretary at War went to Pulteney.[4]

Sweeping as were the changes in favour of the Whigs, the new king's administrative arrangements were made primarily with an eye to his own considerations, and thereby caused Whig dissatisfaction. By placing the Treasury and the Admiralty in permanent commission the King was consciously returning to the policy of William III, not only to avoid overmighty ministers but also with the object of sharing among several men the burden which these large and responsible departments imposed. But the thwarting of Halifax's ambition of at last obtaining the white staff of Lord Treasurer made him a discontented element in the new Ministry's first year. Similarly, the appointments as Secretaries of State of a diplomat and a soldier–diplomat rather than of full-time politicians gave considerable offence, though the move was useful for George's foreign policy. Moreover, time was to show that the appointment of Stanhope to partner Townshend did not result in a good team.

More immediate, however, than the reaction of dissatisfied Whigs was the Tories' anger at the unmistakable evidence of their low standing in the King's eyes. One of the first ominous signs of their disgrace appeared on the second day after George's arrival, when the still hopeful Oxford secured admission and was allowed only to kiss the royal hand; without conversation the King then contemptuously turned his back. Day after day the evidence of Tory decline multiplied. Only in the proposed junior appointments at the Treasury, where Halifax's recommendation carried weight, was there some sign of concession. For four years the former financial wizard had been dickering intermittently with Oxford with a view to forming a Ministry of moderate complexion. While he waited confidently in September to be made Lord Treasurer, Halifax made no secret of the fact that as chief minister he hoped to retain some Tories, just as Oxford had retained some Whigs after 1710. Though such hopes were disappointed, offers were made to Hanmer of the Chancellorship of the Exchequer and to Bromley of a seat on the Board and a Tellership of the Exchequer; but both men demonstrated their solidarity with their excluded friends by refusing the places offered. Bromley, indeed, would have taken the Tellership if it had been obtainable for life, but mindful of his Oxford constituents he refused to put himself in the position of being a court placeman holding office at the King's pleasure.[5]

Henceforth all Tories, whether Hanoverian or Jacobite, drew together in prospect of a general election and a new Parliament. They needed all the unity they could manage, for during the last three months of 1714 they were the subject of a purge of offices which was carried through with unprecedented ferocity and completeness. The Whigs, as Perceval admitted, were 'thirsty beyond measure' after their years of exile; he wrote:

'... the Whigs made such fierce application that it disgusted the King, and he could not forbear expressing more than once his surprise that the nobility and gentry of England, who possessed such large fortunes, were so assiduous and covetous of offices'.

From Ireland, where Sunderland's writ ran, Archbishop King reported to Shrewsbury that 'we have abundance of changes here every day'. In the royal household, the Lord Lieutenancies, the Revenue departments, military posts, legal offices and lesser places throughout the land, Tories were swept away by the kinsmen or other nominees of the leading Whigs, in the most complete upheaval which occurred between the accession of Queen Anne and the first two years of George III.[6]

In anticipation of an election Whig preparations were reported by the Tories to be 'made in all places possible, and no money spared'. From the August prorogation onward there had been a concerted campaign of addresses to the King, condemning the last government with a sameness of wording and sentiment which suggests careful collusion. The implication of treasonable behaviour by Anne's Ministry, in the conclusion of the Treaty of Utrecht, was revived early in January by the impounding of Strafford's papers. A few days later Parliament was dissolved by a short but pointed royal proclamation calling for the return of Members 'such as showed a firmness to the Protestant succession, when it was most in danger'. Tory propaganda, by contrast with that of the Whigs, was ineffective and subdued. The one exception was a powerful unsigned pamphlet by Atterbury, *English Advice to the Freeholders of England*, which did not content itself with recapitulating the usual arguments against the Whigs but launched an attack on the King's involvement in German affairs, accusing the Ministry of preparing for war in that area. This was a home thrust which provoked a vigorous search for the author by the government; but on the whole, Jacobite intervention did more harm than good. In particular a widely circulated declaration by the Pretender, asserting the good intentions of Queen Anne and the late Ministry towards himself, did the Tories great disservice with both the electorate and the Hanoverian court. Just as the 1710 election had been fought on the issues of continued war and danger to the Church, so that of 1715 was conducted, as Whig propaganda had long desired, on the issues of peace treaties and ministerial policies allegedly designed to prevent the Protestant succession.[7]

Before the elections had been long under way, in February 1715, it became clear that the returns were exceeding the Whigs' most optimistic expectations. The electors were impressed by the danger to the Hanoverian succession implied in Bolingbroke's activities at the end of Anne's reign, and in constituencies where government patronage or intimidation could play any part the Whigs had left little to chance. The Welsh border country which had been dominated by the Harley and Foley connections for several decades received particular attention. Oxford's son Lord Harley, who had sat for Radnor, was rejected amid violent scenes which included the murder of two of his supporters. The amount of government interest which could be exerted in Wales, however, was limited, and the conservative, gentry-dominated principality as a whole retained a Tory majority which was not reduced until the beginning of the next reign. Very different were the cases of Scotland and Cornwall. Scotland, which even in the last election had returned two Whigs for every Tory, now sent up only seven Tories among its forty-five Members. The pliable Duchy, its patronage now firmly in Whig hands, could find seats for only twelve Tories amongst its forty-four Members, though in 1713 it had returned thirty-six.

Though the result of the election was a reversal of the majority in the last two Parliaments of Anne's reign, the swing of the electorate against the Tories was not so great as that against the Whigs in 1710. But the floating voters who had opted for the Tories in 1710 and 1713 had deserted them to a considerable extent.* Commentators were well aware of a disparity, implied in the somewhat different strengths of the two swings, between the numerical basis of party support in the nation and the size of the parties in Parliament; and at least one foreign observer in England in 1715 asserted, as many other commentators were to continue to assert, that 'the majority of the populace of this kingdom are Tories'. In fact, in terms of the total number of votes cast on each side in the 1715 election, the two parties appear to have been approximately equal. But the constituencies nevertheless returned 341 Whigs to 217 Tories even before consideration of petitions made for a greater Whig preponderance in the Commons. The discrepancy arose from the circumstance that the counties, which together with the relatively few large-franchise boroughs held the majority of the voters, returned only a small proportion of the Members at Westminster. The English counties returned forty-nine Tories to thirty-one Whigs, and even where Tory candidates were defeated they often obtained far more votes than did successful Whig candidates in borough seats.[8] It was the larger number of English boroughs, where dissenting influence was now unchecked and where government patronage could often be exerted if the dissenting vote were not sufficient, together with the Presbyterian votes in the Scottish boroughs and counties, which returned the Whig majority.†

When Parliament assembled on 17 March a well-publicised set of instructions given by the citizens of London to its new Whig Members set the scene by demanding extensive inquiries into the conduct of the last Ministry. The Ministry's plans for exacting retribution and cowing further resistance called for some finesse in the choice of a Speaker. Hanmer had been reported to have some hopes of re-election to the Chair with court support, and his undoubted loyalty to the new dynasty lent substance to his claims; but the presence of a Hanoverian Tory

---

*For the importance of the floating vote, the reader is again referred to the illuminating work of Dr W. A. Speck, *Tory and Whig*. Dr Speck adds much further information on the swing to the Whigs in the open constituencies in 'The General Election of 1715', *EHR*, xc (1975), 507–22.

†English boroughs of under 1,000 voters returned 234 Whigs and 124 Tories, while those of 1,000 voters or more returned 29 Whigs and 22 Tories. In Scotland the boroughs returned 13 Whigs and 2 Tories, while the counties, where landowner influence was more marked than in England, returned 25 Whigs and 5 Tories (Sedgwick, i, 79).

Speaker would have been a considerable handicap. The government's choice fell upon Spencer Compton, who was proposed by two Members ostensibly unconnected with the extreme Whigs, Hertford and Finch. Compton himself, though an impeccably Whig associate of Walpole, came of a strongly Tory family, a fact which many times in his career caused rumour and his Whig rivals to attribute Tory sympathies to him, though he did little enough to justify the accusation. His reputation, when taken together with that of his sponsors, was sufficient to secure his uncontested election. This hurdle over, Walpole on the 23rd moved an address which condemned the peace of Utrecht and other measures of the Tories and proposed 'to bring the authors of them to condign punishment'. In the ensuing debate the Tories stood together, Perceval noting that the Hanoverian Tories 'fell in again with their former party'. The extent of their weakness was glaringly revealed, however, on their motion for recommittal, which was lost by 244 votes to 138. The House then turned to the business of election petitions, with the Whigs selecting as chairman of the Committee of Elections Richard Hampden, grandson of William III's minister of the same name and great-grandson of the resister of Ship Money. As well as standing as a symbol to intimidate all Tories by his very name, Hampden managed his task competently, for none of the forty-six Tory petitioners was successful, though thirty-one Tories were unseated by Whigs. The extent of this deflection of justice exceeded even that of 1708, when petitions had been heard at the bar of the House.[9]

These ominous signs were only a beginning, for the remainder of the session saw a mounting tide of violence by the Whig majority. The first Tory whose nerve broke was Bolingbroke, who slipped quietly out of England at the end of March and shortly afterwards enlisted with the Pretender under the title of Secretary of State; his prudence subsequently seemed justified. His friend Wyndham, the leading Jacobite in the Commons, had the temerity to take a major part in the session's debates, and was roughly handled on several occasions even before he was arrested in the autumn on suspicion of treason. The initiative in the attack which now began on the former ministers was taken by Stanhope and Walpole, the latter still burning with resentment at his expulsion and imprisonment in 1712. The main purpose of the Whigs, however, was not so much personal vengeance as the destruction of the Tory leadership, as the Tories had tried to destroy the Junto in the impeachments of 1701. There was every prospect of success, for the Tories, unlike the Junto on the former occasion, had no king to turn to.

On 9 April Stanhope produced a large quanity of documentary evidence relating to the behaviour of Queen Anne's last Ministry, and moved that it should be referred to a secret committee to prepare a report. The Tories did not venture to divide the House, with the result that most of the court list of committee members was carried without difficulty. Even under the energetic leadership of Walpole, however, the committee took longer to produce results than was anticipated, for several difficulties were encountered. First and most important was the shortage of written evidence to substantiate charges of treason over the negotiation at Utrecht. A fairly good case could be made out against Bolingbroke, with the aid of his own confiscated correspondence. Oxford, however, proved more elusive. As Lord Treasurer he had had no official connection with the peace negotiation, and his considerable unofficial correspondence was not available to the committee. They nevertheless pressed ahead with their task, and Walpole was able to present their report on 9 June. Despite the outspoken doubts of one member of the committee, Jekyll, as to whether charges could be sustained in the case of Oxford, motions were carried for the impeachement of both this former minister and Bolingbroke for high treason. A few days later Ormonde was voted guilty of treason while Strafford was charged with high crimes and misdemeanours. In the debates on these matters the Tories were reported to be notably quiet and subdued, and even on the dubious charge against Oxford only Edward Harley and Thomas Foley stood up to make a defence. The fury of the Whigs' attack at this point was such, indeed, that anyone who stood between them and the former Ministry was in danger of arrest, if not worse.[10]

It was soon evident, however, that lack of evidence of anything which a judicial examination in the upper house would construe as treason was running the prosecutors into deep waters. Fortunately for the Whigs, Ormonde broke and ran to join Bolingbroke in July, giving the government an excuse to supersede both men's impeachment by more easily obtainable attainder proceedings. The cases of Oxford and Strafford were more difficult. The former's defence was that he had, in carrying out all his ministerial functions, simply obeyed the Queen's commands; and this simple argument carried much weight. Thus by August, though only a few Tories continued in the Commons to raise their voices against the prosecution proceedings, the mood both inside and outside the walls of Westminster was changing. Opinion at large found difficulty in swallowing charges which condemned ex-servants of the Crown for carrying out measures which not only had been fully approved by the monarch but also had been repeatedly ratified by a former Parliament. For reasons such as this the Lords moved with extreme caution against Oxford and Strafford, and had still not settled a date for their trials when all existing business was set aside in September by the news that the Pretender's standard was aloft in Scotland.[11]

During the period of the 1715 Rebellion and its immediate aftermath, both parties were to undergo considerable change. For the Whigs the transition was aided by the passing of the generation of leaders who had served the party since the Revolution; the deaths of Halifax and Wharton in the summer of 1715 were to be followed in the spring of the succeeding year by that of Somers. The much younger Sunderland was brought nearer to the achievement of his desire, the recovery of a Secretaryship of State, when he took over Wharton's post of Privy Seal. But the greatest change was that which in October involved the promotion of Walpole to First Lord of the Treasury, in place of Carlisle who had taken Halifax's place for a few months; with his new post Walpole combined that of Chancellor of the Exchequer. Sunderland and Walpole were both good men to face the immediate crisis of the insurrection, but in the long run they were not easily compatible with each other; for if the former's advancement represented a gain for what was sometimes called the Marlborough group, Walpole's placed the Townshend faction in an even stronger position, as now holding two of the three most important offices of state. The rivalry of the two groups was to play a decisive part in the breakup of Whig party unity after the Rebellion.

For the Tories the effect of the Pretender's move was far-reaching, forcing them to decide whether to give him active support. What the decision would be was the subject of a realistic assessment by the Earl of Mar as early as July, when the Whig assault on the Tory leadership was at its height. He held that:

'those who are only enemies to the set of men now in power and not thoroughly engaged for the King [James] (which is the case of many of the Tory party), will either stand at a gaze and expect the event, or join with the present government.'

So it proved. The romantic haze through which many uncommitted Tories liked to see the Chevalier de St George—provided that he kept his distance—was tempered by a cool appraisal of his chances of staging an effective bid for the restoration of his dynasty. Above all, nearly all English Tories save the relatively few Catholics found the Pretender's religion an effective bar to his return. In 1688 their rejection of James II has been the result of his abandonment of the Church of England, and the only way in which King James's son could have regained their support was by accepting that Church. Bolingbroke had been well aware of this fact in the last months of Queen Anne's life, and as the Pretender's Secretary of State he was still certain of it. In the atmosphere of uninformed optimism which characterised the exiled court he strove to introduce the voice of reason. The only chance of success, he wrote to James, was to 'link unto your own cause that of the Church of England, of the Tory party, and of your sister's memory'. But Bolingbroke struggled in vain against the ill judgment and mismanagement which surrounded his new master, and above all failed to obtain any substantial concession to Tory religious sentiment. In the absence of any such concession, the Tories reluctantly rallied to King George.[12]

As early as the King's first announcement to Parliament in July that an invasion was known to be in preparation, the Prussian Resident was able to report with satisfaction to his court that 'the King has recovered his authority, the two parties are united in supporting him'. Extraordinary sums to meet the emergency were voted without opposition, and in September both Houses authorised the arrest of several of their Members, the most important being Wyndham and Oxford's friend Lord Lansdowne, who were suspected of planning risings in the west of England and elsewhere. Wyndham gave himself up, but suffered only imprisonment for the duration of the crisis; there was little evidence against him, and the extortion of confession by torture was, as Bonet felt impelled to explain to Berlin, out of the question in England. Wyndham was to live to be converted into the chief pillar of non-Jacobite toryism in the Commons. The Rebellion which its sponsors had hoped would rally the Tories to the Stuart cause simply confirmed their decision of 1688 and further weakened the Jacobite section of the party, whose hopes were finally destroyed when the major rebel force under Mar was held at Sheriffmuir and a minor insurrection in northeastern England was defeated at Preston.[13]

When Parliament reassembled in January 1716 the Tories at first remained co-operative, or at least quiescent. Even a four-shilling land tax proposed by Walpole to meet the costs of suppressing the risings only caused a few discontented mutterings. Early in February, however, the Tory leaders in the Commons stirred themselves against a bill intended to transfer the trials of prisoners from the areas in which they were captured, where the juries were considered by the government to be overlenient, to London. Though reported to have summoned all their forces, and even to have been assisted by some Whigs, the opponents of the bill did not muster more than 100 votes. With the first small signs that moderate Whigs were relenting, however, the nadir of Tory fortunes was passed. Stronger resistance was encountered by the government when six rebel Scottish peers who had been impeached without much difficulty in January were sentenced to death. Hitherto the accused men had evoked little sympathy, but the imminence of their execution stirred the Tories into action. In the upper house on 22 February Nottingham unexpectedly swayed moderate opinion in favour of an address to the King, asking for clemency where possible. In the end only two peers went to the scaffold, a compromise between deterence and a growing national aversion from further retribution.[14]

The Tories' best opportunity came with a governmental proposal to replace the Triennial Act by a measure permitting Parliament to sit for up to seven years. The Ministry's thinking, as explained with brutal candour by Perceval, was 'that the only way to destroy Toryism will be to establish the present Parliament for some years to come'. In public the Whigs contended that the Triennial Act had permitted excessive popular participation in politics, tumults at elections, and—a potent argument with many members—the ruin of candidates by frequent electoral expenses. The bill was introduced in the Lords, where all the traditional arguments for and against frequent elections were once more rehearsed at length. The old protagonists of the Triennial Act were able to state their views again, and even Somers, in a lucid spell during his last illness, was able to give his blessing to the removal of the measure whose original passage he had tried to prevent. Shrewsbury, who had greater responsibility than anyone for its enactment, spoke strongly for its retention. Similar resistance to the Septennial Bill was forthcoming in the Commons, where there was still feeling among many Whigs that long Parliaments were 'departing from Whig principles and perpetuating a Ministry though they serve their country ever so ill'. Others feared that their constituents would object to the proposed reduction of their electoral privileges. With such assistance the Tories, in over fifty speeches according to one account, opposed the bill as an infringement of national liberties, and forecast the future subjection of the Commons to the government's powers of patronage. There was, nevertheless, never any doubt that the bill would pass, and the closest division in the Commons gave the government a majority of 122 votes. As in the case of the latterday airing given in the Sacheverell trial to the Whig theory of contractual government, the old-fashioned whiggery which wished to reduce executive influence by such means as frequent elections received, in the Septennial Bill debates, its last major demonstration for many years, and proved to be distinctly unacceptable to the great majority of the party. The work of the Junto in transforming pre-Revolution doctrine into a practical philosophy of power was complete.[15]

The events of the session also saw the end of the distinction between the Hanoverian Tories and the main body of the party. Since 1713 the term 'Hanoverian Tory' had served the purpose of delineating Hanover's more active Tory supporters, though it had never comprehended all the Tories who desired the Hanoverian succession. With the dismissal of Nottingham and Aylesford in February 1716, for trying to save the lives of the Jacobite peers, the limited royal favour hitherto enjoyed by Hanoverian Tories came to an end, and there remained little to distinguish them from other non-Jacobite Tories. Henceforth the appellation 'Hanoverian' to describe a distinctive type of Tory was not much needed. The only Hanoverian Tories who remained in office were absorbed by their own choice into the Whig ranks. The moral of the Finches' dismissal was clear: ambitious Tories must conform completely or perish. There began a steady trickle of Tory defections, led in April 1716 by the wealthy Sir Richard Child. Such changes of party were usually signalled by a vote on some important division, or at the beginning of a session. The usual method was to preface party conversion by a period of withdrawal from notice on the part of the individual concerned, to allow a decent interval for his transformation. Over the next quarter of a century the rate of conversion averaged about one or two party members a year. To this number must be added men who came of Tory families but had themselves never sat as Tories. Thus while Sir Stephen Fox was to be a convert in Parliament, his brother Henry entered it as a Whig, though he had once stood unsuccessfully as a Tory. With the Foxes went, at various times, Dartmouth's Legge kinsmen, the Winningtons and other prominent Tories. Not all leading Tory families succumbed to temptation. Though Nottingham's branch of the Finches returned to the government fold after an interval, Aylesford's fell back among the Tories. A few prominent families remained loyal to toryism because they had to; it was ironic that the Harleys, whose party affinities had been minimal in the great days of toryism, were precluded from office by the prejudice of the first two Hanoverian monarchs, while their friends the once-Jacobite Harcourts were to perform the transition to courtiership under the new monarchy in less than a decade.[16]

But the drift of Tory defectors, scarcely noticed except on a few occasions when it was accelerated by some fresh setback to the party, needs to be seen in perspective. The loss of numbers was largely made good by the election of new Tory Members. Even the more serious weakening at leadership level, especially by the loss of some great families, was to be largely offset for at least a generation by the recruitment of able speakers who made up in energy what they lacked in great affiliations. Down to the 1740s the party proved far from being a rump without a head, and would probably have regained many of its old members if the House of Hanover could have been persuaded to break with the Whigs. Perhaps the best attestation of this possibility came from the Whigs, who regarded the new converts with lifelong suspicion as crypto-Tories whose aim was to oust good Whigs from the favour of the dynasty and to bring their former friends back into office. Such was the imputation under which John, Baron Carteret, the ablest of the Tory converts in the Lords, was to labour after he became a Whig adherent of Sunderland. The fact that such men as Carteret and the Nottingham Finches were often devoted to the personal interests of the royal family was hardly usable as an argument against them; but it was to become a source of deep resentment among the Old Whigs.

In comparison with the solidity of the great bulk of the Tory party which remained in opposition, the Whigs suffered from serious fissures in the course of 1716. The steps whereby their divisions came about were complex and often unedifying, involving a number of related issues and a considerable diversity of interests. In foreign affairs the issues involved the shifting relations of Britain with its allies Austria and Holland and with its old enemy France, as well as the new complicating factor of the King's diplomacy, as Elector of Hanover, with the nations of the Baltic. In domestic affairs the interest centred upon a number of groups in the party and at court, among which were: the King and his entourage of German advisers and mistresses; Prince George and his able wife Caroline, who were on distant terms with the King; the Marlborough faction, which included Sunderland and Marlborough's friend General Cadogan; the powerful heads of the Campbell clan, Argyll and Islay; the Walpole brothers with Townshend; and the somewhat unknown figure of Stanhope.

Until the Septennial Act was passed and the parliamentary session came to an end in June all these interests maintained a common front, in public at least. Immediately afterwards their fragile unity began to shatter. The King proposed to go to oversee his interests in Hanover, taking Stanhope with him but leaving Townshend behind. Before leaving, George felt obliged to invest the Prince of Wales with the title, though hardly the power, of Regent. The Prince was further offended by being forced to dismiss Argyll from the post of his Chamberlain. This was done at the insistence of the Marlborough group which, having succeeded in getting Argyll replaced by Cadogan in Scotland during the later phases of the Rebellion, now feared his friendship with the junior court. But it soon became clear that the Prince and Princess not only intended to continue favouring the Campbells but also were prepared to welcome the presence of Tories. This last development had been maturing for some time. At the final passage of the Civil List in May 1715 the Tories in the Commons, by proposing an independent list of £100,000 for the heir to the throne, had tried a variant of their attempt to please the King on like occasion in 1714. Though the move was defeated by the Whigs, enough was said in the Commons to ensure that the Prince and Princess would, theoretically *ex gratia*, obtain out of the Civil List a substantial annual sum. Having thus realised the usefulness of a party in opposition, the young royal couple never thereafter lost an opportunity to drop hints of their favour towards the Tories, or at least towards nonparty government in which Tories might participate. Early in 1716 Caroline, asked by Lady Cowper if 'she continued in the resolution of being a Tory', provokingly replied that she wanted 'convincing arguments that a Whig was more than a Tory for the King's prorogative'.[17]

From July onward reports of the open favour shown by the young couple to Tories who flooded to their court at Windsor were the subject of agonised scrutiny by Walpole and Townshend. Unable to control the Prince, these ministers were anxious to avoid the imputation at Hanover of being implicated in his dabblings; for they were concerned, with reason, about their standing with the King, whose foreign policy they distrusted. George, as Elector, needed diplomatic support against Sweden in the Baltic, and proposed to get it from France where the Regent Orleans had succeeded Louis XIV as ruler in 1715 and was gradually slowing down French support for the Pretender. In July 1716 a rapprochement was reached at The Hague between Stanhope and the French minister Dubois, and preparations went ahead for a treaty in which the participants confirmed and guaranteed the successions to the thrones of Britain and France which had been agreed at Utrecht. When Sunderland left England quietly and turned up in Hanover he willingly supported the King's foreign policy and united with Stanhope against Townshend and Walpole. The drastic reversal of British alliances implied in the new policy could not but upset Walpole, whose career was based on his sensitivity to opinion in Britain and who feared the reaction of Whig backbenchers to a sudden alliance with France and the virtual abandonment of the Allies.

From this point grievances mounted rapidly on both sides of the North Sea. Townshend and Walpole took an excessively traditionist stance, begging for the inclusion of Holland in the treaty and attacking interference by George I's German advisers in British politics. Walpole also strongly opposed the grant of a peerage to Child, though this had been promised by the King's chief mistress, the Duchess of Munster, in return for a bribe. Stanhope defended the King vigorously; as to the need for British money and naval support in the Baltic, he wrote, 'I believe it may not be impossible even to put this northern business in such a light as may induce the Parliament not to look upon it with indifference.' Sunderland asserted that the King was surprised at the notion that Parliament should not concern itself with affairs in the north; 'and indeed,' he concluded, 'this notion is nothing but the old Tory one that England can subsist by itself, whatever becomes of the rest of Europe, which has been so justly exploded by the Whigs ever since the Revolution'. Such a jibe must have embittered the Walpolites.

A climax came in December, when Townshend was dismissed and offered Sunderland's old place in Ireland as a consolation. Stanhope, anxious that this disciplinary measure should not weaken the Ministry by provoking Walpole's resignation, wrote to him that Townshend's dismissal 'was the only measure which could secure the continuance of a Whig administration with any ease to the King'. Walpole retorted:

'I find you all persuaded the scheme is so adjusted that it can meet with no objection from the Whigs. Believe me, you will find the direct contrary true with every unprejudiced Whig of any consequence or consideration.'

In the end Stanhope's plea 'is the Whig interest to be staked' on Townshend appeared to prevail; Townshend consented to take the Lord Lieutenancy and Walpole remained at the Treasury. But Whig unity was nevertheless at an end.[18]

The real reason for the Walpolites' agreement to accept Townshend's translation to Ireland lay in their desire to be certain of making good Walpole's boast of the strength of his support. Such certainty could only be obtained by intensive preparation, and by finding a stand upon which he could rally the House of Commons. From December onward Walpole's sympathisers were making their case known in the best possible light. To Whig listeners it could be pointed out that Stanhope and Sunderland, in abandoning the traditional Whig policy of opposition to France, had in fact adopted the pro-French proclivities of Bolingbroke. For good measure the Walpolites added that they themselves stood for resistance to the desire of the King's German advisers to obtain a repeal of that clause in the Act of Settlement which prevented foreign-born nationals from taking office in England. To backbenchers of both parties they used the argument that Stanhope and Sunderland desired to keep up the strength of the standing army on behalf of the King's Electoral interests. Finally, the Walpolites claimed —apparently in Tory circles only—that they were resisting a move to proceed against Oxford by attainder. By January both groups of Whig ministers were reported to be 'making their court to the Tories'. The Tories, for their part, were delighted at the prospect of fanning the flames of their opponents' disunity by negotiating with both factions. Since the meeting of Parliament one year earlier, in the aftermath of Rebellion and repression, the prospects of the parties had changed drastically.[19]

Before his bid for control of the party, Walpole had one more task to carry through which he hoped would greatly increase his popularity with it. This was a scheme to reduce the interest on the national debt and to set up, out of the taxes thus freed, a sinking fund whereby the whole sum might eventually be paid off. The greater amount of the redeemable debt stood at 6 per cent or more; an essential part of Walpole's scheme was the reduction of this interest to a uniform 5 per cent. The conversion of unredeemable annuities and a good deal of consolidation of miscellaneous debts were also envisaged. The scheme was a logical extension of Oxford's South Sea consolidation, though at a rate of interest appropriate to peacetime, and could be expected to be received with satisfaction by taxpayers.

By April 1717, therefore, the Walpolites were ready, and they chose to make their stand on 'Hanover counsels'. When Stanhope on the 8th moved for supplies to make subsidy treaties against Sweden, citing that country's recent involvement in supporting a projected Jacobite invasion, he found himself with a party insurrection on his hands. It was to be expected that the Tories would lash royal policies and argue that the treaties were actually required to defend George's seizure of Swedish territories on behalf of Hanover; the shock was that many Whigs joined them, led by Smith and Speaker Compton. An equally unexpected development was that they were supported by a demonstration from the Prince of Wales, whose friends in the Commons expressed his long-standing grievances by withdrawing themselves before the division. The government carried the day by a mere fifteen votes. Walpole himself voted in favour of the supply, though his gesture was intended only to allow the King to save face if forced to employ him in the case of a ministerial defeat. But the Walpolites' action, and that of the Prince, was regarded by both the King and Stanhope as a challenge. It was accepted, and Townshend was dismissed on the following day.[20]

The response of the Walpolites was the same as that of the Harleyites to Harley's ejection in February 1708: mass resignation. Walpole led the way on 10th April and was followed by an impressive section of the Ministry: Methuen as southern Secretary, Orford at the Admiralty, Devonshire as Lord President and Pulteney as Secretary at War. Many lesser office holders gave up their posts, while others such as Smith retained them but continued to support Walpole. For a few days the fate of Stanhope's Ministry seemed to be in the balance; but with the energetic support of the King, who was reported to have accepted 'with all my heart' Orford's tender of his resignation, a Ministry was patched up and the placemen were rallied. The great majority of the office holders stayed with their bread and butter, and Stanhope's weakness was most visible in the higher offices. If Sunderland fell naturally into one of the places of Secretary of State, no-one more experienced or forceful could be found for his colleague than Joseph Addison, a brilliant literary polemicist but a Member of Parliament with no talent for leading, or even speaking in the Commons. Stanhope felt the need, against his inclination, to take the Treasury himself. At best this arrangement was weak in experience and talent, but to the mortification of the Walpolites its held together.

The remainder of the session resolved into a close struggle between the two factions of Whigs for the support of their as yet uncommitted colleagues and of the Tories. Stanhope and Sunderland set about rallying independent Whig support by holding private meetings with Members to bring about a repeal of the Occasional Conformity Act and perhaps even of the Test and Corporation Acts, a project dear to a number of the party. Walpole, on the day of his resignation, produced a bill to implement his financial scheme, but the government managed to get it deferred until Stanhope had time to produce a similar scheme and get the credit. The first open bid for the Tories' support was made by the Walpolites on the following day, when Smith attacked the Ministry for omitting to bring in an Indemnity Bill after the Rebellion. The information received by Mar, now in exile, was that 'both parties court the Tories, they being able to cast the balance to whatever side they join, but they are resolved to join entirely with neither'. This resolution was to be implicit in the Tories' activities throughout this and subsequent Whig schisms.

The difficulties involved in trying to combine the activities of the Tories with those of the dissident Whigs were immediately demonstrated in the struggle which continued to be fought out in committee concerning the supplies for anti-Swedish treaties. Walpole tried to agree a course of action in concert with Bromley, but this arrangement broke down on the Tories' reluctance to co-operate with Whigs and their preference for outright assault on the proposals rather than for the harassments favoured by Walpole. Finch launched a bitter attack on the Hanoverian minister Bernsdorff, now the King's leading adviser in England, as the person whose personal properties in Mecklenburg were the chief interest to be defended against Sweden. Thus Walpole and some of his adherents, unwilling to be involved in an attack so close to the King, were forced into the position of voting for the sum proposed by Stanhope. Walpole could only take consolation in having the assistance of the Prince's followers, who either withdrew or voted against the motion. Henceforth, in any criticism of the King's ministers, the Walpolites were assured of the support of the 'reversionary interest' of the Prince's court, an important factor in persuading public opinion that any Whig opposition was not necessarily disloyal to the new dynasty or tainted with Jacobitism.[21]

As long as the Walpolites still hoped to defeat the government and so to force their way into office in the near future, however, they had to choose issues carefully with a view to embarrassing Stanhope and Sunderland rather than further alienating the King. Soon after the Easter recess such an issue arose on an apparently minor matter. On 13 May Wyndham moved that the preachers before the Commons on the 29th should be Dr Andrew Snape, a High Churchman whose recent pamphlet controversy with the Whig Bishop Hoadly of Bangor was about to contribute to the government's permanent suspension of

Convocation as a mouthpiece of the Tory lower clergy. In this audacious proposal the Walpolites put out their full strength on the Tory side, with the result that the motion was carried by ten votes. The government's defeat made impracticable for the remainder of the session their scheme for repealing the penal legislation against dissenters' holding office, for to court defeat on such a matter would be disastrous.

Encouraged by this success, the Walpolites were careful to select an issue which they hoped would bring about the government's downfall by obtaining a maximum of Tory support; but in this they again miscalculated the extent of the Tories' willingness to co-operate. Marlborough's friend General Cadogan, whose ruthless vigour had completed the mopping up of the Scottish rebels, had alienated not only many Tories but also a number of Scottish Whigs, mainly the adherents of the Duke of Argyll whom he had replaced as commander in mid campaign. Cadogan thus seemed to be the most vulnerable government figure and as such suitable for personal attack in the Commons, nominally on the ground of corruption. The opposition attack was opened by Pulteney on 4 June, and he was ably answered by his successor as Secretary at War, James Craggs the younger. Another ministerialist who performed well was the former Tory Aislabie, whom Addison coldly noted as speaking 'with as much decency as a man could do who is just detached from the party'; the Secretary's memory for Tory origins was as tenacious as that of most Old Whigs, for Aislabie had held an office in the Whig Ministry for over three years. The opposition Whig leaders spoke with all their force, but nearly all the usual Tory debaters were unexpectedly silent. Even more significantly, Finch and Hanmer absented themselves and let it be known that they had no intention of breaking Cadogan in order to help Walpole back into office. In this abstention they were joined by fifty-five other Tories, with the result that the government carried the final vote by 204 to 194.* Among those who voted against Cadogan were seventy-eight Whigs, who thus committed themselves unequivocally to opposition without any immediate prospect of being raised to power with Tory assistance.[22]

For the moment the Ministry was saved. Two days later Stanhope signalised his triumph by introducing proposals concerning the national debt. The interest-reduction and sinking fund were to go through, but some of Walpole's more ambitious and constructive schemes were abandoned for the moment; Walpole was reduced to claiming a share

---

*As often seen in this study, the theoretical impossibility of abstaining from voting was easily circumvented by absenteeism, except in the rare instance of a 'call' of Members. Although abstention through calculated absence could sometimes work against party solidarity, its commonest motive was probably silent disapproval of tactics which appeared to set aside party principles in order to obtain short-term ends.

of the credit for ideas of his own devising. In another matter, however he had the better of the First Lord. On Stanhope's bland suggestion he reassumed the prosecution of Oxford, whose trial had been long deferred; but Walpole refused to let this transparent manoeuvre embroil him with the Tories. When the case came on in the Lords, the Commons' managers for the impeachment failed to make an appearance, and Oxford was formally acquitted. After nearly two years in the Tower he was released, the last man to suffer from a purely political impeachment.[23]

When the session ended on 15 July Walpole had learned some important lessons which were to determine permanently his political stance and methods. One was that any attempt to use the Tories was fraught with dangers for a Whig in opposition. Walpole was also to show later that he had learned how important was control of patronage by a Ministry; Stanhope and Sunderland had leaned heavily on the votes of the Whig placemen, dismissing a number of the minority who had joined the Walpolites in divisions. Finally, Walpole had learned that his appeal to 'every unprejudiced Whig of any consequence or consideration', to those in fact whose economic independence made them politically largely independent of government or other patronage, had been only moderately successful by reason of his mistakes. The government's remaining supporters were far from being confined to the placemen, for a large number of those independent Whigs whom Walpole had confidently expected to rally to him in his attack on the pro-Hanoverian policies of Stanhope and Sunderland had been unconvinced of the cogency of his arguments. In later years, when the menace of rebellion was no longer a very recent memory, Walpole would be in unison with the beat of this independent heart of the party, and would be able to change the direction of government policy under George II back to the traditional Whig one of distrust of the Bourbon. Later still, his pupils and successors in office, the Pelhams, would successfully appeal to the same heart of the party against that king's 'German' foreign policy. But for the moment the Stanhope Ministry, despite the encumbrance of German advisers about the throne, had succeeded in retaining most independent Whig opinion. Over the next three years the struggle between the Whig factions would centre on their appeals to that opinion.

In the rivalry between the two Whig groups, the Tories had so far gained more than either. 'The three parties subsist separately without any sort of understanding with one another,' wrote one of Mar's correspondents, 'so that hitherto all projects for drawing the Tories into either of these parties, notwithstanding all offers, have been entirely defeated.'[24] Eagerly courted, though greatly feared by both Whig groups, the Tory party had recovered from its drastic setback between

1714 and 1716, when even extinction had seemed a possibility, to the position of an uncrushable opposition. This standing was assured by the continued loyalty of the electorate in the counties, was exploited in successive Whig schisms, and was given the formidable appearance of a jumping-off place for the formation of a Tory government if Hanoverian monarchs tired, like William III and Anne before them, of Whig pretensions. That neither George I nor George II did in the event see fit to turn to the Tories has given the party after 1717 a retrospective appearance of futility and lack of coherence which was not equally apparent to contemporaries over the quarter-century which saw the rise, dominance and fall of Walpole.

CHAPTER 10

The Whig Compromise
1717-24

Over the next three years the Tories' determination to favour neither of the Whig factions exclusively was weakened in practice by the Ministry's strongly anti-Church measures and party policies. A desire to obtain the dissenters' relief from the Occasional Conformity and Schism legislation was accompanied, in ministerial proposals, by attempts to remove the religious tests and to loosen the Anglican control of the universities. Further, Stanhope and Sunderland proposed to perpetuate the Whig control of the upper house, which had been re-established by new creations of peerage since 1714, and to extend the life of the existing Commons beyond the span permitted by the Septennial Act. Some of these schemes were almost as unacceptable to independent Whigs as they were to the Tories, and resulted in the return of the Walpolites to office by 1720.

The struggle between the two Whig groups for the Whig independents' allegiance continued in Parliament and the press for several years. A government tract claimed to be 'for a limited monarchy in the House of Hanover, for the Church and regal supremacy as by law established; for tolerating the Protestant dissenters and freeing them from those hardships they were lately put under'. The dissident Whigs tended to avoid such generalisations; as the originators of schism they had to justify their action. Moreover, Walpole intended to extend his recently adumbrated favour of churchmen, both to conciliate the Tories and to bid against them for the Church's valuable support; and this course inevitably involved disservice to the dissenters. That an element of such disservice had been implicit in Whig practice, if not theory, since the Revolution was not an argument which he could easily use. Nor, in the circumstance of the ultimate need to conciliate the House of Hanover, could the Walpolites say openly that it was they who were the closer of the two groups to the principle of limited monarchy, the most basic of party doctrines. It is not surprising, therefore, that they preferred to base their case on a good Whig record and on personal reputation. Could men of untarnished party reputation, such as Orford the victor of La Hogue, asked a Walpolite tract, be thought capable of acting against party interests? 'Ministers of state', remarked another, attributed to Walpole himself, 'have always a right of preserving their own principles, and a liberty of adhering to what, in their judgment, they think is for the service of their country and the interest of the master they serve.' In spite of the guarded language the dissident's case was well directed towards the sort of independent opinion which, in William's reign, had often caused high office holders in a Whig Ministry, like Thomas Pelham, or independent Whigs as eminent as Sir Richard Onslow, to vote with the Tories against the policies of the court. For the successors of such men, and for the ordinary Whig in the coffeehouse, there emerged from the pamphlet warfare the conviction that the Walpolites had at least as good a claim as Stanhope and Sunderland to represent true party principles and to censure deviationism in their rivals.

Median Whig opinion soon afterwards found its best exemplar in Arthur Onslow, a nephew of Sir Richard, who for his thirty-four years as Speaker was to stand as the foremost representative of the Whig country gentlemen. For the younger Onslow, as for the elder, party behaviour and party principles were not synonymous. Of his early years in Parliament, from 1720, he wrote: 'I kept firm to my original Whig principles, upon conscience, and never deviated from them to serve any party cause whatsoever.' The Stanhope–Sunderland Ministry, he believed, made excessive use of government patronage. Of their administration he wrote, after chairing the House through Walpole's and much of Pelham's, that he 'never knew so corrupt a time'. In the long run, independent party opinion saw the management of the Commons by Stanhope and Sunderland, on behalf of the King's foreign policies, as a worse divergence from principle than Townshend's and Walpole's criticisms of a Protestant monarch and their growing tendency to conciliate the Church of England. But in 1717 both sides had a tenable case, and both had to be taken into account. Before the party could be reunited, agreement would have to be reached both upon the limits of security which could be allowed to the dissenters and upon the limits of action permissible to the monarch and his German advisers. Such agreement came only after years of intensive debate which ended in compromise when both factions were exhausted; but since the alternative was Tory resurgence, compromise had to come eventually, because the basic affinity which bound all Whigs together against toryism was not destroyed. As the ministerial writer put it:

'. . . there are but two grand parties in the nation, and scarce a man or woman which is not of one or t'other; and though there may be several things done by their own side which some may dislike, yet if they do not dislike them more than they like their party, they will come into everything essential to it'.[1]

With the approach of Parliament's meeting in the autumn of 1717 the Prince of Wales broke openly with his father, soon setting up a rival court at Leicester House where he daily entertained the Tories and dissident Whigs. The King responded by embarking on the expensive course of opening a public table for government supporters, going out of his way to demonstrate his confidence in the Ministry. But beneath the calm of this ministerial surface there were disturbing undercurrents. Stanhope and Sunderland were increasingly worried about the direction in which Hanoverian foreign policy was leading them, while the German advisers were again pressing for a repeal of the clause in the Act of Settlement which kept them out of office and Parliament. Berns-dorff, indeed, was reported as so discontented as to be 'looking out for new men to come into the aid of the Court'. Such rumours did not assist the prospects of the Ministry in the Commons. Nor did the fact that Stanhope had seen fit to take a peerage just before the end of the last session. As an expression of the King's approval the gesture had been helpful at the time, but it left the Ministry's party in the Commons to be led nominally by Addison, actually by the junior ministers Craggs and Aislabie.[2]

Thus hampered and weakened, the Ministry was fortunate that one section of its opponents, the Tories, were not fully prepared to take advantage of the situation. The Jacobites among them were for an early attack on the Ministry, but the party as a whole was in a state of un-pleasant indecision. Some Tories looked to the recently liberated Oxford for an indication of their future course of action, but his attitude was enigmatic. Forbidden to attend at court, and spitefully excluded from the Act of Grace extended to the prisoners from the Rebellion, he had no cause to love the government; but though he dabbled anew with the Jacobites as an insurance, his private correspondence re-affirmed, as always, his loyalty to the Protestant succession. More decisive was the influence which Bolingbroke was beginning to exert in a new direction. As early as 1716 he had been urging the Tories, via Wyndham, to avoid at all costs any further entanglement with the court-in-exile and its futile intrigues. Further than this Bolingbroke's advise was in favour of alliance with the government, rather than with the Walpolites. There were signs that the Tories were taking the former advice and avoiding Jacobite entanglement; in December 1717 a small but significant indication of their attitude came at a by-election for Oxford University, when a Jacobite could not find enough support to justify a poll against the Tory candidate George Clarke. But to support the Ministry just when it was launching a campaign favouring the dis-senters was more than the Tories could stomach. Although a Tory amendment to the address, supported by Walpole, was easily rejected in a thinly attended Commons, the attitude of the Walpolites and the later arrival at Westminster of many more Tories were sufficient factors to put the Ministry in doubt of the wisdom of bringing in legislation concerning the dissenters. The matter was again put aside for a more propitious occasion.[3]

The Walpolites' next vote with the Tories occurred on 4 December in an attempt to reduce the land forces, swollen by the emergency of the Rebellion, to a peace footing of 12,000 men. As Walpole's motion for this—to Whig eyes—obviously factious proposal failed by over fifty votes, he concentrated more circumspectly during following days on putting forward what he claimed were more efficient methods of making such disbandment as the government offered, promising by these a cash saving of £100,000. This approach succeeded on the 9th in reducing the Ministry's majority to fourteen votes. And a month later the Walpolites again joined the Tories on a military issue, with a full-dress attack on a clause of the Mutiny Bill for punishing mutiny or desertion by death. By choosing a point well calculated to arouse the humanitarian instincts of many Whigs, Walpole was able, in a full House, to come within eighteen votes of defeating the government.

This result, though a disappointment to the opposition, was quite sufficient to make the Ministry take further stock of its prospects. Stanhope and Sunderland had before them the possibility of a war with Spain, with which Britain's relations were becoming increasingly strained. But any policy requiring war expenditure was bound to be closely examined by the Tories and Walpolite Whigs. On 17 March, when the King experimentally asked for extra contingency supplies for the fleet, Walpole spoke ominously of 'the air of a declaration of war against Spain'. His likely opposition made further revelations on foreign policy inexpedient, and four days later the session was brought to an unusually early end.[4]

New ministerial arrangements were urgently needed to avoid the problem of leadership in the Commons which had become all too obvious since Stanhope's departure. Addison was quietly shunted back to the realm of literature, where he would be of more service, and the southern department was taken over by Craggs. By mutual consent, Stanhope took over the northern department from Sunderland in exchange for the Treasury, but his office of Chancellor of the Exchequer was given to Aislabie, a change which futher strengthened the ministerial bench in the lower house.

In the summer of 1718 the opposition press concentrated upon drawing the attention of the nation to difficulties which Stanhope, in his anxiety to include the Empire in his alliance with France, was bringing by involving Britain in the Habsburg's quarrels with Philip V. But Admiral Byng's victory at Cape Passaro over a Spanish fleet was popular, and the argument of the Whig opposition that the battle contravened the law of nations, being unaccompanied by a declaration of war, was defeated by sixty votes on the address on 11 November. Despite speeches in support of Walpole by Wyndham and the Jacobite William Shippen, a substantial number of Tories led by Bromley contributed to the government's victory by their absence. And on the 17th, in a debate on another address to the King approving his belated declaration of war, the government's majority rose to seventy-one. After the narrow majorities of the last session this was an extremely encouraging start for the Ministry. Not only the Tories were wavering; one of the leading Walpolites, Pulteney, was voting erratically after making overtures to the Ministry, and he might well be followed by others if Walpole continued to have small success.[5] For these reasons, Stanhope decided that the time was ripe to attempt his proposed changes in the status of the dissenters. In December he introduced in the House of Lords a bill for repealing the Occasional Conformity and Schism Acts and for nullifying the effect of the Test and Corporation Acts.

With this measure the relationship of the Whigs as a whole with both Dissent and the Church reached a watershed. Both Whig factions saw the party's control of elections as the stake, but they differed as to the measures needed. Stanhope and Sunderland were inclined to the view that, as one dissenter put it, there was hardly 'one place in England where the Whig interest could carry an election if the dissenters should be angry'. This, however, was only one opinion, and a highly biased one. Perceval's view of the attitude of the dissenters in the last session, when the measure had been deferred, was that 'the most reasonable of them have been cool in setting their friends upon doing anything for them, acknowledging that if ever the Tories get uppermost they shall be used the worse for any favours done them now'. Many of the actions of the Whigs for more than a quarter of a century had shown, in contradiction of Stanhope's view, that they believed the Anglican vote to be far more important in electoral matters than that of the dissenters. The lesson of the Sacheverell affair reinforced this view. After 1715 a considerable feeling grew up in the party that further conciliation of the Church was expedient. A widely circulated pamphlet of that year, *The Whigs Vindicated*, undertook to prove the Whigs to be 'the best friends of the Church'. Indeed, the author went so far as to maintain 'that the Church of England owes its preservation and very being, next under the providence of God, to Whiggish principles'. Had not the principle of excluding Charles II's Catholic heir, he asked, been anathema to Tories, and were not the Whig gentry as devoted members of the Church as the Tories? Was it not possible for an honest Whig gentleman who went to Church twice each Sunday to be railed at during election time as a Presbyterian, while his rival, who was never seen there more frequently than at monthly or six-weekly intervals, was greeted as a friend and patron of the establishment? Professor Plumb has remarked of Walpole that 'his Church policy was scarcely distinguishable from Nottingham's'. Many thoughtful Whigs shared Walpole's attitude.

The ministerial view that the dissenters should be protected thus clashed with a growing Whig belief that the Church should be allowed to retain its privileged status. The result was a compromise, though one which leaned towards the latter point of view in that the position of the dissenters was restored only to that which they had enjoyed in 1711, before the passing of the Occasional Conformity and Schism Acts. Stanhope's plan to suspend the sacramental tests embodied in the Corporation and Test Acts was dropped while it was before the Lords, in face of strong Whig opposition and as a result of Sunderland's assessment that the Commons would reject it in any case. The sweeping nature of the proposed change roused even the usually staid upper house to a frenzy of activity. No fewer than fifteen of the twenty-six episcopal votes cast, including that of the newly appointed Archbishop Wake of Canterbury, went against the Ministry. When the bill came down to the Commons in its truncated form the opposition was led by Walpole, who claimed in his speech that he had been turned out of office for not consenting to the repeal of the penal legislation. He further maintained that the bill was 'against the judgment of even half of the Whigs'. Though, as was no doubt the ministers' hope, some of Walpole's usual Whig followers left him on the issue, his unequivocal stand was justified when he was joined by government Whigs as normally reliable as Castlecomer and Hinchinbrooke, along with Stanhope's two Pitt in-laws. A government victory by 243 votes against 202 at the committal on 7 January 1719, the crucial division, could not conceal a strengthening of Walpole's case. In all, sixty-nine Whigs had voted against the bill, and of these twenty-two were placemen. In addition, the unusually large number of fifty-seven Whigs, including fifteen placemen, had absented themselves and thus avoided making the difficult decision. Finally, it was noticeable that among the ministerial majority were all but about four of the Scots, including the followers of Argyll who dared not flout Scottish opinion by coming out against the dissenters; but for this fact, it could be argued, Walpole's moral victory might have been converted to an actual one.[6]

The session was not to be concluded without one further cause for intense excitement. This was no less than a proposal by Stanhope and Sunderland to tamper with the constitution of the House of Lords in order to secure their own future position. Since the accession of George the creation of nearly twice as many peers as Anne had approved in December 1711, together with the appointment of Whig bishops when vacancies occurred, had ensured the re-establishment of a substantial

Whig majority which was also a working majority for the present Ministry on most occasions. This situation might, however, easily be changed. All Whigs were well aware that the precedent of Oxford's dozen creations could be repeated if ever the Tories came to power with the King's approval. A possibly more immediate danger for the Ministry was the King's early death and the formation of a Walpolite Ministry under his successor. The Prince had been at pains to show his personal adherence to the opposition by voting in the upper house against the repeal of the Occasional Conformity and Schism Acts, while Walpole himself, in the course of debate on the same measure, had given a clear hint of possible future impeachments.

The outcome of these considerations was the Peerage Bill, which proposed to limit the number of English peerages to only six more than the existing total. Scottish representative peerages, usually providing a safe block of government voters, were to be increased to twenty-five with hereditary membership. Further accessions to the upper house would be confined to royal titles and replacements of peerages which became extinct. The bill met no check in the Lords, where it was introduced, but soon ran into difficulties in the lower chamber. A detailed assessment by Sunderland and Craggs showed, in addition to the usual dissident Whig opposition, well over 100 Whigs whose support for the bill was at best doubtful. A struggle for the minds of these doubters, and for the approval of public opinion, began immediately. The argument which most impressed the independent Whigs was Walpole's one that 'the House of Lords will be a fixed independent body, not to be called to account like a Ministry, nor to be dissolved or changed like a House of Commons'. Another consideration which weighed with most Members was that the bill would reduce every commoner's personal chance of elevation to the peerage. Stanhope was forced, owing to what he called misunderstanding of the bill's purpose, to let it lie upon the table at the end of the session. Its final failure—to anticipate the result of its reintroduction the following year—ensured that any future clash between the two Houses could, in the last resort, be resolved in the Common's favour by Oxford's expedient of creating new peers.[7]

The Ministry's determination to pass the Peerage Bill did not flag in 1719 and brought about a showdown with the King's German advisers, who had worked strongly against the measure as deleterious to the authority of the Crown and to their own trade in peerages. By the end of June, Craggs reported Stanhope to be, on this account, 'on the point of resigning every day'; and almost simultaneously Stanhope himself was able to announce that the King had agreed to the disgrace of Bernsdorff. By November the ministers could report to their supporters a complete success against the remaining foreign advisers with 'the resolution the King has taken not to suffer his Germans to meddle in English affairs'. The announcement was true; the foreigners had little influence thereafter, so that the Ministry was at last free from the damaging imputation of favouring them and their policies. This victory, taken together with the settlement over the dissenters, removed in fact the main genuine differences between the two wings of the Whigs. Before they came together in nominal amity, however, the impetus of their quarrel carried it on for a further session.[8]

While in attendance upon the King in Hanover during the summer, Stanhope and Sunderland concocted a programme for the reduction of opposition which was so far-reaching as to surprise and alarm even some of their colleagues. In addition to bringing in a revised Peerage Bill they proposed to break the Tory control of higher education in England by reform of the universities, in which appointments down to college level would be brought ultimately under government control. Such a proceeding had been in the air for several years and was likely to please many Whigs. More extreme still was the ministers' intention to obtain a repeal of the Septennial Act in order to extend indefinitely the life of the existing House of Commons, hopefully to increase the ministerial majority by pleasing the Whigs. But the King's speech, when Parliament opened on 23 November, cautiously contained only a recommendation 'to complete those measures which remained imperfect the last session', a phrase which could certainly be taken to allude to the peerage issue but which left other intentions vague and open to adaptation. Much depended on the reception given to the revised Peerage Bill.[9]

So closely had the Ministry kept its own counsels about its plans that when the bill was rushed through the House of Lords in the first week of the session it took the Tories by surprise. Oxford, who had emerged from his semiretirement to play a part in opposing the bill in the last session, wrote from the country on the opening day that he saw no reason to hurry to London. Bathurst a fortnight later expressed himself as 'surprised to the last degree that the Ministry should bring in the peerage bill without a probability of carrying it'. But the Ministry's hope of rushing the bill equally speedily through the Commons, before the dilatory Tory Members arrived there, was to be destroyed by the vigilance of the Walpolites.

The bill had its first reading in the Commons on 1 December, but an opposition motion to put off the second reading for a week, while the latecomers were rounded up, was passed despite the government speakers' efforts to get an earlier day. In the decisive debate on the motion for committal, which took place on the 8th, the Tories turned out and voted in force. But the Tory leaders did not speak, and it was the Walpolite Whigs who bore the brunt of the debate, while defectors from the ranks of the government turned the balance of voting. Walpole had been making intensive personal efforts to sway the doubters. On the day, with well over 450 Members present, he gave one of the most effective speeches of his life. Forcefully he recapitulated the opposition arguments, especially the two which weighed most: Stanhope, he told the House, 'having got into the House of Peers, is now desirous to shut the door after him', while the House of Lords would be only too glad to have its powers increased at the expense of the Commons. He asked in peroration for gentlemen to:

'recollect that the overweening disposition of the great barons, to aggrandize their own dignity, occasioned them to exclude the lesser barons, and to that circumstance may be fairly attributed the sanguinary wars which so long desolated the country.'

Against his oratory the ministerial arguments of such as Craggs, who did not believe them himself, rang weakly. About 144 Whigs opposed the motion, and it was rejected by 269 votes to 177.[10]

Few doubted that so decisive a defeat for the government would necessitate some new ministerial arrangements to accommodate the Walpolites. In fact, four and a half months were to pass before this came about. Meantime both sets of Whigs manoeuvred in Closet and on backstairs, with the ultimate threat in the offing of more defeats for the government in the Commons if suitable arrangements were not made. The Universities Bill and the repeal of the Septennial Act could not be attempted. Nor, without the support of Walpole, did the Ministry dare to put before the Commons another more delicate matter: a project to obtain the vote of £500,000 to pay off an accumulated debt on the Civil List. In one matter, however, the Ministry was able to win a point and to improve its bargaining position. This was a scheme by Sunderland to settle the problem of the government annuitants by the aid of the South Sea Company. Walpole managed to occasion some delay by pressing a rival scheme which involved using the Bank of England rather than the company, but the ministerial bill was carried through by Aislabie and Craggs, aided by the support of the Commons for any proposal which would help to control the national debt. By this time Stanhope and Sunderland were ready to parley with Walpole. Their first impulse, immediately after the defeat of the Peerage Bill, had been to strengthen their government by the inclusion of some selected Tories. But Harcourt, who was entrusted with an approach to Bromley, met no success. The Tories refused to enter into employment except as a party, and after Christmas many of them even followed Bromley's lead and stayed away from Parliament; for as the latter explained, 'we could only have joined with them, and no further than they thought fit to go, in whom we could have no confidence'.

Continued Tory unity furthered the cause of Whig reconciliation, for each set of Whigs became increasingly fearful that the Tories were secretly negotiating with the other set. Quietly the Whig leaders came to an understanding; Stanhope and Sunderland undertook to obtain the King's consent to a reconciliation with the Prince, while Walpole similarly undertook the Prince's compliance. On 23 April 1720 a family reunion was staged publicly, with great embarrassment to all who observed the mutual frigidity of the royal participants. But the thing was done, and on the same day Walpole announced 'that a bargain was made for those Whigs who had resigned their employments to be put in again by degrees'. Shortly afterward, Walpole fulfilled his part of the bargain by supporting an address promising to pay the Civil List debt; and at the end of the session, in June, the first instalment of the Ministry's part of the bargain was paid in appointments. Walpole and Townshend became Paymaster-General and Lord President respectively, Grafton was announced as Lord Lieutenant of Ireland, Methuen received a household post as Comptroller, and two Walpolites were admitted to a reconstituted Treasury Board. Thanks to the Ministry's successful delaying action the gains of the opposition Whigs were not as great as might have been expected in December, but they were as substantial as they could be without an unacceptable degree of loss of face for the King, Stanhope and Sunderland. On the surface at least, the Whigs were again a united party.[11]

The summer of 1720 and the parliamentary session which followed it saw no topics of political interest to compare with the South Sea bubble and the subsequent attempts to apportion the blame. The recent South Sea Act had permitted the company to take over most of the remainder of the national debt in return for a fixed 5 per cent interest payable by the government until 1727, after which the rate would be reduced to 4 per cent. Thus far the arrangement bore some resemblance to Oxford's original scheme, as did also the inducement to annuity holders to take South Sea stock in exchange, namely the prospect of high rates of interest as a result of trading. The difference between the two schemes arose out of the motives behind them, for whereas the earlier one was honest the later was not. Aislabie, Craggs and his father the joint Postmaster-General James Craggs the elder, Sunderland and even Stanhope, with varying degrees of foreknowledge and success, invested in South Sea stock which began to rise rapidly even before the end of the session. Some, like Aislabie, were given stock in return for their service in making possible the barely legal devices which swiftly enriched the directors of the South Sea Company. The directors deliberately used the initial rise as an inducement to the holders of government securities to come in even at increasing cost, on the expectation of quick capital gain, with the result that the company made a profit out of the terms of the exchange of stock. By June, South Sea stock stood at over 1,000. Speculation became a national fever; 'party feuds seem to be laid aside and utterly extinct by the rise of South Sea stock' wrote one observer, as Tories joined Whigs in the rush to buy this or other bubble scrip.

By early September the bubbles had burst, and Prior reported: 'Walpole and Townshend sent for, that they may settle matters'. Modern historiography has modified the traditional glowing account of Walpole's part in the crisis, by demonstrating that he showed no sign of foreseeing the crash and displayed no particular financial acumen in his personal investment; even the scheme whereby he sought to salvage some of the wreckage was not of his own devising. Nevertheless two points stand out concerning his part in the affair which was to bring him back to the Treasury within a year. The first is that, in common with his friends, he had opposed the great weakness of the South Sea Bill while it was under debate on 23 March: namely the failure of the government to insist that the South Sea Company should, as the Bank had proposed to do, state in advance a fixed rate for the exchange of annuities for South Sea stock. The second point is that when the bubble burst no-one had any confidence in Sunderland and Aislabie at the Treasury, and few saw any hope of salvation unless Walpole could produce it.[12]

When Parliament assembled on 8 December the wrath of bewildered parliamentarians was fully apparent. Thomas Brodrick, an Irish Member, wrote that 'this not being a party cause, arrows in full volleys are let fly from every quarter'. The lawyers Cowper in the Lords and Jekyll in the Commons led the way, the latter voicing a general desire for ministerial blood when he hinted broadly that 'some were highly criminal who were not directors' of the company. Against such opposition Walpole strove hard to lower the temperature of debate, maintaining that undue heat and the indiscriminate pursuit of scapegoats would only delay remedial measures. Waiting until 21 December, when most of the Tories had left London for Christmas, he presented his scheme in the Commons. The company's large surplus stock, which arose from its manipulation of the terms received by former government annuitants, was to be distributed among stockholders in partial compensation. This rough and ready measure was not the hoped-for panacea for all losses sustained by the public, and most of Walpole's other proposals proved to be impracticable. But little could be done apart from allowing him to go ahead. After Christmas there began in earnest the searching out and punishment of those responsible for the suffering, and as Walpole took unofficial control of the Treasury he became more and more involved as a 'screenmaster general' in an attempt to protect the late administration, much as Harley had done in similar circumstances in 1711. But the government was unable to prevent the setting up in the Commons of a secret committee to investigate the company, and it had the mortification of seeing the 'court list' of candidates for this body defeated in a ballot by a list consisting of Tories and discontented Whigs.

Before the full wrath of Parliament had expended itself, however, fate took a hand to divert it from some of the ministers. On 4 February 1721 Stanhope 'burst a blood-vessel' while defending himself in the Lords, and died the following day. His death was accompanied by the demise of the two Craggs, the elder probably by suicide and the younger by smallpox. Aislabie was expelled from the Commons and sent to the Tower on 8 March; but this event saw the climax, for Walpole's first victory came on the 15th when Sunderland's case was before the Commons. The First Lord claimed to be innocent of making profit on bubble stock; but, as Brodrick bitterly noted, the 'sheet anchor' of the ministerialists' argument was the warning to Whigs that 'if you come into this vote against Lord Sunderland, the Ministry are blown up and must and necessarily and will be succeeded by a Tory one'. At the same time many of the Tories held back from the attack, being unwilling to see Sunderland overthrown for the benefit of Walpole, though others including the Jacobites went ahead to Shippen's bugle call of 'overturn, overturn all Whigs'. Sunderland was acquitted by 233 votes to 172; but as a young Member remarked, '172 was a great number against a Prime Minister'.[13]

Even before the sudden deaths of Stanhope and the Craggs the Treasury had been earmarked for Walpole, though Sunderland was rumoured likely to be compensated with a Secretaryship while Stanhope fulfilled a long-standing ambition to replace Marlborough as Captain-General. The opposition's attack on Sunderland greatly altered the situation in favour of the Walpolites, for he could hardly be transferred with safety while his fate was under debate. The northern department was accordingly given to Townshend, while the southern was occupied by Sunderland's protégé Carteret. When Parliament rose for Easter at the end of March, Walpole was duly given the Treasury, together with the Chancellorship left vacant by Aislabie's resignation. He had been overseeing the work of both offices since early February, if not earlier, and was to retain them for twenty-one years. Sunderland bowed before the storm but remained Groom of the Stole, retaining also his place in the Cabinet. The remaining year of his life was to be devoted to intrigues for the recovery of his position as soon as the

temper of Parliament made this possible. Sunderland's fall removed
him from the position of chief scapegoat, especially as the attack on
him had revealed mismanagement rather than criminality in his conduct of the Treasury. Indeed, a fortnight after his dismissal he was
reported as being 'in much better esteem than Walpole, especially
with the Tories'.[14]

As soon as Parliament rose and the new First Lord disappeared to
his home in Norfolk, the simmering intrigues of Sunderland came to
the boil. He was still in a strong position. Though affairs in Parliament
had forced his retirement he was still favoured by the King, who was
also increasingly pleased with Carteret, one of the few politicians who
spoke German fluently. Since the Walpolites' promotion a struggle had
been carried on over Sunderland's desire for an early general election,
before his opponents had time to consolidate Treasury patronage in
their own interest. But the need to settle public credit, together with
the King's desire for an enactment of a new Civil List scheme, had
been enough to resolve the argument in favour of the Walpolites. Early
in August some kind of reconciliation was staged between the two
factions, though Carteret hastened to write that as a result of this
'neither Lord Sunderland nor I have lost any ground with the King'.
The first overture for the pacification was portrayed by Carteret as
proceeding from a sincere Townshend, who might however have difficulty in controlling Walpole in an undertaking that 'all South Sea
matters shall be kept out of Parliament next sessions'. In fact it was
Sunderland and Carteret who, already at the time of this letter, were
setting about betraying Walpole.

The leading element of the Sunderlandites' scheme was a desire to
make alliance with the Tories and to bring some of them into a new
Ministry. By what processes of thought the once most extreme member
of the Junto had reached the stage of contemplating a Tory alliance, to
exclude a hated Whig rival, is a subject for surmise. Some ambitious
leading politicians had always been more anxious to manipulate party
principles for their own purposes than to be guided by them. Carteret,
originally a Hanoverian Tory, was one such. The supreme example
was Bolingbroke, who like Sunderland had been the extremist of his
party only when party extremism seemed the path to success, but who
was now ready to abandon party for his own purposes. There were
other recent precedents. By 1721 Cowper was deeply involved with
the Tories; Harcourt, on the other hand, was now firmly established
as a Whig. It was left, ironically enough, to the Jacobite son of Wharton
to utter the pleasantry that ' 'twas very odd Lord Cowper should be
head of the Tories and Lord Harcourt the tail of the Whigs'. With
such an atmosphere in high places it is not surprising that Sunderland
thought he could arrange a Ministry to suit his own taste. But the

adaptable political outlook of a few great men had not extended to the great bulk of the parties, or even to their most respected leaders; and when Sunderland in August made explicit the hints he had been dropping to Tories intermittently since the end of 1719, he was firmly rebuffed. Bromley, who was approached as leader of the Oxfordites in the Commons, reported to Oxford:

'I absolutely declined the opportunities offered and pressed upon me of receiving all possible assurances from the first. Promises were made to me so extravagantly large, that it was affronting me to imagine I could think them sincere and be imposed upon by them.'

Shippen later related that the Tories had decided to reject a proposal which might lead to some of their number's taking office, 'resolving to enter into no concert with any of the two contending powers at court, but to stick together'. Shippen's motive, though not Bromley's, was to serve the Jacobite cause by playing off the two Whig groups as usual, but from Sunderland's point of view the result was the same: failure to secure the co-operation of the Tories.[15]

By contrast with the marathon nine months of sittings during the South Sea crisis, the session of 1721–22 was to be cut short at three and a half months. Under the Septennial Act an election was due early in the new year, and in order to get the necessary business transacted in time Parliament had to be recalled in October. Attendance down to Christmas was accordingly extremely low, especially among the Tories. In January 1722, however, activity revived a little. In the Commons the Tories took the initiative with a bill to reduce government manipulation of elections by regularising the issue of electoral writs and punishing false returns. The bill represented good opposition tactics, as it received the support of many Whigs who felt the eyes of their constituents upon them. In the time-honoured manner for such embarrassing issues, the bill's rejection was reserved for the government majority in the Lords. Further than this the short session saw little of moment, with Members of Parliament slipping away early, as they had come late, to prepare for their elections.[16]

The elections which began soon after the dissolution on 10 March showed that, though the Tories had preserved their integrity by holding off from Sunderland's overtures, they had not thereby improved their chances at the polls. While the Whigs benefited for the first time from the capacity of Walpole at the head of the Treasury, their opponents were reported to be listless and despondent in the campaign. In Scotland the Tories rarely bothered to contest seats, from an expectation that even if they won the returning officers would fail to declare them elected; hence of the forty-five Members returned north of the border only one was a Tory. As in 1715, Wales returned a Tory majority, and so did the English county seats. But in the numerous small English boroughs the government's consolidation continued. In Cornwall the Whigs gained a further five seats over the figure of 1715, making a total of thirty-seven out of forty-four seats. On the other hand, the borough seats of London and Westminster returned Tories, reflecting, as in the counties, the still insecure position of Whig candidates in the more popular constituencies. The elections were not a success for the Jacobites, and at Oxford University Bromley and Clarke easily repeated Clarke's success of 1717 against Jacobite opposition by substantially defeating Dr William King. Overall it was thought at first that the Tories had held their ground, and at the end of April L'Hermitage had access to an estimate of their strength as 189. This, however, overstated the Tories' numbers; the final result, before the consideration of petitions altered the picture in the coming session, was 379 Whigs to 178 Tories, representing a gain for the Whigs of thirty-eight over their numbers at the same stage in 1715.[17]

On 19 April, while results were still coming in, Sunderland died. How far he might still have succeeded in furthering his nebulous schemes if he had lived is a matter for speculation, but his death did not entirely put an end to them. Carteret was still much in the King's favour and evidently hoping for a change of heart in his master, for he thought fit to point out to the Tories that they had lost 'a very good friend' in Sunderland. The Secretary, a diplomat whose dexterity as Ambassador to Sweden had smoothed the way to peace in the Baltic in 1720, was a typical member of the administrative coterie with which Stanhope and Sunderland had latterly surrounded themselves. Carteret himself was descended from cavaliers and Tories on both sides of his family, a fact which had not prevented him from deserting to the Whigs as soon as possible after 1714. Other members included Trevor, Boyle, now Baron Carleton, and Harcourt, all of whom were former associates of Oxford and had long balanced between the parties sufficiently to be considered sometimes as moderate Whigs and sometimes as moderate Tories. Their standing with those Whigs who had never truckled with the Tories was well expressed by the architect Sir John Vanbrugh, when he wrote of Carteret and Carleton that 'I find it the opinion of many that it will be difficult for the Whigs to act in confidence with them.' Though the Sunderlandites were certainly not Tories they were clearly, for Vanbrugh, not Whigs either.

The dubious party antecedents of such men were to be fully capitalised by Walpole in mustering the Whigs against them. While Sunderland had lived they had acquired, in the eyes of the party, a share of their leader's aura, as a former associate of Somers, Halifax and

Wharton. Shorn of this protection, Carteret and his friends relied upon the King's favour alone. Lord Chesterfield was later to relate

'. . . that on the death of Lord Sunderland Lord Carteret had applied to the late King to support him, as he was then surrounded by his enemies; that the King promised it him, but told [him] the necessity of the time forced him to temporize; that hereupon Lord Carteret spoke to the Duchess of Kendall, who bid him have patience, and told him the King hated his other ministers'.

Even allowing for the possibly apocryphal nature of the story, it accurately represents the situation which was to exist for several years after Sunderland's death. While still misliking any alliance with avowed Tories, George was anxious to use amenable men of Carteret's stamp rather than those politicians who had assailed his Baltic policies once and who might take a similar stand any time the Whig back-benchers so dictated.[18]

The attitude of the King forced Walpole to place his emphasis where his inclination in any case lay: on the necessity of a fully Whig Minis-try. Though he had been willing enough to use the Tories' support when in opposition he never, neither now nor later, seriously considered giving them a share of power. His purpose was twofold: to prevent his rivals from ejecting him with the aid of the Tories, and to prevent the Tories from forming a government of their own with some assis-tance from Carteret's set. The way to both these ends lay in isolating the Tories, and for the next two sessions he concentrated on humbling them and making them appear too much a dangerous party for any good Whig to dabble with. At the same time he undermined his minis-terial colleagues whenever possible. As they were noticeably weak in the Commons, especially since the death of Craggs and expulsion of Aislabie, he conciliated party opinion and prejudice there; as they had the King's ear in household appointments, he continued to build Treasury patronage into a massive Walpolite concern, turning out any Whig who was not his own follower.

The methods which Walpole pursued at this time to consolidate his personal entourage were to continue for the rest of his career, not always to his advantage. The need for loyal, if not particularly able, adherents in office at all levels not only further alienated the Tory-tainted men but at times enraged many whose Whig credentials were as good as Walpole's own. And his emphasis on personally dominat-ing the House of Commons excluded from it able men whom he would tolerate in the Ministry only if they were in the House of Lords. But in one matter, and the most important, his touch was sure; he always aimed, in Onslow's words, 'at the uniting the Whigs against the Tories as Jacobites . . . and making therefore combinations between them

and any body of Whigs to be impracticable'. This policy of appealing
to party loyality succeeded in keeping him in office for twenty years,
and when it failed he was to fall with it.[19]

The initial means to carry out his policy were presented to Walpole
by the Pretender and Bishop Atterbury. The bishop was discovered to
be at the centre of a conspiracy for a well-planned rising in London,
combined with an invasion from France by Irish-officered troops, due
to take place as soon as the King set out for his summer visit to
Hanover. A beehive of panic was thoroughly stirred with the stick of
government propaganda. Within a fortnight of the new Parliament's
meeting on 9 October 1722, the Habeas Corpus Act was suspended
for a year and the senior English peer, the Duke of Norfolk, was sent
to the Tower by his fellows. Not even the 1715 Parliament opened
with greater Whig *éclat*.

In the Commons the Tories' first test of strength came with the Suspension Bill, when their amendment on 16 October to reduce the
period to six months was supported by the Whigs still in opposition,
including Smith, Jekyll, Brodrick and Spencer Cowper, and divided
193 Members against the Ministry's 246. However, when the Tory
leaders called for the outright rejection of the bill on its third reading,
their allies remembered their Whig identity; some left the House and
others went over to the court side, with the result that the Tories were
reduced to only 124 votes. Ten days later, however, they were again
joined by some Whigs on a government proposal for an augmentation of
the army by 4,000 men; the Dutch Resident, L'Hermitage, reported that
'many Whigs, to make themselves more popular, joined with the Tories
in this opposition'. It was a salutary reminder that the old magic
formula of a 'standing army' could still, as in the later 1690s and during
the period of Walpole's opposition after 1717, cause embarrassment
to Whig governments. Walpole's enemies took note.[20]

Whig doubts about the expediency or justice of the course being
pursued by the First Lord were most strongly expressed towards the
end of November in narrowed voting upon his proposal for an extraordinary tax on Roman Catholics, to defray the cost of the recent
measures against the plot. The Tories were joined on this issue not
only by the usual Whig dissidents but even by so respectable a Whig
independent as the future Speaker Onslow, while others expressed by
their absence a disquiet at the injustice of the plan. Only forty-nine
votes carried Walpole to success on 23 October.[21]

After Christmas the investigation of the Atterbury plot proceeded
in a secret committee of the Commons, and at the beginning of March
1723 Pulteney presented the committee's report on the evidence. Bills
of Pains and Penalties were accordingly brought in against Atterbury
and his principal agents, Plunkett and Kelly. On so clear a party issue

the Whig dissidents could hardly fail to vote with the government Whigs, and Jekyll, Smith and Brodrick took a leading part in the prosecutions. Their opponents, left to themselves, voted manfully but made a poor showing in debate; 'the Tories never had less to say in their lives' and 'the Tories spoke sadly as if they were mumbling thistles' went the gleeful reports. In Plunkett's case the Tories had to argue that there was, including the testimony of the necessary two witnesses, too much evidence to justify a parliamentary trial; in Atterbury's case they urged that there was too little evidence for such a proceeding. Despite accusations of inconsistency they managed to put up a solid party front, as in the case of the impeachments of 1715. The price of their stand, however, was that public opinion convicted them of Jacobite sympathies, and their unsupported votes appeared so denuded as to cause Onslow to reminisce twenty-five years later that this time saw 'the greatest disproportion in the numbers upon the divisions in the House of Commons I ever knew there'. This writer's view of the importance for Walpole of the Atterbury affair was equally definite: 'it fixed him with the King, and united for a time the whole body of the Whigs to him'.

In fact, Walpole was still not 'fixed' with the King when the session ended in May; nor, while Carteret remained in office, could the Cabinet be said to be principally Walpolite. But Parliament was well under control, with the Whigs more elated and the Tories more subdued than at any time since 1716. Of the two years which followed the exile of Atterbury and the imprisonment of his chief abettors, a historian has written that they 'probably exhibited as few ripples on the surface of English politics as any equal period in English history'. However, not far beneath the surface, changes were taking place which greatly affected the future of the party alignment.[22]

Shortly before the end of the session Walpole had reluctantly acquiesced in a royal pardon for Bolingbroke, who for several years had been plying royal favourites with bribes and Whig politicians with promises of support. Returning at once to England, the former arch-Tory immediately began to preach in person what he had long advocated by correspondence: namely the abandonment of parties with a view to making possible the entry of Tories—doubtless including himself—to office and power. He was soon surrounded by a new coterie, of which the most prominent were his friends Wyndham, Gower and Bathurst. Bolingbroke revealed to Walpole that he had received approaches from Carteret, and had rejected them. In July he began to press the Ministry to accept his group's support, for which the first return would have to be a repeal of the act of attainder against himself. Walpole had never needed Tory support less, and was only embarrassed by the offer. He was encountering considerable criticism from his own party even at the suggestion of a repeal, and gave Boling-broke no hope of the fulfilment of his wish in the near future. Towns-hend agreed that 'it will be absolutely necessary for us to rest on the Whig bottom'. But the Secretary was obliged, no doubt wryly, to inform Bolingbroke of the King's continued good intentions. The brothers-in-law had to temporise and step warily under provocation from court.[23]

Another undercurrent favoured the Walpolites, however, with the possibility of recruiting an important new supporter of indisputably Whig principles and of good parliamentary support. The young Duke of Newcastle, who already commanded a well-trained phalanx of twelve or more supporters in the Commons in addition to several friends in his own House, had recently drawn himself away from Car-teret and his Tory intrigues. Newcastle's new adherence more than compensated for the potential loss of an abler, if less influential politi-cian. Pulteney, since his resignation with Walpole in 1717, had always tried to keep one foot in the Sunderlandite camp, sometimes in person and sometimes through his relation Daniel Pulteney, Sunderland's brother-in-law and follower. Disappointed of any important office, Pulteney was giving the Walpole family cause for alarm, particularly by threatening to raise the Bolingbroke affair in Parliament.[24]

The main interest of the political world of Westminster as a new session approached was the backstairs Walpole–Townshend tussle with Carteret, now reaching its final stage. While this conflict went on, Parliament's meeting was delayed, reflecting Walpole's desire to avoid unnecessary 'cabals' between his opponent and parliamentarians. He hardly need have worried, for the session which at last began in January 1724 was exceptionally quiet, with Jacobite Members still cowed and other Tories discouraged after the prosecutions of the last session. The address went unopposed, and a proposal to continue the extra 4,000 troops for another year rallied only 100 opponents, including Jekyll and some other Whigs. Much of the session was taken up with taxation changes proposed by Walpole to make the customs and excise services more profitable and efficient, and thereby to relieve the strain on the land tax. Such a desirable change could meet little opposition, and further divisions were few and spiritless. So little menacing did the Tories seem that when a Whig lawyer tried towards the end of March to raise the matter of Bolingbroke's pardon a general laugh was raised and no seconder was found.[25]

Before the session sighed to its end in April, Members learned that the great struggle in the Closet was over. Carteret had overreached himself and been outwitted by Townshend in a court intrigue. A patent sold by the Duchess of Kendal to William Wood for minting Irish coinage had crystallised Irish indignation at English rule; and Carteret's manoeuvres, with the help of the Brodrick family, to deflect the storm towards Walpole were exposed. Carteret was sent to Ireland as Lord Lieutenant to sort out the trouble he had helped to stir, and the Secretaryship was taken by Newcastle. Another Sunderlandite, George Treby the younger, was removed as Secretary at War to make way for Newcastle's brother Henry Pelham. Only in an attempt to neutralise the disappointed Pulteney, by encouraging him to take a peerage, were Walpole and Townshend unsuccessful. Pulteney became an increasingly troublesome figure in the Commons. But on the whole the ministers could reflect that the party schism begun in 1717 was at last over, with the King's preferred English advisers dead or disgraced, the German advisers departed for Hanover, the Tories isolated and government upon a solidy Whig basis. Moreover, the outcome of ideological debate within the Whig party had been a satisfactory compromise between principles and practicality; the dissenters were secure but the Church was not endangered, Baltic or Hanoverian policies were laid aside, and the new monarchy was largely observing the limitations laid down for it.[26]

CHAPTER 11

Walpole Whigs, Tories and Patriots 1724-34

Walpole—Sir Robert, as he became in 1725—differed from his immediate predecessors as principal minister by remaining as government leader in the Commons, choosing, like Pulteney, to refuse a peerage. Walpole's managing ability arose out of the talents which not even his enemies denied that he possessed. In the opinion of Chesterfield, himself a shrewd parliamentary tactician, Walpole was the 'best parliament man, and the ablest manager of Parliament, that I believe ever lived'. After 1727 a new monarch shared this high opinion. According to the courtier Lord Hervey, in his memoirs, George II and his consort 'were possessed with an opinion that Sir Robert Walpole was, by so great a superiority, the most able man in the kingdom, that he understood the revenue, and knew how to manage that formidable and refractory body, the House of Commons, so much better than any other man, that it was impossible for the business of the Crown to be well done without him'.

Walpole's control of Parliament arose out of his determination to keep his administration exclusively Whig. The price which both George I, in his last years, and George II paid for smooth-running affairs and an adequate Civil List was party control. While nonparty government probably had a good deal of appeal to both monarchs as an abstract proposition, neither could afford to lose the goodwill of the bulk of the Whig party. Thus though, as is often said, Walpole owed his authority to both the Commons and the Closet, the balance was not an even one. George II began his reign by rejecting the minister but came to accept him because of his acceptability to the Whigs. When a sufficient number of the latter finally turned against Walpole in 1742 to secure his defeat in the Commons, the King reluctantly had to let him go. The following minister, Granville (Carteret), lasted only two and a half years because, unlike Walpole, he failed to secure the adherence of the Whig old corps. 'This Parliament', rejoiced Speaker Onslow after the fall of Granville, 'has torn two favourite ministers from the throne.' Impregnated, like all Whigs, with principles forged to fight the Stuarts, Onslow had no doubt that in the last count the Whig party controlled the monarchy.

Walpole's dominance of the parliamentary party derived in the first place from his insistence on Whig principles and in the second from his attention to detail in policy and management. Like Oxford before him, he was often accused of taking too much into his own hands, and the charge had much truth. After 1724 the direction of government became more personalised. The Cabinet met less frequently, and its place as a decision-making body was taken by Walpole and Townshend, with Newcastle and one or two others participating as needed. Townshend had a mind of his own, but Newcastle in his early years of office probably lived up to the report which the French Envoy Chamonel sent on his appointment: 'It suffices [his colleagues] that he has the docility to do and say as they dictate.' After Townshend's departure in 1730 no individual minister stood up to Walpole. But the price of omnipotence was omnipresence, which in its turn brought criticism. Nowhere was this more true than in the Commons, where Walpole constantly had to make in person the adjustments necessary to keep a court party running smoothly. As the socially conscious Perceval wrote, on an occasion when the First Lord attempted to defend one of his unofficial Whips against an independent gentleman in a disputed election case,

'. . . it is this meanness of his (the prostitution of the character of a first Minister in assisting and strenuously supporting the defence of dunghill worms, let their cause be ever so unjust, against men of honour, birth, and fortune, and that in person too), that gains him so much ill-will'.

But as every eighteenth-century minister knew, the dunghill worms, or placemen, were an important ingredient of management and worthy of constant attention.[1]

The machinery of court patronage in Parliament has been so often described as to need little comment here. It is sufficient to point out that by 1724 Walpole was well on the way to turning the Whig majority in Parliament into a more specialised Walpolite Whig majority. In the House of Lords this continued to be assured through the household office holders, who numbered between twenty-five and thirty, and through most of the sixteen elected Scottish peers; to these, by Walpole's judicious use of a promotion system which took advantage of the very unequal incomes of the various dioceses, were added the regular votes of nearly all the twenty-six archbishops and bishops. Thus not only did the Lords remain an essential longstop for those bills, especially place and pension measures, which sometimes caused independent Whigs in the Commons to side with the opposition, but also it could save Walpole in what amounted to censure debates. The most spectacular example occurred in 1733 when only one bishop voted for an attempt to revive the South Sea issue.*

In the Commons the First Lord's most useful acquisition was in Scottish votes, for Argyll had drawn nearer to him since the last election, bringing control of most of the Scottish Members. In 1725 the alliance was cemented by the dismissal of Roxburgh and the abolition of the Secretaryship for Scotland. For over a decade Argyll and his brother Islay became virtually Walpole's managers for the northern kingdom, though without the status which a Secretaryship would have conferred. Officially, Scottish business went through Newcastle's hands, and in this way Walpole was able to keep some control over the Campbells. Scottish patronage was joined with court and Treasury patronage, which by the beginning of George II's reign accounted for around 130 Members in the Commons and was to draw in still more later. But in this assembly which could gather together over 400 Members, and in extreme cases over 500, the court party lacked the assured working majority enjoyed by its counterpart in the Lords. Patronage, of itself, was never enough to control the lower house even on routine business; for this the support of the independent Whigs was always needed.[2]

Fortunately for Walpole there was rarely a stable or united opposition, though the prominence given to setpiece debates on certain issues sometimes gives another impression. From 1726 to 1739 Parliament assembled about the third week of January and debated the same annually recurring matters at about the same calendar date. Procedural regularity, however, concealed a real disunity among the opponents of the government. The Tories might have formed a stable opposition but for the complicating presence of an increasing number of Whig opponents of Walpole. In practice a united and continuous opposition was made impossible by the repeated refusal of both the Tories and 'patriot' Whigs to act together on important issues, making even tactical co-operation impracticable for any length of time. When the Tories joined the dissident Whigs in December 1741 to bring down Walpole, they did so only after repeated refusals stretching over many years, after three years of ill-conducted war, and after a general election which overrode government control for the first time since 1710.† The Tory

---

*Nevertheless the importance of the Lords' powers for the executive did not enhance the authority of the House itself in Walpole's time. In April 1726 Strafford complained that a royal message concerning the raising of additional supplies had been sent to the Commons only, but even on so sensitive a matter the ministerial majority easily defeated a motion by fifty-nine to thirty-one, and the minority were reduced to a written protest, 'lest any mistake of this kind should be attended with such evil consequences as to encourage evil ministers hereafter to a total neglect of this House'. A precisely similar case occurred again in February 1740 (Turberville, *XVIIIth Century* 22–3).

†Thus Professor Foord has written that ' "patriots" never included the Tories,

refusal to overthrow Walpole for the benefit of opposition Whigs was countered by the patriots' loathing of the necessity which forced them to work with Tories whenever this became possible. The archdissident Pulteney professed in public a desire to end 'the senseless division of Whig and Tory', but privately he always insisted that 'Whig principles' were inconsistent with 'Tory notions'. When his friends entered office in 1742 he was reported to have said: 'now, I thank God, we are out of the power of the Tories'.

The main hope of a successful opposition to the government Whigs lay, after 1724 as well as before, in a full muster of Tory voting power in support of the dissident Whigs. This was feasible on normal occasions because the Tories rarely voted for the government; Sedgwick's detailed study of the division lists shows that in the four issues for which lists survive from the first ten years of George I's reign, only six Tory votes had gone astray out of a total of 527 cast, and that the picture remained similar at least as late as 1754. But, as has already been seen, joint activity was bedevilled on occasions when a Ministry was in serious danger of being outvoted, because many Tories would vote in its defence, or abstain by absence, in order to prevent its Whig opponents from overthrowing it in order to form another Whig Ministry. Such behaviour was not required while the number of Whig dissidents was low, but it was to be revived in the 1730s after Pulteney had gathered a substantial body of discontented Whigs.

Less difficult for the Tories than the question of whether to combine with opposition Whigs was the problem of their relations with the Pretender. This prince, like his son later, never received substantial support from English toryism, despite the hopes of Jacobite exiles and the assertions of Walpolite propaganda. If vague assurances conveyed by clandestine routes to the court-in-exile were a sufficient proof of Jacobitism, a good many Tories might, it is true, have been implicated. A Jacobite list of supposedly probable supporters of Atterbury's attempted rising in 1722 had included 106 current members of both Houses. But the great majority of these were, from their records in the more hopeful ventures of 1715 or 1745 or from other indications of their outlook, palpably fence-sitters quite disinclined to risk their necks. The opinion of Hervey was that by the early part of George II's reign the Jacobite section of the Tories 'was fallen so low . . . that in reality it consisted only of a few veterans (and those very few) who were really Jacobites by principle, and some others who, educated in that calling, made it a point of honour not to quit the name'. Atterbury, who knew his men from the bitter experiences of 1714 and after, believed that if

who persistently rejected identification with the dissident Whigs. This probably helps to account for the rapid development of "the Opposition", which could be employed to describe all the various factions of Walpole's enemies' (Foord, 154).

Tories had been taken into office by George II in 1727, as they hoped, they would not have assisted the Pretender.

English Tories had a shrewd knowledge, much of it derived from Bolingbroke, of the puerile feuds and blinkered euphoria which characterised the Jacobite court and rendered it incapable of devising an effective policy for staging a restoration. Even the lifelong Scottish Jacobite George Lockhart sickened of such an atmosphere and bought his return from exile in 1728 by agreeing to dabble no more in plots against the government. As he passed through London on his way north he found that the Tories knew too much for the Pretender's good; and being unable to give them a better opinion of the chances of Jacobitism than they already possessed, he kept silence and passed on. His reticence did nothing to further the Pretender's cause in the reign of the second Hanoverian monarch. The little band of parliamentary Jacobites under Shippen kept their faith, and pinned upon the easy sympathy they received from other Tories the exaggerated hopes which they duly recorded in crude ciphers and sent to their master. But the great majority of the Tory party was Hanoverian by conviction or caution, and had better hopes to pursue than the will-of-the-wisp of Stuart restoration. Under George I the Tories were fortified by constant rumours that the heir to the throne, or perhaps even its present in-cumbent, would tire of whiggery and turn to the natural allies of monarchy. After these hopes were disappointed in 1727, many Tories derived a measure of hope for the future from the ideal of nonparty government which fascinated Bolingbroke for the rest of his long life. Foremost among such men was Wyndham, now fully converted from Jacobitism. The greatest obstacle they found was, in Onslow's words, Walpole's 'plan of having everybody to be deemed a Jacobite who was not a professed and known Whig'.[3]

The two years following the fall of Carteret saw little revival of effective parliamentary resistance to Walpole's Ministry, for though Pulteney moved into opposition he was able to take only a handful of personal friends with him and made little contact with the Tories. With the latter still subdued, there was not much reaction to the passage of supplies in the Commons in the autumn of 1724. Just before the Christmas recess Walpole took advantage of the usual thinning out of Tories at this season to pave the way for a measure to their disadvantage: the altera-tion of the franchise of London. In the 1722 election the capital city had shown its traditional independence of government by returning four Tory Members. One of these, John Barnard, was already demon-strating himself to be the well-informed and hard-to-please parliamen-tarian he was to remain for nearly fifty years, first as Tory and later as a very independent Whig. The implementing bill for the change received its third reading in the Commons on 19 March 1725, with only eighty-three votes cast against it, and passed in the Lords without difficulty. As a result the government gained two of the City's four seats in the next general election, though the new act was less effective in long-term electoral results, for London was not easily cowed. But there was a considerable gain in immediate prestige for Walpole, for the Tories had again been isolated over the issue.

From early in the session, however, Pulteney and his chief supporters Samuel Sandys and Sir John Rushout showed signs in small matters of trying to annoy the Ministry. Their efforts broadened in the new year in the impeachment of Lord Chancellor Macclesfield for peculation and the taking of bribes. Pulteney was joined by Wyndham in trying to obtain a parliamentary investigation which could be turned into a general inquiry into government practices, but they were frustrated by the ministerialists' participation in the prosecution, Walpole having no objection to sacrificing a guilty colleague whose appointment had in any case been made under Sunderland. And early in April Pulteney committed himself irrevocably to opposition by cavilling at a proposal to meet new royal debts on the Civil List. By the end of the session he was the recognised leader of a small new band of dissident Whigs, a position which was regularised by his dismissal from the household office of Cofferer. His long exile was begun.[4]

In later years Pulteney may have regretted making his break over the Civil List. He always preferred, indeed, to postdate his first opposition by a few months to a subject far more worthy of his talents for oratory and pamphleteering: namely the treaty concluded at Hanover with France and Prussia in September 1725. Pulteney—'this Achilles' of Hervey's envenomed phrase—was to criticise the renewed French alliance as long as it lasted, and to castigate it long afterward as the root of all subsequent ministerial errors. Townshend's main reason for reviving a policy over which he had himself virtually resigned in 1717 was laudable, if somewhat alarmist: a possible future union of the crowns of the Empire and Spain. But the Treaty of Hanover achieved no popularity, and became a gift of great value to Pulteney. He immediately began to strive for an understanding with the Tories, and was reported in December to be boasting that they 'came in so fast he knows not what to do with them'.[5]

This piece of bravado was not, however, borne out by the experience of the session which began on 20 January 1726. The King's opening speech called for increased naval forces in view of the imminence of war with Spain, but though Pulteney joined the Tories in criticising the address he aroused their suspicion by not pressing his attack. And in a debate on army estimates on the 28th Pulteney found himself unable to divide in the absence of many Tories, while Wyndham actually supported the enhanced forces on the grounds of national safety. Not until 9 February did Pulteney risk a division, on a motion for an investigation into the national debt, and the attempt was lost by 262 votes to 89. After this discouraging start the dissident Whigs' campaign had little success. Even on a government motion on the 17th to assure the King that the Commons would stand by him if Hanover were attacked, a suggestion which would normally have been sufficient to alienate a large number of independent Whigs, Pulteney and the Tories were able to muster only 107 votes. In general, parliamentarians showed themselves to be reluctant to risk factious voting in time of emergency, and the Tories in particular were not anxious to ally themselves with a former persecutor.[6]

Before the next session, however, there occurred a spectacular union between Pulteney and Bolingbroke. The latter had remained quiescent in the session of 1726, vigorously denying to the Ministry, through Harcourt, that he had any understanding with Pulteney. His denial was probably true at this time, and arose out of his remaining hope of obtaining a reversal of the act of attainder which still prevented his sitting in the House of Lords. However, Walpole employed all his arguments with the King against this reversal, and at last won the tussle by citing the reluctance of the Whigs to countenance any such action. With hope gone by the end of the session, Bolingbroke bitterly turned to active opposition.

The first fruits of Bolingbroke's decision were seen in December when, in preparation for Parliament, there appeared the first number of *The Craftsman*, to which he contributed jointly with the two Pulteneys. This publication was, in its early years, the chief organ of its founders, and had a circulation which considerably exceeded the circulations of its opposition predecessors and its government rivals such as Walpole's *London Journal*. In anticipation of government muzzling the writers proclaimed the 'liberty of the press', by which term was meant, they wrote, 'an unreserved discretionary power for every man to publish his thoughts on any subject, and in any manner, which is not forbidden by the laws of the land'. Parodying the prevalent advertisements of the day for quack medicines, *The Craftsman* began in its third issue a pleasant satire on a cure-all 'specifick' obtainable only from 'Dr Robert King'. Its main business, however, was to put forward its own remedy for state ills: namely the 'coalition of parties' in which 'names of distinction' were to be set aside. Against the *London Journal*'s constant emphasis on the continuance of party differences, its rival urged: 'let the very names of Whig and Tory be for ever buried in oblivion'. The message was mainly that of Bolingbroke, who was to develop it in a series of writings. This series began with his

Remarks on the History of England, first published in *The Craftsman* in 1730; continued in *A Dissertation upon Parties*, which likewise first saw light in that journal; and culminated with the most famous of his pamphlets *The Idea of a Patriot King*, published in its final form in 1749 to justify the Tories' alliance of 1747 with Frederick, Prince of Wales. The message, with its emphasis on a nonparty monarchical government, was one which would have been very familiar to Queen Anne; for it was no less than Oxford's old cry for the abolition of parties under an ideal monarchy.[7] The attempt to revive deep-rooted 'country' instincts, however, had more effect in the long run in a general subversion of Walpole, whose corrupt practices were be-laboured year in and year out, than in bringing about a union of Tories and dissident Whigs. And if the 'patriot' philosophy was the polemical contribution of Bolingbroke, the soubriquet of Patriots settled down largely to denote Whig dissidents.*

At the opening of Parliament on 17 January 1727 the international situation was ominous, with undeclared war with Spain taking place at sea and on Gibraltar. The national danger minimised the effectiveness of opposition. In the debate on the address Pulteney sought to defer a reference to the need for putting the nation into a posture of defence, urging that Parliament needed time to carry out an investigation of the state of the nation. But though he was supported by Hanmer, Shippen, Wyndham and other Tories, the 'minority' (as the government's miscellaneous opponents were called with increasing frequency) mustered only 81 votes against 251. Eight days later a motion by Pelham to increase the size of the army by over 8,000 men was opposed by about the same number. The turnout of the opposition rarely exceeded 100 throughout the session, with 81 votes against doubling the two-shilling land tax and 109 against a vote of credit. In the course of the debates at least one Tory, Sir Edward Knatchbull, went over permanently to the government; and, on average, barely more than half the party was present for divisions, indicating a continuing doubt about the line taken by the Tory leaders. Pulteney himself carried with him, by Horatio Walpole's computation, no more than ten Whigs. As the beginning of a joint opposition these results were not encoura-ging.[8]

*A recent trend among students of politics and political thought has stressed that Bolingbroke's writings, while inspired by his political opportunism, repre-sented a genuine strand of contemporary thought and a development of traditional political doctrines. Some suggestive contributions are: J. G. A. Pocock, 'Machiavelli, Harrington and English Political Ideologies in the Eighteenth Century', in *Politics, Language and Time*; Isaac Kramnick, *Boling-broke and His Circle*; and Quentin Skinner, 'The Principles and Practice of Opposition', in Neil McKendrick (ed.), *Historical Perspectives . . . in Honour of J. H. Plumb* (1974).

Three sessions of Pulteneyite intransigence had come no closer to shaking Walpole's hold on the Commons than the preceding ones of Tory quiescence. There occurred in 1727, however, an event which in many people's belief might have removed the minister by shaking his position at court. In June the King died on his way to Hanover, and the Prince of Wales, now George II, promptly desired Walpole to take his instructions from a favourite, Spencer Compton. For several weeks the possibility of a Compton Ministry, or alternatively of a Tory Ministry, was widely discussed. In fact, the continuance of Walpole's administration was not in doubt after a three-week session of Parliament convened on 27 June.

Tories flocked to court as soon as the news of George II's accession arrived in England. Over the years they had received encouragement of a vague nature, and the royal couple had some intention of relaxing the rigid barrier against them, if only to curb the pretensions of the Whigs. The King certainly tried through Lord Chancellor King to get some Tories put into commissions of the peace, but his determination was not very great and it crumbled completely when the orthodox Grafton protested that some of the men recommended by Hanmer for Suffolk were 'jesuits'. The King's greatest failure, however, was his attempt to make Compton his first minister. In this resolution he was weakened by Queen Caroline's opposition to the Speaker, by Compton's own self-doubts, and above all by Walpole's obviously superior ability to get a good Civil List from the House of Commons. The First Lord's proposals were shepherded through to give George £100,000 a year more than the £700,000 his father had received, together with £100,000 for Caroline and any excess produced by the taxes provided. This achievement, rather than Walpole's improved draft for the King's closing speech, decided the contest with Compton. It was a victory not only over the Speaker but also over the Tories, discouraging their last hopes. When Parliament ended they had largely fallen off from attendance at court. Walpole's earlier decision to remain in the Commons, with its vastly greater problems for a party leader but its overriding control of money to assist a First Lord, was triumphantly vindicated in his tussle with Compton.[9]

The elections of the autumn, which seemed tame after the Closet struggles of June, presented few surprises. Before the summer session, when Tory hopes had still been high, there was report of heavy candidatures, especially in the counties. But in the event the situation appears to have been normal in all but a few constituencies. Scotland returned no Tories but included three opposition Whigs in its numbers. In Wales the Tory majority was at last overbalanced by Walpole's patient spadework, and fourteen Whigs were returned for the twenty-four seats. The English counties returned their usual Tory majority, including in

Herefordshire the talented Edward, son of Auditor Edward Harley, who was soon to assume a leading place in the parliamentary party. In Kent, Knatchbull's desertion to Walpole was punished by his failure to secure his return, forcing him to fall back ignominiously upon a Cornish borough provided by the government. In Cambridgeshire, however, where in 1722 two Tories had been returned by majorities of over 500 each, the sons of Townshend and Nottingham were now able to secure their own return by much larger margins while a Jacobite candidate, Sir John Hynde Cotton, received only thirty-two votes. The English boroughs continued their trend towards domination by the Whigs, with Newcastle securing no fewer than thirteen personal seats and influencing elections in many other instances. London, however, continued to show a measure of independence by returning Barnard and another more extreme Tory among its four Members, despite the strenuous electoral efforts of the Ministry in co-operation with the three great corporations of the Bank, the East India Company and the South Sea Company. And the obstinately Tory corporation of Cambridge insisted upon returning that city's near neighbour Cotton, despite his total failure to appeal to the freeholders of the county.

Jacobites, and even other Tories, had need of such loyal pockets of resistance as Cambridge in this year, which produced their lowest returns for any general election between 1714 and the fall of Walpole. When the dust had subsided they were in possession of only 131 seats, a number which was to be reduced to 128 after petitions. The massive majority of Whigs contained fifteen men, led by Pulteney, who were to be largely in opposition, leaving Walpole a phalanx of 400 who could usually be relied upon to support the government.[10]

The first two sessions were conducted in a low political temperature. In divisions the Tories and Pulteneyites rarely succeeded in obtaining more than 100 votes and were therefore reluctant to divide frequently. Before Parliament assembled, Compton was sent to the Lords with the title of Baron Wilmington, and his removal dispelled any doubts about Walpole's ascendancy. On 23 January 1728 the ministerial nominee Onslow was elected to the Chair of the Commons without opposition. He was a generally acceptable choice, and though he did not entirely live up to Walpole's desire for an amenable Speaker his adherence to Whig principles was to make him an invaluable intermediary between Ministries and the party in the House for five successive Parliaments. His duties began in a highly government-dominated Commons. By early 1728 war was virtually at an end; but when, on 9 February, Pulteney ventured to divide the Committee of the Whole on the Ministry's desire to keep up the level of the forces for a further year, he found himself defeated by a crushing 290 votes to 86. Successive divisions on the national debt early the next month showed little change in this majority; the government seemed unshakable on any issue.[11]

Better success was obtained by the opposition in its journalism than in Parliament. Gay's *Beggars' Opera* popularly portrayed Walpole as a highwayman, and its still more scurrilous successor *Polly* had to be banned from the stage by Grafton in his capacity of Lord Chamberlain. In the session which began in January 1729, however, Tories and opposition Whigs found themselves unable to maintain the unity which their press demonstrated and enjoined. On the address the Tories divided only eighty-seven votes; Pulteney, having criticised the address himself, withheld his support in the division and was openly taunted by Shippen with inconsistency. The Tories were quick to take their revenge. On 31 January the two Pulteneys and their group spoke strongly, William Pulteney several times, against Pelham's motion for retaining the army at the same number as in the last year. But this time it was the turn of most of the Tory orators to hold back. The disunited state of the opposition was plain for all to see, and it was reported that Wyndham and other Tories had left London because of the difficulties encountered.

Later, however, the prospects of effective attack revived over the delay in finally concluding peace with Spain. The result of ministerial prevarication, due to the reluctance of Townshend to hazard the Treaty of Hanover, was the immediate defection of many independent Whigs from the Ministry on this issue, so that the opposition mustered numbers which rose in successive debates from 129 to 145. On the last occasion, 13 March, the court party was reduced to a majority of thirty-five, which indicated considerable absenteeism as well as outright opposition from some of its usual supporters. Opposition leaders took heart, for what could happen once might happen again with greater intensity. Walpole and most of his ministerial colleagues took alarm and set about preventing such an event.[12]

In May the King set out for Hanover, accompanied by Townshend, and Walpole set in motion behind his brother-in-law's back a negotiation which resulted by November in the conclusion of the Treaty of Seville. Though not as yet a decisive break with Townshend's pro-French policy, this marked a step in the right direction. Spain ceased to harass Gibraltar and restored the Asiento. But in return, Britain had to guarantee the aspirations of the Spanish royal family to territories in Italy, some of which were claimed or held by the Emperor; this was a concession which Walpole would later have to atone for by the reconciliation with Austria which alone would satisfy Whig opinion. Thus, by the opening of the next session in January 1730 Walpole had gone some way towards conciliating his Whig critics, both by pacifying Spain and by putting a final blow to the Austro–Spanish alliance; but

Pulteney was still left with certain dangerous levers for pressure. Townshend remained in office and an embarrassment to his colleagues. And the Treaty of Seville had done little to safeguard Britain against new signs of French discontent at a time when the birth of a Dauphin was opening the way, by lessening fears that Philip V might yet succeed to the French throne, to the possibility of a revival of the alliance of the Bourbon monarchies.

It was thus with greater than usual preparation and expectations that Parliament assembled on 13 January for what was to prove an eventful session. Pulteney had come to a working agreement with Wyndham, and even the Jacobites were urged by the Pretender to move in harmony with the dissident Whigs in order to overthrow Walpole. The Treaty of Seville was attacked by Pulteney, Cotton and others as contrary to the interests of the Emperor. The first major success in reducing the government's majority came, however, on a ministerial proposal to keep 12,000 Hessian troops in pay despite reductions in British forces. After a long and angry debate on 4 February, in which this attempt was denounced as advantageous only to the Elector of Hanover, the minority was about 169, of which only half was accounted for by the Tories.[13]

Having found the independent Whigs willing to listen to pro-Austrian and anti-Hanoverian arguments of considerable strength, the elated opposition now received an even better reception for anti-French sentiments. The opposition completely roused the Commons and surprised the Ministry on 10 February with a new topic, announcing and bringing witnesses to prove that the harbour at Dunkirk, a privateering base in time of war, had been rebuilt by the French in violation of the Treaty of Utrecht. Pulteney pressed hard for an immediate debate leading almost certainly to a motion of censure, but to his chagrin he now found that the Tories led by Wyndham were prepared to give the Ministry time to prepare its defence. On 27 February, the day set for the major debate, over 450 Members were accordingly assembled in the lower house, with half the House of Lords reported present in the visitors' gallery. The only important evidence produced by the Ministry was a copy of a hurriedly obtained order by the French for the demolition of the harbour, but this proved sufficient to stiffen the government's independent supporters. Walpole adroitly diverted the debate from a planned censure by launching an attack upon Bolingbroke as an instigator of strife. This in turn called up Wyndham in defence of his friend and Edward Harley in justification of the Tory Ministry which had obtained the Treaty of Utrecht. After a fifteen-hour sitting the Ministry carried 270 votes against 149. About thirty paired Members had been constrained by heat and the crowding to leave the House before the vote, and both the diarists present felt the effect of the packed atmosphere. Knatchbull was carried out fainting at about midnight and was thought to have then caught the fever which, though he attended further sittings, killed him a few weeks later. Perceval caught a cold and wisely kept indoors for the next two days.[14]

The parliamentary storm over Dunkirk provided the first major challenge by a near-united opposition. Though it did not produce the extremely close voting and unprecedentedly high attendance which was to be achieved two years later, over the Excise Bill, it shook any complacency which the ministers retained. From the opposition point of view, however, the result was not entirely satisfactory. From the first, according to Perceval's observation, the opposition leaders had been held back by their followers from obtaining votes of censure. The Tory backbenchers were still not, and never would be, reconciled to destroying Walpole for the sake of Pulteney.

Nevertheless some opposition gains were seen. At the height of the Dunkirk excitement, on 16 February, Pulteney's henchman Sandys had unexpectedly defeated Walpole by ten votes with a motion to bring in a bill making more effectual the legislation for excluding government pension holders from the Commons. Although the Pension Bill and its several successors were rejected by the Lords, it scored a moral victory against the government on a court–country issue, detaching sixty or more independent Whigs to the opposition side in the division. Other government defectors appear to have followed the example of Knatchbull, who went away before the motion was put.

Even before Parliament was prorogued in May ministerial changes were under way. Townshend had for some time been isolated among his colleagues, and was now replaced as Secretary by William Stanhope, Baron Harrington, the diplomat who had carried through the Treaty of Seville. The way was now clear for Newcastle and Harrington to revive the Austrian alliance, even if this meant cooler relations with France. At the same time Carteret, who had been showing signs of restiveness in the Lord Lieutenancy of Ireland, was dismissed. He was replaced by the Duke of Dorset, whose post of Lord Steward was used to conciliate the able and ambitious Chesterfield. Wilmington was given the Privy Seal to make available the post of Paymaster-General for Pelham, Walpole's favourite follower. The changes represented the biggest reallocation of posts since 1724; and they were soon further improved by Wilmington's removal to the Lord Presidency on the death of Trevor, which made room for Devonshire as Privy Seal. Finally, Horatio Walpole was brought back from Paris and made Cofferer and a privy councillor to strengthen the government frontbench debaters in the Commons. The Ministry was now almost wholly composed of Walpole's nominees.[15]

Before Parliament met in 1731, the First Lord set out to achieve two diplomatic ends: to ensure the demolition of Dunkirk, by means of pressure on the French court, and to conciliate the Emperor. Both purposes were formulated with an eye to the Ministry's independent Whig supporters. Neither matter could be hurried, however, and neither had come to fruition when the two Houses reassembled. Nevertheless the new policies eased the way. The address brought on a smart debate but no division. On 3 February the Hessian troops were again retained, by a slightly larger majority than in the previous year; and on the 23rd the government went on to obtain a majority of 122 against a motion reflecting upon its handling of relations with Spain, with 121 Members going out with the opposition. In March, Walpole concluded his treaty with Vienna on the basis of confirmation of Spain's right to put troops into the Italian duchies. The apparent miracle of combining a confirmation of the provisions of the Treaty of Seville with the conciliation of Austria had been achieved by Britain's undertaking to guarantee the Pragmatic Sanction promulgated by Charles VI in 1713, to ensure the succession of his daughter Maria Theresa to the undivided Habsburg estates. Time was to show that Walpole held this guarantee lightly, but the alliance it brought had an immediate effect on parliamentary affairs. Thus when the opposition Whigs tried to stage another Dunkirk on 5 April, this time alleging the rebuilding of Spanish military works before Gibraltar, the attempt fell flat. Pelham and Walpole triumphantly gave details of the new treaty, and had the satisfaction of hearing Wyndham welcome it, albeit with the reservation that he wished it had taken place some years before. Pulteney and Jekyll tried to save the day, but went unsupported by the Tory orators. The debate was put off by the ministerial speakers without a division. Thus petered out, for the moment, the opposition Whigs' hope of continuing to fault the Ministry on its diplomacy.[16]

During the summer and autumn the dissident Whigs made renewed efforts to conciliate Tory leaders, even appearing in public with them despite an ever-present fear of the propaganda use which the ministerial press would make of this behaviour. Pulteney referred to this dilemma when he wrote to a correspondent, knowing that his letter would be opened in transit by Walpole's post office: 'I will be extremely careful what I say, not to give offence and bring you into any disgrace for continuing your friendship with such a Jacobite as I am.' Fortunately for the shaky opposition alliance some fresh cement for its unity was to be provided by a revived overconfidence on the Ministry's part, and the battles of the next two sessions were fought mainly on fresh ground concerning domestic issues.[17]

Parliament assembled quietly enough in January 1732, for the settlement of foreign alliances which was trumpeted in the speech from the throne could be countered by little but nominal criticism. In February, however, there loomed a new iceberg for wrecking the Walpolean galleon. The First Lord had set the Treasury in motion towards reorganising the entire fiscal system, a move designed mainly to conciliate the Whig independents and the gentry. The land tax was to be reduced to one shilling in the pound, and the deficit was to be made good in other ways. This would be done in part by a new salt duty, and in part by bringing wine and tobacco out of the customs into excise jurisdiction, in order to obtain greater revenue by the reduction of smuggling. The opposition took its stand on the immediate proposal to reimpose the salt duty, and speaker after speaker rose to denounce this measure as mulcting hardest those sections of society, the poorer ones, which were least well fitted to pay; even government supporters remembered that they had to face a general election in two years' time. On successive days the Ministry's majority fell alarmingly to thirty-nine, then to twenty-nine, amid taunts that it was preserved only by the Scottish votes. Nevertheless the Salt Bill passed both Houses before the end of the session.

Before Parliament met again the public's views were invoked more vigorously by the political press of both sides than they had been at any time since 1714. The *Craftsman* and a host of ephemeral publications thundered their message that the government had struck at the poor man through the salt tax and now intended to set up new excise duties which would lead to a general excise on all the essential commodities of life. Even free handbills circulated by the Ministry could not counter the simple but basic contentions of the opposition, whose effectiveness was seen in increasing pressure but upon Members by their constituents. Horatio Walpole was instructed by Norwich, for which he intended to stand in 1734, to oppose his brother's intended measure. Perceval, thinking that 'the people were so possessed against it that it would unsaddle a great many of the government's friends who should vote for it', trembled for his seat at Harwich. Many other boroughs were reported to be writing to their representatives to oppose the scheme. Nevertheless the ministers professed to remain hopeful.[18]

At first their optimism seemed to be borne out. On 14 March 1733, with over 500 Members present in the Commons at times, Walpole moved that, by way of a preliminary to the proposed excise, the duty on tobacco should be removed from the customs. The opposition speakers put their main effort into the contention that extending the excise would result in the loss of British liberties, through the additional government patronage created, and in the ruin of the majority of the nation by taxation. In the stifling heat of the House both sides paused at one point to agree on a need to build a new and larger chamber to discuss such matters. In conclusion, 98 Whigs joined 106 Tories in the minority, but the Ministry carried the day by a fairly healthy majority of sixty-one votes. However, over the next three weeks this situation was changed by the increased clamour from press and constituencies, stirred up by the opposition leaders. When the Excise Bill for tobacco was introduced on 4 April a second reading was authorised by only 236 votes against 200; and on the 6th the Ministry succeeded in rejecting a motion for printing the bill by a mere sixteen votes. Walpole had now seen enough, and on the 11th, amid ostentatious opposition demonstrations of joy, he announced the dropping of his scheme for both tobacco and wine.

The Ministry had faced defeat but not actually experienced it. Once the Excise Bill was given up many of the Whigs who had deserted rather than risk their seats swiftly demonstrated that they had no intention of going into permanent opposition. This was seen in the appointment of a committee on customs frauds, initially proposed to embarrass the Ministry. For membership of this body the First Lord named five independent Whigs who usually supported the Ministry, together with a ballast of government placemen. At a Cockpit meeting with over 250 party members present he urged his hearers to vote, in the interest of party solidarity, for his entire list. 'Lord Bolingbroke', he told them solemnly, 'was at the bottom of it all,' and if they did not carry the list they might open the door to that menacing figure. Pulteney had foreseen an appeal to party instincts and had attempted to forestall it by drawing up a rival list composed entirely of opposition Whigs, which would have made a mockery of Walpole's argument that the government's continuance was threatened by resurgent toryism. Unfortunately the Tories refused pointblank to accede to this strategem, and Wyndham insisted that a number of them should be included in the opposition list. Walpole's contentions thus seemed somewhat confirmed, and the court list was carried to a man. And a fortnight later the Ministry drove yet another wedge between its opponents on the occasion of a request by the King for a marriage portion for the Princess Royal. While Tories rose one after another to remonstrate at the proposed sum of £80,000, and to point out that this was twice the sum which had been given at the marriages of Queen Mary and Queen Anne, the Pulteneyites supported the proposal. The Tories did not venture to press a division unaided; but the dissension within the opposition was clear for all to see in the bitten lip and angry shout of indignant Tories.[19]

Although the Excise Bill did not reach the House of Lords, the following month saw the first serious challenge there to Walpole's control. Inspired by events in the lower house, the Tory peers led by Bathurst took the initiative with an inquiry into the uses made of estates confiscated from South Sea Company directors. Aided by dissident Whigs under Carteret and a number of ministerial deserters, Bathurst obtained on 24 May an equality of votes, seventy-five to seventy-five, on a government motion, which was accordingly lost. Walpole treated this threat even more seriously than that in the Commons. Intense lobbying defeated the opposition on 2 June, and punishment of the government rebels was set in motion. At the height of the short-lived opposition successes in both Houses, the opposition leaders had, if the King's information was correct, assigned themselves places in a Ministry which was to succeed Walpole's, with Pulteney at the Treasury and Carteret and Wyndham as Secretaries of State. George, angered by the implication that he would have had no say in the matter, blurted out to Hervey a sentiment which must have been more often in his mind than on his lips: that rather than submit to dictation he might have preferred to take in the Tories alone. He added:

'I know one of my family supported by a Tory Administration would be but lame work, and Jacobites round the throne of a King that sits there upon the revolution establishment and principles must in time grow very troublesome and dangerous, but if I was pressed, I had rather try to oblige a whole party.'

The Tories might have come nearer to power in 1733 than they had reason to expect.

His fury expended, the King bowed once more to the dictates of necessity. Walpole demanded and obtained a full measure of retribution against those placemen who had defected over the excise scheme. In the fervent desire of the minister to make examples in high places, all caution was thrown aside. Patronage in the House of Lords did not, as in the Commons, simply maintain a useful cadre for government majorities; it virtually provided Walpole's majority, and was of commensurate importance. Chesterfield, Bolton and Cobham were deprived of their posts and commissions. Argyll, who had wavered, was too powerful in Scotland to be thus disciplined, and his brother Islay had remained loyal; but no mercy was shown in the case of other Scottish peers, among them Marchmont, Stair and Montrose. The dismissal of serving military officers like Cobham and some Scots, though not unprecedented, was regarded as particularly severe; but control of the upper house, Walpole's longstop, was of supreme importance. Within the next few months the government side there was strengthened also by the elevation of some useful debaters. At the end of the session Hervey was raised to his father's peerage of Baron Hervey of Ickworth; and at the end of the year fortunate vacancies allowed Attorney-General Sir Philip Yorke and Solicitor-General Charles Talbot, who had both performed well in the Commons during the crisis, to be appointed as Lord Chief Justice and Lord Chancellor respectively, Yorke taking the title of Baron Hardwicke and Talbot becoming Baron Talbot.

By the dismissals a host of dragon seeds was sown. Chesterfield was followed into opposition by three Stanhope relations in the lower house, and Bolton and Stair led off similar followings. Cobham was doyen of an important group of future Members of Parliament including William Pitt, the Grenville brothers and George Lyttelton. But the immediate effect of the removals was a stabilisation of the political scene. Before the session ended on 13 June Pelham wrote complacently that 'by the steadiness of the party, which appeared in a ballot in the House of Commons, and by the firmness of our master in the main point, we are now got pretty firm in our seats again'.[20]

In the autumn of 1733 most of Europe became involved in the war of the Polish succession; but when the Emperor appealed for British assistance under the Treaty of Vienna made two years earlier, he met a polite refusal. Technically he was the aggressor against Poland, France and Spain, and the Ministry pointed out that the Austrian alliance was a defensive one. When Parliament met for a short session in 1734 its debates did not centre upon foreign affairs, and calls in both Houses for war on behalf of Austria found little popular support. Attempts to revive indignation over the excise affair proved equally unsuccessful, so the opposition Whigs in both Houses concerted an indirect approach, striving to make certain military officers irremovable except for professional misconduct or by parliamentary address. Lord Morpeth, formerly the hammer of the Hessians, introduced the matter in the Commons on 13 February during the passage of the Mutiny Bill, while Chesterfield led the attack in the upper house on the same day; but as an attempt to vindicate the peers who had been deprived of their commissions the matter failed to warm either House. And a vote in the Lords on 28 March giving the government a majority of 101 to 58 on a contingent raising of army strength in the recess demonstrated that the Ministry's ascendancy there was firmly re-established.[21]

In the Commons debate on the officers, the motion had to be dropped after Shippen and the Jacobite squadron refused to join Wyndham in support of Morpeth. Nor was the next attempt at a combined opposition there more successful. On 13 March William Bromley, son of Oxford's old friend who had died two years earlier, introduced another attempt to repeal the Septennial Act and restore the Triennial Act. Debate ranged widely over old party scores, and a few Whigs who still saw intrinsic merit in the proposal were nevertheless influenced by ministerial emphasis on the danger of resurgent toryism. It was clear, as Tory after Tory rose to support Bromley's motion, that they believed their proposal to be a popular one with the electorate; Bromley indeed specifically claimed that in calling for a bill to end Septennial Parliaments he was 'supported by the common voice of the people, and have it particularly recommended to me by the great majority of those I have the honour to represent in Parliament'. Pulteney professed to share the Tories' belief, and speaking near the close of the debate he decided to go one better by recommending annual Parliaments. But his elaborately drawn parallel between the check imposed upon government by frequent elections and the resistance offered to the Stuarts by the first Whigs made little impression. As to resistance doctrine, he wrote vindictively: 'the Whigs clamoured against me, forgetting that the Revolution to which we owe the present establishment was founded upon it', while 'the Tories did not much approve of it, being so contrary to their notions of passive obedience and seeming to justify the Revolution'. The government prevailed by a comfortable 247 votes against 184, of which but seventy-seven came from dissident Whigs.[22]

As the climax of several years of uneasy co-operation, this result left a good deal to be desired; but it represented a semblance of unity with which the opponents of the government could go to the polls against the greatest electioneer who had yet arisen. One observer, at least, believed that the opposition 'now seem convinced of the folly of their mutual jealousies and are taking measures to act everywhere in concert against Sir Robert'. In contrast to the relatively hurried election caused in 1727 by the death of George I, preparations for that of 1734 had been long and thorough. The government press, if still less effective than that of its opponents, was by now much more numerous. In addition to the *Daily Courant*, now in its fourth decade in the Whig service, and the *London Journal*, Walpole had William Arnall's vigorous *Free Briton*, the *Weekly Register, Read's Weekly Journal*, the *Flying Post*, the *Hyp-Doctor*, the turncoat *British Journal*, and a newly created political organ, the *Corn-Cutter's Journal*. In support of the opposition there were regularly the *Grub Street Journal, Fog's Weekly Journal* and, above all, the *Craftsman*; the latter, in the last winter, had been printing the essays of Bolingbroke which were subsequently published as *A Dissertation upon Parties*, a tirade against the survival of parties provocatively addressed to Walpole. Among the party-orientated provincial newspapers one at least, *Howgrave's Stamford Journal*, owed its creation to the needs of the Tory Cecils in this election. In addition, the Tories printed the memoirs of the pre-Revolution Tory Sir John Reresby and circulated a list of those who had voted against repealing the Septennial Act.[23]

Stirred up by such publications the elections proved unusually energetic, and in many cases violent. The shadow of the Excise Bill still lay over the government. Up and down the country Walpole was burned in effigy with all the enthusiasm once devoted to performing the same service for the Pope. It was the Tories who, as in the last session in the Commons, were usually reported as making the running in opposition to established government candidates; Newcastle's incoming and outgoing correspondence was particularly full of complaints about their activity and their lack of regard for his past 'civilities and good usage' of them. Newcastle himself was able to report his usual success in every one of the seats he customarily controlled, 'notwithstanding the strongest and most violent opposition from the Tories that ever was known in Sussex'. The government as a whole, however, was less successful than Newcastle in both counties and boroughs. In Yorkshire, which had the largest electorate of all, the freeholders had long been assailed by a Tory campaign of literary persuasion and detailed canvass; after a poll which aroused nationwide interest a Tory contender stood in the lead with the aid of an opposition Whig who, though not himself elected, served to split the Whig vote. Metropolitan Middlesex returned Pulteney and a Tory unopposed. Kent, where a Tory had been returned in place of a Whig in 1733, now re-elected him with an opposition Whig, the latter in place of a government candidate. In general it was the already-strong Tory interest which gained ground in the counties: Gloucestershire, which had rarely sent up Tories since the Revolution, now returned two; Hampshire untypically elected a Tory, who topped the poll with an opposition Whig second; Essex elected two Tories instead of the usual one; and Cheshire likewise replaced a Whig by a second Tory. As a final blow to Walpole, two Tories were narrowly returned in his home county of Norfolk, which in each of the last two general elections had returned two Whigs unopposed. But in Norwich Horatio Walpole and his fellow Whig candidate just managed to stem the tide and secure their return, despite the warning which the former had received at the time of the Excise Bill. On the whole the English boroughs, except those with a very wide franchise, proved as safe for the government as always, with the west country and especially the Cornish boroughs well to the fore. In Scotland the Ministry lost some ground, but with the continued assistance of the Argyll interest it retained control of the great majority of both county and borough Members. Overall government numbers fell from 342 before the dissolution to 326 after. The Tories obtained 149 seats, nineteen more than at the dissolution, while the opposition Whigs lost three and dropped to eighty-three. When petitions had finally altered the position in the Ministry's favour, by taking four seats from Tories, the ministerial majority early in the new Parliament was 102 in theory, if absenteeism and defection were not taken into account.[24]

The result was undoubtedly a serious fall in prestige for the Ministry. By comparison of the number of its supporters before and after the election, losses appeared small, but by other criteria the figures were ominous. Compared with the position immediately after the 1727 election, the government majority had fallen by no less than 170, the losses being largely accounted for by a great increase in the number of opposition Whigs. Clearly, further defections on the scale which had taken place since about 1730 would place the government quickly in jeopardy. Walpole professed to be satisfied with the result of the elections, but Newcastle more frankly thought that the new Parliament 'will require great care'. One factor which neither foresaw was the changing character of the opposition Whigs. In the elections there had been a heavier-than-average turnover of Members in this group. Among the crop of new recruits who were quickly to make their mark in opposition were Cobham's coterie of able young protégés or nephews, namely William Pitt, Richard Grenville and George Lyttelton, together with the disobliged Marchmont's able twin sons Lord Polwarth and Alexander Hume Campbell. Against such men, Walpole could set little in the way of good recruits of the younger generation. The best was Henry Fox, who having stood unsuccessfully as a Tory in 1727 was now returned as a Whig, following the conversion in the Commons of his older brother Stephen at about the time of the excise crisis.

A final source of sober reflection for the Ministry was the unconsoling attitude of the King, who as usual took the opportunity to point a moral and,

'. . . too publicly, accused the Whigs of negligence; saying at the same time, that if the Tories had had a quarter of the support from the government that the Whigs had received from it for twenty years together, they would never had suffered the Crown to be pushed and the Court to be distressed in the manner it now was'.

Maliciously George added: 'for the honour of the Tories, that they were always much firmer united, and much more industrious and circumspect, than the Whigs'. The King's attitude, as was feared by his reporter Hervey, may well have furthered the interests of the Tories. At the least it helped to keep them out of the hands of the Pretender, and also provided the possibility of an alternative government which could be dangled, spectre-like, before the eyes of the Whigs in the hope of reducing their more extravagant claims to control. Queen Caroline remarked on the same subject: 'This is always the way of your nasty Whigs: though they themselves are supported by the Crown, they are always lukewarm in returning that support to the Crown.' However, despite electoral losses and royal lunges, it remained for a further full-term Parliament to show that whiggery in the hands of Walpole was not easily diverted from its course.[25]

CHAPTER 12

Party Distinctions Preserved
1734-42

The Parliament of 1734 came closer than its two predecessors to being dominated by placemen, in that these stayed constant in number at now just over 180 while the independent Whig element of the ministerial party was diminishing. Nevertheless the charge that the governmental Whigs were a corrupt and compliant court party, while their opponents represented the uncorrupted and independent section of Parliament, does not stand up to examination. Nearly 150 of Walpole's customary supporters among the Whigs in 1735 held no place, and both these and many of the placemen were probably economically and socially as independent as the Members who opposed them. Bolingbroke's assertion that the true division was between 'constitutionalists and anti-constitutionalists, or of a court and a country-party', and his many similar remarks on this theme, have often been quoted as a description of mid eighteenth-century politics rather than as what they were: part of a campaign to deny the reality of party differences which were obstructing his own advancement. Within a year of publishing these words in 1734, Bolingbroke despaired of forming an effective country party out of two disparate elements, neither of which, he came to believe, really intended a coalition of parties. He retired to France in 1735, and from there bombarded his correspondents with denunciations of royal treachery, ministerial corruption, Tory stupidity and Whig perfidy. His hope of constructing a country party has been described by Plumb as being 'as utterly futile, as ridiculously unrealistic, as the rest of Bolingbroke's political philosophy'.[1]

In 1734 most Whigs and Tories remained, both politically and socially, almost as far apart as ever. Among both government and opposition Whigs the united response always elicited by any suggestion of danger from Jacobitism was undiminished, while an increasing desire to repeal the Test and Corporation Acts was reviving a charged party issue. On the Tory side an undiminished anxiety to safeguard the Church's privileged position was shortly to be given striking demonstration. Moreover, the Tories' attachment to the ideal of shorter Parliaments and their dislike of penal legislation continued to unite Jacobites with their fellows against Whig parliamentary dominance or attempted political persecution. Socially the two parties had little, if any, more intercourse than they had in the time of what two historians have called the 'divided society' of William's and Anne's reigns. In the Commons the Tories sat together, and the parliamentary diarist Edward Harley, whose account illuminates their activities from 1735 onward, gives virtually no indication of tactics concerted with opposition Whigs but plentiful instances of mutual resentment and lost opportunities for co-operation. The Liberty or Rumpsteak Club, founded by dissident Whig peers in 1734, pointedly excluded the Tory lords even though they possessed one necessary qualification for membership: the experience of having had the King's back turned upon them.

In one respect, genuine juncture in opposition should in theory have become easier after about 1733 or 1734. Some of the newer Patriots, despairing of bringing down Walpole without Tory assistance, were ready to modify the Pulteneyites' commitment to party. In the upper house Chesterfield led the way in attempting to obtain a 'broad-bottomed' opposition plank, while in the Commons the new Members who owed their allegiance to Cobham were amenable towards the new philosophy. William Pitt, indeed, was to be in 1756 the first minister to be supported by the Tories since 1714. That such men were more willing than the original Patriots to work with Tories was to make possible the final sudden decision of the Tories, in the autumn of 1741, to assist in bringing Walpole down. But the broad-bottom Whigs in that year amounted, on their own computation, to no more than a third of the dissident Whigs and had little chance of support from the independent Whigs who had always supported Walpole. It was for this reason that the advocates of a broad-bottomed administration were swept aside after Walpole's fall in 1742, and that a new Whig Ministry was established.[2]

For the opening of the new Parliament's first session in 1735 the opposition Whigs planned to make a demonstration in the Lords, on the score of corruption in the election of the Scottish representative peers, hoping to repeat the success of 1733 in that House. The careful preparations of Walpole and Islay had resulted in the return of all sixteen of the court list, despite the energetic efforts of Chesterfield and the Scottish opposition to carry at least some of a rival list. A petition from several Scottish peers complaining of misconduct of the election was presented by an important recent adherent to the English opposition, the fourth Duke of Bedford, who had inherited the title in 1732 and abandoned his predecessor's support of Walpole. Nevertheless the attempt to arouse the House had no success, and with the aid of the Scots the government side held firm with comfortable majorities. Once again Walpole's punitive measures were shown to be effective.

Henceforth the main hopes of Chesterfield and other opposition peers were pinned on their efforts to influence events in the lower house, though a steady if unsuccessful pressure continued to be exerted by them in the Lords.

In the Commons the initial opposition likewise showed no sign of making an indentation in the Ministry's majority. Pulteney had hoped that the Tories might be induced to support Sandys for the Chair, but he found them 'out of humour' with the latter on account of some unspecified action during the elections; Onslow's nomination thus went unopposed. The Tories nevertheless received Pulteneyite assistance over the election petitions, which were heard at the bar of the House. With a number of good cases against highly partisan returning officers a fair measure of success was achieved; and in addition a petition against two Tories returned for the borough of Marlborough was beaten off by the assistance of Jekyll and other opposition Whigs. But the Ministry quickly asserted its control otherwise. The address was carried by eighty votes, and contentious calls for an increase of 10,000 seamen and an augmented land force achieved majorities of seventy-three and fifty-three respectively. These three debates exhausted the possibilities of discussion on foreign policy. 'Peace without rest, and war without hostilities' concluded Pulteney on the address. 'Not one drop of English blood spilt, or one shilling of English money spent' contended Walpole in the navy debate. That the Place Bill on 22 April was rejected by only twenty-six votes was considered less remarkable—such bills never being a government strongpoint—than was the preceding debate on it, in which were presented the maiden speeches of the young hopefuls of the opposition Whigs: Grenville, Pitt, Lyttelton and the Hume Campbell twins. In coming years the first three, commonly known as 'Cobham's Cubs' or simply as 'the cousinhood', were to eclipse most older opponents of the government in their vitriolic attacks on corruption, on Walpole personally and even on the King.[3]

In spite of heavy attendances the ministerial majority had been established in the all-important first session, and was therefore unlikely to crack in coming ones unless national circumstances changed. In Europe hostilities had largely ceased, though a formal peace did not take place for a further three years. Pulteney professed himself 'weary of contending with corruption' and announced that he would largely absent himself from Parliament in 1736; and as a result of general apathy the first two months of this session were poorly attended. Pulteney kept his promise, and Wyndham was so unusually subdued as to give rise to unfounded suspicions that he was about to defect to the Ministry. The real reason for both men's inactivity may, however, be surmised from what in March became the chief subjects of parliamentary business: three proposals affecting the Church. Despite many brushes the two men had striven in public over a number of years to bring their followers into some form of co-operation. This endeavour promised to be ended by the revival of religious issues.

For some years the dissenters had again been pressing for a repeal of the religious tests, a project which still had the sympathy of many Whigs. On 12 March an opposition Whig moved for the repeal of the Test Act, and party passions were at once excited. Walpole, fearing to arouse the sleeping Church, threw against the attempt the placemen and such independent Whigs as he could command on such an emotive occasion. Edward Harley noted that 'most of his creatures, though in their hearts for it, voted against the repeal', though 'many of them in their speeches reflected on the Church establishment'. In defeating the proposal by 251 votes to 123 the Tories thus found themselves unwontedly alongside ministerialists against many of the opposition Whigs. A few days later there came on a second bill whose purpose was to prevent the undue harassment of Quakers in their conscientious stand against paying tithes. The timing of this measure allowed Walpole to demonstrate politic sympathy for a dissenting cause on a matter much less damaging than that of the religious tests; but in supporting the bill he came up against the bitter opposition of his principal ecclesiastical adviser, Gibson of London, and most of the bishops. The bill passed in the Commons, with Harley grimly noting that 'all the discontented Whigs joined with the Court', but was rejected in the Lords where fifteen bishops voted against it and eleven more abstained. The legal peers Lord Chancellor Talbot and Newcastle's close friend Hardwicke were also active in opposing the bill.*

The matter which brought forth the strongest indignation of the Tories with their erstwhile Whig collaborators was a bill brought in by Jekyll 'to restrain the disposition of lands, whereby the same become unalienable'. The real purpose of Jekyll, Sandys and the other Patriot Whigs who supported the Mortmain Bill was, in the opinion of the Tories, to strike at the universities, charity schools and other Church institutions which customarily received estates by will in mortmain. In the upshot the government agreed to except the universities from the act, but the Tories remained highly dissatisfied with it. Deserted again by the Patriots, they had a new injury to brood upon. Once more party distinctions had triumphed over any possibility of opposition unity.[4]

*Dr H. T. Dickinson notes that Walpole 'had succeeded in appearing as the friend of the radical Whigs and Dissenters, had divided the Opposition along Whig and Tory lines, and had freed himself from an embarrassing ally' in Gibson, who was replaced as adviser on ecclesiastical patronage by Newcastle (Dickinson, *Walpole*, 176). It might be added too that Walpole had done all this without substantially advancing the cause of the dissenters or, in the long run, alienating the Church.

Tory revenge duly followed in the next session, though not in the first contentious debate, which took place on 18 February 1737. On this occasion the Ministry announced its intention of keeping the land forces at 18,000. After a long and bitter debate, with the Prince of Wales in the gallery, the government obtained a respectable majority of 246 to 177. This debate, however, was merely a curtain raiser. In its course had been mentioned the desire of Prince Frederick for a parliamentary allowance of £100,000, the sum which his father had enjoyed as Prince of Wales. Pulteney now had hope of obtaining the permanent support of the reversionary interest as an important step in making his opposition more respectable and in countering the damaging governmental imputations of his association with Tories and Jacobites. An alliance with the Prince would render the Patriot Whigs less dependent on Tory support in forcing their way into office as Walpole himself had done in like circumstances in 1720. But in relying upon blind Tory opposition to the government both Pulteney and the Prince miscalculated. Many independent Whigs joined them, remembering that the Civil List obtained by Walpole for George II in 1727 had been unofficially envisaged as including £100,000 for the use of the Prince's household. But in the end the government was saved from humiliating defeat by the reluctance of some of the Tories, especially the Jacobites, to vote alongside the opposition Whigs on behalf of a member of the House of Hanover. Wyndham was almost alone among his party in speaking on behalf of the Prince, and some forty-five Tories absented themselves from the division, allowing Pulteney's motion to fall by a margin of thirty votes, 234 to 204.[5]

Much of the session was taken up with a bill pressed on by Carteret in the Lords to make an example of the authorities in Edinburgh for permitting the Porteous riots. The opposition peers' intention was to force a quarrel between the Ministry and its Scottish supporters, and in this they succeeded admirably. Newcastle and Hardwicke, the latter newly Lord Chancellor on the death of Talbot, chose to pursue a quarrel with Argyll by supporting the Edinburgh Bill, with the result that he gradually drifted thereafter into opposition. In the Commons the Tories objected to the measure on their usual principle of opposing bills of 'pains and penalties'. They found unfamiliar allies in the Scottish Members, who deserted the government side for once to defend the honour of their capital city. Walpole was probably not sorry that the bill, when it emerged from committee, was modified out of recognition; but in terms of damage to his government its work was already done, and the result was to be seen in his loss of control of Scotland in the next general election.[6]

In September the King made his final break with Prince Frederick, expelling him from St James's Palace. Amid a blare of publicity the

Prince took his wife and infant daughter with him, shortly setting up a new establishment at his father's old opposition headquarters of Leicester House. In the expectation that the question of the Prince's allowance would be raised again in the following year, both courts began to bid for the support of the Tories. The King led the way, giving a pension of £600 to Lady Kinnoul, the first Earl of Oxford's youngest daughter, telling her that 'he was sensible [that] by not knowing Lord Oxford much he had not behaved to him so well as he deserved'. The Prince soon attached some Tory followers to his small entourage. But the most systematic effort to cultivate the Tory party came from some of the newer members of the Whig opposition, led by Chesterfield. Out of their willingness to conciliate the Tories came, over the next three sessions, the more positive philosophy of interparty collaboration which was beginning to be denoted 'broad bottom'. The chief difficulty which its supporters faced was that Pulteney, Carteret and many of the original Patriots wished only to stage a reunion with the Ministry under the aegis of a reconciliation between the King and the Prince; such a step, like its predecessor in 1720 when Walpole and Townshend had rejoined Stanhope's Ministry, would certainly exclude many opposition Whigs as well as the Tories from the fruits of office.

Despite the descent of the Prince to opposition, his hopes of obtaining a parliamentary allowance were not fulfilled and opposition was slow to rally under his flag. The Ministry noted with satisfaction that 'the opponents being a body composed of men of different principles and of different views are much disjointed, and have not any set scheme of opposition'. At the outset the Bishop of Chichester heard that 'the Tories will not come into the Prince's party, unless he will join with them in opposing the army'. A meeting between Wyndham and the Prince's representatives with a view to a 'treaty' broke down before it was well under way, over the Prince's stolid Hanoverian refusal even to contemplate joining in the annual motion for the reduction of the land forces to 12,000 men. In the subsequent debate on 3 February 1738 the opposition was defeated by eighty-five votes, which was a slightly higher government majority than in the previous year. After this bad start there was no possibility of reviving the matter of the Prince's allowance with the Tories' support.[7]

The main hope of united opposition came in March from a new source: the renewed tension which was developing between Britain and Spain. On the 3rd a petition was presented to the Commons by merchants trading with Spain and the West Indies, complaining of depredations committed at the expense of British seamen and property by the Spanish navy in the course of its searches for contraband goods. On the 28th, after the House had heard the merchants in person for several days, Pulteney concluded by offering several resolutions particularising upon the cruelties experienced from the Spaniards and upon the trading rights claimed by Britain under various treaties. It was evident that the merchants had the sympathy of the Commons. To avoid being forced deeper into quarrel with the Spanish court, Walpole offered a more moderate motion and obtained a majority of 256 to 209.

This reduced ministerial margin in a well-attended House was a reminder that since 1730 some of the opposition's greatest demonstrations of unity had been on foreign affairs. But for the moment little more could be done on this ground, and before the end of the session one further incident emphasised a basic lack of shared interests among the opposition. On 13 April the Speaker complained of press misrepresentation of Members' speeches and of journalists' discourtesy to Parliament. The ministerial speakers, Yonge, Winnington and Walpole, then called for a resolution reasserting that the reporting of speeches was a breach of privilege. Wyndham and Pulteney, the only two opposition speakers whose views were recorded, could not agree on a stand. The former told the Commons that, if he could be sure that misrepresentation could be avoided, he would be against depriving the public of a knowledge 'so necessary for their being able to judge of the merits of their representatives within doors'. Pulteney, on the other hand, though claiming to uphold the liberty of the press, was against the reporting of speeches. Bereft of the support of the Patriots the Tories made no further effort, and a resolution was passed promising the 'utmost severity' towards any newswriter presuming to report debates or other parliamentary proceedings, whether during session or in the recess. Though the latter restriction was not strictly upheld, parliamentary reporting was set back for a generation, in strong contrast with the press conditions which had done so much to further party causes in the last half-century. Of the two parties the Tories, who had since 1714 gained more from equal access to the press, were to suffer more from the ban.[8]

One polemicist, indeed, was undaunted. Bolingbroke paid a visit to England in 1738 and began, in the hope of appealing to the Prince, to redesign and refurbish his blue print of a political society from which Tories were not excluded. The result was *The Idea of a Patriot King*, which was circulating among the Prince's circle in its earliest manuscript form soon after. The old politician's hope of an impartial 'Patriot' monarchy was an admission of defeat, in that it transferred his vision of a partyless political scene from the present to the undefined future. Though he continued to exhort opposition leaders to unite, his private assessment was gloomy. The spirit of Jacobitism 'rises anew among the Tories', he wrote, 'and that of the narrow, interested party, knaves and fools, among the Whigs'. He was not alone in his view. Wyndham bewailed a loss of sight of the opposition's original aim as he saw it, namely a change of measures, and suspected that some of his former Whig allies wanted only a change of men by getting themselves into office as quickly as possible. This suspicion was shared by Cobham, Chesterfield and Marchmont, who early in 1739 discovered grounds for their belief that Carteret and Pulteney were trying to make the Prince of Wales personal rather than opposition property.[9]

Nevertheless, February 1739 saw all the government's opponents for once acting in tolerable unity over the subject which had come closest to aiding them in the previous year: Britain's relations with Spain. The speech from the throne announced the recent conclusion of a convention with Spain, to settle outstanding differences and avert a new war. But though the Ministry had secured some compensation for past depredations, the right of search upon which the Spaniards insisted had not been renounced. The opposition seized with new vigour upon the vague nature of the arrangements, and on 23 February the ministerial majority sank to thirty-five, then to twenty-nine, and finally to thirteen. On 8 March, when the Convention was due to be debated again, both government and opposition brought up their lame and halt for a sitting at which about 500 Members were at times in the Commons. In the outcome, 260 Whigs voted for a government address of thanks, and 132 Tories together with 100 opposition Whigs voted against it. Prominent among the last were three Scottish followers of Argyll, though the Duke himself did not formally break with the Ministry until a year later. The crowded debate continued for over seventeen hours, and at the end the House was not only reduced by pairing but also extremely tired. The following day one elderly placeman was actually asleep when his friends went out for a division, and was perforce counted as voting with the minority.[10]

In the course of debates on the Convention of Pardo, Pulteney, Sandys and Wyndham had announced their intention, if defeated, of absenting themselves from further business in protest. They were followed in their withdrawal by the opposition Whigs and most of the Tories, though about thirty of the latter refused to follow Wyndham's lead. No sooner was Parliament prorogued on 14 June, however, than heartsearching began among the secessionists. Pulteney was ascertained by a dismayed Wyndham and Polwarth to favour a return by the absentees; moreover he told Wyndham that a projected City petition to applaud the secession must be the responsibility of the Tories alone, lest it should ruin the Whig party. Bolingbroke, when he read of this, raged in a letter to Wyndham:

'what has he, and you, and every honest man meant by the opposition

you have carried on, and by your coalition, but to break the Whig
and Tory faction both? The whole body of the Whigs must be reunited, he says.'

It was decided to end the secession, though neither those who opposed
nor those who favoured the return were thereby put in a good frame
of mind for the coming session. 'Union among ourselves', lamented
Chesterfield, 'cannot be expected where our views are so widely
different.'[11]

The opening stage of the new session bore out such fears. Parliament
assembled on 15 November, before Christmas for the first time in
fourteen years. For this unusual step an outbreak of war with Spain
was responsible. The declaration of war was urged by Newcastle to
satisfy national and parliamentary feeling, and Walpole acquiesced
reluctantly. Pulteney's strong support for the war ensured that there
was no opposition to the address or to naval and military supplies,
though he greatly offended the Tories by a slighting reference in the
address debate to 'those that he had acted with'. Early in the new
year Pulteney made an attempt to return to a useful ground of co-
operation by reviving criticisms of the Convention of Pardo. But when
he moved on 21 February 1740 that official papers relating to that
Convention should be produced for examination by a secret committee, Walpole was able to make use of the national emergency to
prevent the rubbing of old sores, and a substantial majority of 247 to
196 rejected the motion. For the remainder of the session the government continued to have good majorities in the Commons on the conduct of the war. But appeal to patriotic feelings in a time of national
danger was a two-edged sword; the Ministry's future depended upon
its ability to wage war successfully and without excessive expense.[12]

In the summer recess some changes of far-reaching importance were
made in the Ministry. Argyll, whose uneasiness at his colleagues' behaviour had found vent as early as 1737 in open rejection of the
Edinburgh Bill, was dismissed from his several military offices immediately after the end of the session. The desire of the second Earl of
Godolphin to give up the Privy Seal, which he had held since 1735,
gave Walpole an opportunity for promoting Hervey, one of the government's most effective speakers in the upper chamber. The appointment
would have been made earlier but for the objections of Newcastle,
who saw in the advancement of the able Hervey a challenge to his
own and his brother's positions. In fact, Walpole's regard for Henry
Pelham was undiminished, but his relations with Newcastle had become extremely strained when the Secretary had seen fit to press for
war with Spain. It took all Pelham's and Hardwicke's tact to keep the
Duke from resigning over Hervey's appointment, and henceforth the

Walpoles were well aware that they had a potential rebel in their camp. As a final ministerial change, just before the next session, the commission of the Treasury was remodelled to exclude George Dodington. The decision was taken reluctantly, and only after much provocation while this politician, who controlled a useful five votes in the Commons, had dithered as to whether to defect before the Ministry foundered. Henceforth Dodington joined permanently with Chesterfield and the broad-bottom Whigs to give them some badly-needed assistance in the Commons.

The accession of Dodington to the opposition did little to offset the loss of a greater man. In June 1740 death removed Sir William Wyndham, leader of the main body of the Tories since the mid 1720s. Latterly Wyndham had moved closer to the position of the opposition Whigs. Two years after his death, indeed, his son Sir Charles and his friends Bathurst and Gower proved to have closer links with Pulteney and the Prince than with the Tories. But Wyndham, while he had lived, had remained Tory, and by so doing had often brought his party to work with Pulteney. Well might Bolingbroke bewail the loss of his chief disciple, and well might broad-bottom Whigs foresee as the result of that loss further moves by the Tories towards party isolation and by Pulteney's group towards a future understanding with the government.[13]

Their gloomy expectations were borne out in the session which began on 18 November, the last before a general election was due to take place. Pulteney, in a presession discussion with Chesterfield, showed reluctance to attack supplies, on the ground that it 'might shake the King's throne'. Thus the precedent of the last year was followed in that no major issues were opened before Christmas. January 1741 passed equally quietly, for the Ministry allowed a Place Bill to pass in the Commons, 'it being', as Harley noted, 'so near a new general election'. The Lords could be relied upon to throw the bill out. By the time this had happened, however, Walpole had met and triumphantly survived the major threat of a censure motion.

This project was from start to finish the work of the leading opposition Whigs. It gained much of its impetus from the grudges borne by such recent adherents as Argyll, but it was also very acceptable to the Pulteneyites because it could be directed against the minister without directly involving the King or threatening the war effort. Identical motions were made simultaneously in both Houses on 13 February for an address requesting that Walpole might be removed 'for ever'. In the Lords, Carteret's motion was defeated without difficulty, by 108 votes to 59. In the Commons the honour of opening the case against the minister was given to Sandys, who proved himself worthy of the occasion in a powerful speech ranging over the whole period and all aspects of Walpole's administration. Sandys' main contention was that the minister had taken over all functions of government, either in person or by immediate direction. Walpole defended himself energetically against the charge of being 'sole' and 'prime' minister.* His acquittal by a large majority, however, had little to do with his denials, for he was saved by the Tories, who had no doubt about the culpability of his administration. Harley, Cornbury, Shippen and others rose to state that they could not agree to censure Walpole alone. Harley recorded that 'many of the Tories whose principles abhor even the shadow of bills of pains and penalties, or to censure anyone without evidence, refused to vote in the question and withdrew'. Of the remaining Tories some actually voted for Walpole and some few against. The result of the Pulteneyites' care to select Walpole as the sole scapegoat, leaving the rest of the Ministry unscathed to be joined in office by themselves, was a staggering defeat with only 106 votes cast for the motion and 290 against it.

After the result came the inquest. Egmont noted that Walpole had derived some benefit from the fact that his 'personal behaviour towards the Tories has always been obliging although an enemy to them as a party'. There was general agreement that the incident was a further setback for the future chances of unity among the opposition. Bolingbroke ranted: 'the conduct of the Tories is silly, infamous, and void of any colour of excuse'. The culprits, however, remained unrepentant in face of criticism. The refusal to censure Walpole, remarked a Tory apologetic pamphlet, marked the difference between a party, which was based on principles, and a faction, which was based on self-aggrandisement; a party

'. . . act from the dictates of their conscience; and conformable to a certain system of opinions, which they take to be right. A faction again is a body of men acting upon no principles, but from a selfish scheme of interest, which allows them to go to any length with any party, provided they may thereby serve themselves.'[14]

One further incident before the end of this session illustrates the care which the government's opponents had to take to avoid further publicising their disunity on the eve of elections. On 8 April the Commons was asked for a vote of credit of £300,000, in view of a

*Though Walpole has often been described as charged with being a 'prime' minister, it should be noted that contemporary accounts of this debate gave priority to the term 'sole' minister; his offence, in the view of his accusers, was not so much that he was principal minister as that he virtually superseded his colleagues' authority even in their own spheres (see Coxe, *Walpole*, iii, 559–61; Cobbett, xi, 1,232; and Sedgwick, i, 91–5, for Ryder's account).

worsening situation in Europe which might involve Britain in aiding Austria under the second Treaty of Vienna. Pulteney immediately strongly supported the government motion, thus forestalling the Tories' usual objection to this form of vote. A belated attempt later by some of the broad-bottom Whigs to bring the matter up again, and thus to open the way for further dissension, was prevented on the advice of Chesterfield, who thought that 'it would be almost only a Tory opposition, and that Pulteney would have carried two-thirds of the Whigs present with him'. Disunity, in fact, was decently veiled where possible.[15]

Parliament was dissolved on 27 April, two days after prorogation. Dissident Whigs like Chesterfield had pinned their hopes on 'the spirit of the nation' at the polls. In fact the elections were quiet and the open constituencies gave the opposition little cause for optimism. The war with Spain was popular, and no second excise crisis had arisen to stir the electorate. Even in the borough of Westminster, where the opposition Whigs put up the popular naval hero Admiral Vernon against one of the Ministry's soundest men, Sir Charles Wager, the poll was going strongly against the opposition candidates when the high bailiff, a government man, injudiciously called in troops and closed the poll early to prevent any possibility of failure. This was later set right by petition and a new election; but opposition victory on such terms was hardly encouraging. Nor were the opponents of the Ministry helped by the disarray in their own ranks. Thus in Gloucestershire Lyttelton and another opposition Whig were indignant to find themselves opposed by two Tories, who won easily. The greatest gains for the opposition came in Scotland and the Cornish boroughs, where the influence of Argyll and Prince Frederick respectively was for the first time thrown into the scale against government candidates. Argyll's efforts were aided by Scotland's resentment at the Ministry's treatment of Edinburgh over the Porteous riots, and resulted in the return of twenty-one opposition Whigs together with five Tories; this reduced the government's Scottish supporters to nineteen. Compared with the position just before the dissolution, the Ministry lost twenty-one seats altogether in Scotland and Cornwall. This loss was slightly offset by ministerial gains elsewhere, so that the overall result was a drop in the government's Members from 300 to 286. The total number of opposition Whigs rose from 115 to 131, thanks to Scotland and Cornwall, but that of the Tories dropped from 143 to 136. The results thus showed no landslide, but a reduction of Walpole's majority from a pre-election figure of forty-two to a theoretical nineteen, with five seats unfilled because of double returns, promised a fairly even balance.[16]

The narrow margin gave rise to much speculation and planning in the summer of 1741, particularly among the broad-bottom Whigs. Almost sufficient numbers were now available to bring Walpole down if unity could be attained. But to make the Whigs work in harness with the Tories, wrote Dodington, would 'baffle our most serious and most united endeavours'. And as to most of the Tories, 'if the name of Whig comes across them, it locks up all their faculties, and they cannot exert them'. To reach an understanding the solution was, they thought, for half a dozen Whigs to come together with half a dozen Tories to concert measures. The names of a dozen men were accordingly put forward for this purpose, but at this point a major difficulty arose: Pulteney, consulted by Dodington, was very unenthusiastic about pre-session preparations and refused to take the lead. After learning this, Dodington bitterly professed himself to have done with making plans. In reply to his complaints Chesterfield penned what proved, in the event, to be the correct analysis of the Pulteneyites' position: 'they reason quite differently, desire to get in with a few, by negotiation, and not by victory with numbers'. Unfortunately, Chesterfield thought, though Pulteney's aims were narrow the nature of his support in the Commons was wide, owing to his adherence to party distinctions: 'the silly, half-witted, zealous Whigs consider him as the only support of Whiggism; and look upon us as running headlong into Bolingbroke and the Tories'. What then was to be done? Chesterfield saw no hope but in pressing on with the forces available.

But if the Ministry's opponents had their difficulties, these were now more than offset by new problems facing Walpole. The outbreak of war in 1740 between Austria and Prussia brought Britain at last to undertake to support the former; but when Prussia concluded an alliance with France, war between Britain and that nation too seemed likely. To worsen matters, from the Ministry's point of view, George II concluded in August 1741 the Treaty of Klein Schnellendorf, neutralising Hanover and safeguarding the Electoral territories. Walpole advised against the treaty but had to bear the brunt of the general cry of 'Hanover influence' led within the Ministry by Newcastle, who wailed: 'It will be impossible to prevent a parliamentary enquiry into this conduct'. Foreseeing Walpole's fall from office on this issue, the Secretary and Hardwicke redoubled the negotiations which they had carried on for some time with Carteret and Pulteney. If the ministers were tempted to take out an insurance for their own continuance by coming to an agreement with the Pulteneyites, their action could be justified in terms of preserving the Whig party by keeping out the broad-bottom Whigs and Tories. Eventually Walpole himself was to endorse, for this very reason, the treachery he despised.[17]

But these negotiations were as yet only suspected, and at the opening of Parliament on 1 December the weather seemed set fair for a broad-bottom alliance. Chesterfield had succeeded in procuring from the Pretender a letter urging his supporters to join with the Whigs in bringing down the Ministry. Widely distributed, this document arrived in time to mobilise those Jacobites who had refused to support the censure motion of February. But the main body of Tories too, heartened by the prospect of bringing down the whole Ministry and sustained by the broad-bottom Whigs' offers of a joint war Ministry, was now ready to act. In addition, the independent Whigs who normally supported the government were angered by the Klein Schnellendorf Treaty and worried by the uncertainty of the diplomatic situation in regard to France. With supporters still arriving from the country neither side cared to hazard a division on the address, though Walpole conceded a committee on the state of the nation for 21 January. But by 10 December over 500 Members were in London, and 210 were reported present at a meeting of Tories and Patriots while a further twenty-five sent their excuses. The strategy agreed upon was to whittle down the government majority by means of contested election returns, which had been shown to be a ministerial weak point after the 1734 election. On the 16th the opposition brought up its full strength to get its candidate elected as chairman of the Committee of Elections and Privileges. After two vast dinners at rival taverns the opposing sides met in the Commons, where the Ministry was defeated by 242 to 238. Of the majority, 127 were Tories and 115 Whigs. The last included several men previously supposed to be ministerial supporters, and others were absent. Further votes before Christmas showed the same pattern, and by the time of the recess Walpole's position was seen to be desperate.[18]

Parliament reassembled on 18 January 1742, and Pulteney tried to settle the matter quickly. Papers on overseas negotiations had been called for just before Christmas. On the 21st he rose to move for a secret committee of twenty-one Members to examine these documents, a proposal taken as a preface to impeachment. The subsequent debate was long remembered as a classic one in which all the leading speakers excelled. Both Pulteney and Walpole were at the top of their form, while among future gladiators who earned praise were Henry Fox and, for the opposition, the recently elected George Grenville. For the division 508 Members were present, including the Speaker and four tellers. Both the Ministry and its opponents had scraped up every possible supporter. The veteran Sir William Gordon was raised by the opposition from his bed of sickness and borne into the chamber, with a bandage round his head showing beneath his periwig; another Member came on crutches. Ministerial accounts agreed that there were more 'incurables' on the other side, if only because three government invalids who had been secreted in a room with a door to the back of the Speaker's chamber found, when the division came on, that Patriot foresight had stuffed the keyhole with sand to keep them out. The Ministry still managed to carry 253 votes against 250; but the latter were, in Horace Walpole's opinion, 'the greatest number that ever *lost* a question'.

Despite the wavering of some peers, Walpole still had a working majority in the Lords, where a censure motion concerning the conduct of the war was rejected on 28 January by sixty-nine votes to fifty-seven. But on the same day he decided to risk dividing the Commons again, in support of two ministerial petitioners with a strong case for being allowed to represent the borough of Chippenham. He was defeated by one vote on a technical point, and on 2 February the election itself was determined against the government by sixteen votes. By this time, however, Walpole had seen enough; deserters and absentees had made his position untenable, and further petitions would finish the work. On the same day, after nearly twenty-one years in office, he announced his intention to resign. To effect a change of Ministry, Parliament was prorogued on the 3rd for a fortnight.[19]

Walpole made no secret of the fact that his removal had been declared a necessity several days earlier by a number of his colleagues, particularly Newcastle and Hardwicke. He accepted their decision in order to prevent a total change of administration, for as he wrote to his close friend Devonshire, in announcing his departure, 'I am of opinion that the Whig party must be kept together, which may be done with this parliament, if a Whig administration be formed.' Danger lay in the intention of the newer opposition Whigs—whose spokesman was Argyll—to obtain, in Harley's words, 'a coalition of parties, for altering measures, for bringing in the Tories as well as Patriots into place without distinction of party, called the broad bottom'. But by the time of the second vote on the Chippenham election the details of the administration to be formed were cut and dried by private conferences between Newcastle and Hardwicke on the one hand and Pulteney and Carteret on the other. On 11 February Wilmington was appointed as a figurehead First Lord, Pulteney having refused the place to underline his long-standing claim to have been disinterested in his opposition to Walpole's regime. Pulteney's associates felt no such constraint. On the same and following days Sandys became Chancellor, Gybbon and Rushout also joined the Treasury Board, and Carteret took the northern Secretaryship, thus replacing Harrington who was moved into the office of Lord President vacated by Wilmington.[20]

These appointments thus largely preceded and forestalled the purpose of a mass meeting of the late opposition, which was called by Argyll to meet at the Fountain tavern on 12 February. With well over 200 commoners and thirty-five lords present, Argyll and other speakers stated their desire for a broad-bottom administration, casting angry reflections on the Pulteneyites for rejecting that ideal. Pulteney and Sandys defended themselves. Pulteney professed to agree to the aim of extinguishing parties and party names by bringing Tories into the Ministry, but said he was for doing it 'by proper degrees as occasion should happen'. The supporters of a broad-bottom administration had little confidence in this assurance, but so thoroughly had they been outmanoeuvred that there was little to be done. This was made even more clear in a confrontation staged four days later between Pulteney and some of the broad-bottom leaders in the presence of the Prince of Wales; after this meeting the Prince agreed to Pulteney's urging that he should make a formal submission to the King, thus setting a seal to the new ministerial arrangements. On the 17th George II and his son met each other in strained circumstances reminiscent of the reconciliation of George with his own father in 1720. Nothing now remained but for the broad-bottom Whigs to decide whether to accept such crumbs as the new Ministry offered in order to detach them from the Tories. Yet another meeting took place at Dodington's house on the evening of the 17th. Argyll, revealing that he had been offered his old military posts again, reasserted his intention:

'to restore affairs upon so broad a bottom, that the nation might be satisfied, and every person qualified to serve his country, without distinction of parties, should have the opportunity of doing it.'

Such was his evident sincerity that both the Whigs and the Tories present urged him to accept the offer and give them an advocate in the Ministry. The following morning a number of them accompanied him to court to accept office.

Such faith as the broad-bottom advocates still retained in ministerial promises was due to be destroyed in less than three weeks. On 8 March the King deleted the name of Cotton, proposed by Argyll, from the list of a new Admiralty Board. Argyll immediately resigned, leaving the Ministry free of broad-bottom Whigs. That there had ever been any intention on the part of the government to admit Tories on a basis of equality with Whigs may be doubted. Egmont heard 'that the Duke of Newcastle had prevailed with His Majesty not to countenance the Tory party in the least'. Hardwicke discoursed to Bishop Secker on the evening of the Fountain tavern meeting against the taking in of Tories. Walpole was generally and correctly believed to be still active 'behind the curtain', and his view on the admission of Tories needed no publicising. From members of the former opposition now in office the Tories had even less to hope. Carteret had got his friend Winchelsea in as head of the Admiralty, but Winchelsea's branch of the Finches had long ceased to be Tories; in any case, Carteret's head was far too full of his plans for Europe for him to concern himself with Tory aspirations. Pulteney was reported to thank God that he was no longer in the power of the Tories. Thus ended the best chance since 1689, albeit a slim one, of the sinking of 'distinctions of party'.[21]

A Whig Ministry remained firmly in the saddle, and in following years the broad-bottom Whigs were to join it, partially replacing the Pulteneyites, without making more than token efforts to bring in Tories. With the possible exception of Argyll, who died in 1743, the broad-bottom Whig leaders' commitment to cross-party government was less strong than their prior Whig affiliations. Even the possibility of a Ministry including Tories would not have come about in 1742 but for the desperate belief of men like Chesterfield that no lesser outcome could produce the measure of Whig–Tory co-operation necessary to bring Walpole down. With his fall the only possibility of the submergence of party distinctions passed away. Apart from Bedford's brother-in-law Gower, who entered office with a handful of followers who rapidly ceased in the estimation of their friends to be considered Tories, the Tory party remained intact. Not until their leaders made common cause with the Prince of Wales in 1747 did they see much hope of obtaining office, and their support for a Ministry did not come about until Pitt formed his first administration in 1756. After 1744 circumstances favoured the Pelhams' emphasis on the continued integrity of the Whig party, and succeeding adjustments to their Ministry were far from bringing in Tories in order to 'broaden the bottom'. By the middle of the century, indeed, this term had lost most of its former meaning and was used merely to describe the admission of more Whigs to the administration. While Walpole's pupils stayed in office the admission of the Tories remained unacceptable.

Conclusion

The two parliamentary parties whose vicissitudes have been followed in these pages were sustained by the great issues of the day: especially religion, the succession, and the need to settle the problems of government on a new basis in the post-Revolution era. To these matters were added the impetus generated by party strife itself, dividing Parliament and the nation into two largely irreconcilable factions whose bitter clashes built up traditions of mutual exclusiveness at all levels. The absence of modern party organisation ensured that the conflict would be, if anything, more marked than under the nineteenth- or twentieth-century party system, since the moderating element of ritualisation imparted by developed institutions was largely lacking in the early parties.

Down to the fall of Walpole, at least, party differentiation remained intact because the issues which had given birth to it were still very much alive. That the party distinction was artificially fostered after about 1721, by Walpole's insistence that the Tories were supporters of the Pretender, is true only in a limited sense; for, though few Tories were active Jacobites, Walpole's contention embodied the important truth that such hope as the Pretender possessed could be based only on them. And if Walpole benefited from the continuance of the parties, it is equally certain that his opponents stood to gain by artificially hastening party decline. If Bolingbroke, the gamekeeper-turned-poacher of party tradition, had less success than Walpole in attaining his ends, it was because party ideas remained more important in the minds of both Tories and Whigs than did the court–country artefact which Bolingbroke attempted to erect.

The post-1714 fissures in the Whig party should not be allowed to conceal a continued unity of tradition shared by nearly all Whigs, whether in or out of office. Nor should the fact that Walpole built up a formidable patronage system for the benefit of his own section of the party be permitted to overshadow the even more important truth that his administration could not have lasted a week but for the continued approval of the majority of the independent Whigs. The cry which most often rallied these independent Whig gentlemen was the perennial ''Ware Tory' of Walpole and the Pelhams; and it was a cry, as Pulteney fully realised, to which even the dissident Whigs had to respond. Because of the pull of party, on Tories as much as on Patriots, such terms as 'opposition', 'minority' and 'country', used as collective descriptions of the government's opponents, are by no means indicative of a body as coherent and well-established as the parties.

In 1742 the Tory party not only was still in existence and in good heart after twenty-eight years of opposition, but also remained an important and effective part of the political scene. Such was the suddenness of the reversal of party fortunes in 1714 that it is easy to slip into thinking that the Tories ceased to be an important factor under the House of Hanover. Contemporaries, lacking access to the afterknowledge which reveals that the Tories were politically proscribed for nearly fifty years, had only the experience of the past to go on. In 1695 the Tories, and in 1702 the Whigs, had appeared in hardly better case than did the Tories in 1714—and had recovered. To most members of both parties the possibility of a Tory revival, if the circumstances became propitious, remained very real, and with reason. In the eyes of George I and his successor an alliance with the Tories was at times tempting; and though no such step was taken by a reigning monarch, Prince Frederick was to take it while in opposition soon after the failure of the Young Pretender's invasion had diminished the danger of Jacobitism. The Tories' assured place in Parliament was owed not only to their widespread support among the electorate but also to the fact that their existence as a potential alternative administration gave monarchs a useful check upon Whig pretensions.

Together with the physical presence of a substantial Tory minority after 1714, there remained considerable continuity in Tory thinking. The Church of England principle remained, as was seen at the time of the anti-Church measures of 1736, to distinguish the Tories not only from those Whigs who overtly supported Dissent but even from many of those who sympathised with but did not join them. Opposition to diplomacy or to strategy which seemed likely to entail unusual expenditure remained, after 1714 as before, a primary Tory consideration. Support for shorter Parliaments likewise continued to be a feature of Tory thinking, as it had been as early as January 1689.*

For the Whigs the formation of a new party Ministry after the fall of Walpole proved decisive in ensuring party continuity. Though Walpole himself was gone, his concept of political life was preserved. Whig unity was not, indeed, ensured—since 1714 this had never been more than briefly possible in a situation where Whig Members comprised three-quarters to four-fifths of the House of Commons—but a sufficient majority of the Whigs continued, after the fall of Walpole as before,

*Whatever may be the applicability after 1742 of the view of 'the Tories of early Hanoverian England' expressed by Professor J. B. Owen, namely that 'in terms of policy they were indistinguishable from genuine Country Whigs' (*The Eighteenth Century, 1714–1815* (1974) 114), it is certainly not equally valid for the period down to the fall of Walpole.

to provide a solid base, the 'Old Corps', on which successive Whig Ministries could be built. And if complete adherence to Whig principles was, like the unity of the party itself, rarely observable after 1714, the main body remained firm on some major points, while certain fundamental principles and assumptions were still shared by all who called themselves Whigs. The rejection of short-lived Parliaments and of place legislation, though not common to the whole party, was adhered to by the majority under the Junto, Walpole and the Pelhams. The traditional Whig alliance with Dissent, always equivocal, was not broken; for though tactical considerations caused the Junto to permit the passage of the Occasional Conformity Act and Walpole to oppose its repeal, along with that of the Schism Act, Walpole's later government largely protected the dissenters from further harassment. The repeal of the Test and Corporation Acts remained as impolitic as ever, but Dissent continued to see its eventual salvation as likely to come, if at all, from the Whigs.

Of those more fundamental Whig principles to which all Whigs continued to subscribe, the first was continued rejection of the main line of the House of Stuart. In this matter it cannot be said, except in a handful of cases, that the Whigs had in any sense changed in 1742 from the position they had held in 1689 and 1714. The basis of the new dynasty's support was far from being exclusively Whig, but only the Whig party, in the view of George I and George II, could be relied upon absolutely. It was this fact which kept the Whigs in power despite the discontent which these monarchs so often felt with them; and it was this which put their leaders in an impregnable position in their dealings with the Crown.

The challenge to monarchy made explicit in the actions of the first Whigs under Shaftesbury was submerged for a time by the Junto's acceptance of a working arrangement with William III. Many of William's recorded sayings, however, show that he remained aware of the current of antimonarchical thought in the party. Anne, too, was under no illusion as to where she stood with the Whigs, and many heartfelt expressions were wrung from her by their challenge to her authority. Under George I and George II the overt challenge was again transformed into an implicit one. But though the idea that government was the king's was not openly dismissed, and was even fostered so long as the Whigs remained in control, government fell in practice more into the hands of the Ministry. In particular the growing complexity and widening patronage ramifications of the Treasury placed ever-growing power in the hands of those ministers, such as Walpole and after him Pelham, who knew how to run its business to the best advantage. The well-entrenched tradition that Walpole, by his long tenure of this office and by remaining in the House of Commons throughout, was the first modern Prime Minister is not far from the truth. The Whig leaders took into their own hands much of the power which had once been the monarchy's, consciously or unconsciously continuing assumptions of the Revolution which had not been put into legal effect.

Between 1689 and 1742 both parties scouted the claims of monarchy when it suited them to do so. The attempts of William and Anne to retain ministers or favourites were frustrated in the cases of Leeds in 1695, Sunderland in 1697, the Junto lords in 1699, and Harley in 1708, to mention only major figures; while these monarchs had to appoint men not of their choice in 1700, when William accepted a Tory Ministry, and in 1708, when Anne was forced to agree to a Whig-dominated one. That the situation somehow changed after 1714 as a result of one-party government can hardly be maintained. George I was obliged to give up his German advisers in 1719 and to accept the detested Walpole and Townshend in the following year; and in 1724 his favourite minister Carteret was manoeuvred into a harmless office. George II preferred Compton but accepted Walpole in 1727, and gave up the latter extremely reluctantly in 1742 after coming to realise his value. And two years later this king was forced, even more decisively than his father had been, to give up Carteret. Though monarchs could still, after the Revolution, in theory appoint and dismiss ministers at will, experience showed that they often did so at the risk of losing control of Parliament through the activities of one or other of the parties.

It is hardly possible to exaggerate the implications of the Revolution and subsequent settlement for the development of parties. Frequent and regular meetings of Parliament provided the indispensible ground for uninterrupted party development. But over and above this effect, the rich penumbra of political ideas which accompanied the removal of the old monarchy, openly expressed from the first days of the Convention's meeting in 1689, ensured a climate of opinion in which the parties would be able to flourish despite their lack of respectability. Determination to limit the powers of the executive received ideological backing from Whig publicists of the Revolution era; but after 1689 it was more often the Tories, convinced that the post-Revolution executive was dangerous to themselves, who took the lead in clipping back governmental powers, abandoning in practice their original theories of nonresistance and passive obedience. The laws of treason, the dismissal of judges, and above all executive control of Parliament through placemen and by the avoidance of frequent elections, were all attacked by the Tories, assisted by such Whigs as were unable to adapt themselves to the Junto's partial acquisition of a court mentality. Thus the Tories, especially when in opposition, adopted implicitly many of the ideas which the Whigs had pioneered before the Revolution.

The rights generally assumed to have been inherited from the settlement included, for Tories almost as much as for Whigs, that of men to take government into their own hands to a greater extent than had before been possible. These rights also included that of politicians to band into parties for the furtherance of this end. Beyond this the parties differed, in the first generation after the Revolution often violently, on both ideological and practical matters. But in the era of Walpole the violent aspect of the parties began to die down, giving their strife a more tolerant and sometimes even urbane appearance. By 1742 the virtual eradication of the rival party, so long the aim of both, had already been tacitly abandoned, leaving the way open for the peaceful acceptance later in the century of the concept of a constitutional opposition party. That some degree of mutual tolerance had been achieved by the middle of the eighteenth century speaks of a considerable element of development in both parties, based upon many decades of experience. Seen in this light, the heavy emphasis which some twentieth-century historians have placed upon the absence of a modern type of party system may perhaps be viewed in better perspective. Half a century after the Revolution, over sixty years after the names Whig and Tory were first flung at rival politicians, the parties were still much in evidence. Though their history was to pass through a chequered period from the fall of Walpole until the earlier part of George III's reign, the tradition which they had established continued to be too much a part of political life to disappear. Early in the nineteenth century, Tory and Whig parties were to stand as firmly as in the early eighteenth century, rebuilt upon solid foundations.

NOTES

Abbreviated references in the footnotes and these Notes are given in full in the Select Bibliography (*see* authors or short titles alphabetically, except for MSS.). Volume numbers are given in roman numerals, followed by page numbers.

INTRODUCTION

1 Burnet, iv, 287 and v, 285–6, Onslow's notes; Grey, ix, 120; *Chesterfield Letters*, ii, 516; B. W. Hill, 'Executive Monarchy', *HJ*, xiii (1970) 379–401.

2 Trevelyan, i, 154–5; *Private Corr.*, i, 324; J. H. Plumb, 'Growth of the Electorate', *Past and Present*, xlv (1969) 90–116; Burnet, vi, 224.

3 W. T. Morgan, 'Some Sidelights upon the Election of 1715', in *Essays . . . in Honor of Wilbur Cortez Abbott* (Harvard, 1941) 170–1; C. S. Emden, *The People and the Constitution* (1956 edn.) 15–16; Speck, esp. chs 6 and 8.

4 W. L. Sachse, 'The Mob and 1688', *JBS*, iv (1964–5) 23–40; Browning, *Danby*, ii, 187–8; Boyer, *Quadriennium*, i, 13; G. C. Gibbs, 'Laying Treaties before Parliament', in *Studies . . . in Memory of David Bayne Horn* (1970) 125–6.

5 *The Freeholder*, no. 53; *Wentworth Papers*, 470.

6 *The New Association of Those Called Moderate Churchmen* (1702); Paul de Rapin-Thoyras, *Historical Dissertation Upon Whig and Tory* (1717); [Samuel Squire], *Historical Essay Upon the Balance of Civil Power* (1748).

7 Ranke, v, 292; T. B. Macaulay, *The History of England . . .* (1855 edn) iv, 118; Feiling, *Tory Party*; G. M. Trevelyan, 'The Two-Party System', in *An Autobiography and Other Essays* (1949) 184; Sir Lewis Namier, 'Monarchy and the Party System', in *Crossroads of Power* (1962) 231; Walcott, 160.

8 Kenyon, *Popish Plot;* Jones, *First Whigs* and *Revolution of 1688;* Western, *Monarchy and Revolution.*

9 Halifax, 'Of Parties', in Foxcroft, *Halifax*, ii, 505–7; Jones, *First Whigs*, 212 and *Revolution of 1688*, 144; H. L. Snyder, 'Party Configurations', *BIHR* xiv (1972) 39, n. 3; many examples of early party organisation are supplied by Holmes, *British Politics*, and Speck.

10 Holmes, *British Politics*, 34; Sedgwick, i, 81, 86, 89 and 104, tables in nn. V, XII, XVII and XXXII.

11 Cowper, 'An Impartial History', in Lord John Campbell, *Lives of the Chancellors* (1846) iv, 425.

CHAPTER 1

1 C. H. Firth (ed.), 'Memoirs of Lonsdale', *EHR*, xxx (1915) 93–4; J. H.

Plumb, 'Elections to the Convention Parliament', *CHJ*, v (1937) 251–2; Burnet, iii, 373–5; Klopp, iv, 347; *Evelyn Diary*, iv, 614; Lacey, 224.

2   Jones, *First Whigs*, 11–13; Plumb, *Political Stability*, ch. 5.

3   Foxcroft, *Halifax*; Browning, *Reresby*, 550; Krämer, i–iii.

4   Add. MS. 40,621, f. 5; *CJ*, x 9; Grey, ix, 5; *Clarendon Corr.*, ii, 252–4; A. Simpson (ed.), 'Notes of a Noble Lord', *EHR*, lii (1937) 92; *LJ*, xiv, 108.

5   Grey, ix, 7–25 and 29–37; *Miscellaneous State Papers*, ii, 401–12 and 414–25; *CJ*, x, 14 and 15; HMC, *Portland*, iii, 424; Luttrell, i, 499; Firth (ed.), op. cit., 92; Add. MS. 40,621, f. 7.

6   Grey, ix, 51–2; *CJ*, x, 17, 19 and 21–2.

7 *LJ*, xiv, 111–13 and 118–19; *CJ*, x, 19–20; Grey, ix, 54; Browning, *Danby*, i, 430–1 and iii, 164–72; *Clarendon Corr.*, ii, 260–6.

8   Add. MS. 40,621, f. 26; Browning, *Reresby*, 557; Foxcroft, *Halifax*, ii, 202, 205, 221 and 242; Burnet, iii, 378 and iv, 6–7; Sloane MS. 4,223, f. 210 ('Lord Somers'); Cobbett, v, 68–70 and 93–4.

9   Add. MS. 40,621, f. 26; Foxcroft, *Supplement*, 312.

10 Plumb, 'Elections to the Convention Parliament', op. cit., 235–54.

11 Grey, ix, 33, 84–106, 119–20, 123–5, 128–9, 148–50, 150–3 and 153–8; Burnet, iv, 8–9; HMC, *Portland*, iii, 429; Foxcroft, *Halifax*, ii, 225; E. A. Reitan, 'From Revenue to Civil List', *HJ*, xiii (1970) 574.

12 Grey, ix, 111, 190–200 and 218–26; *CJ*, x, 51 and 98; Burnet, iv, 13, 16 and 20–1; Foxcroft, *Supplement*, 315–16; Foxcroft, *Halifax*, ii, 213 and n. 5; *Evelyn Diary*, iv, 637; Lacey, 233 and 236; Horwitz, 88 and 92; Browning, *Danby*, i, 447–8.

13 E. Harley, 18 April, Loan 29/143/1; R. Harley, 1 June, Loan 29/164/2.

14 Add. MS. 29,594, f. 165; *CJ*, x, 165 and 200; Grey, ix, 244–52.

15 Foxcroft, *Halifax*, ii, 218–19, 227–8 and 229; *Clarendon Corr.*, ii, 284–5.

16 Grey, ix, 345–6; Burnet, iv, 28; Oldmixon, 11.

17 *CJ*, x, 286 and 298; Grey, ix, 411–21, 450–1 and 456; Sloane MS. 4,224, f. 83 ('K. W. Character'); *Clarendon Corr.*, ii, 296; Add. MS. 33,923, f. 465.

18 *CJ*, x, 309–23; Grey, ix, 480–8 and 490–3; R. Harley, 14 Dec., Loan 29/164/4.

19 *Shrewsbury Corr.*, 14–16; Dalrymple, ii, app., pt 2, 80–94.

20 Add. MS. 29,594, f. 185; Lacey, 241; Foxcroft, *Halifax*, ii, 243; Feiling, *Tory Party*, 270, n. 3; Grey, ix, 510–20; Browning, *Danby*, iii, 164–72; *CJ*, x, 329–30.

21 Grey, ix, 520–2 and 538–47; *CJ*, x, 332–3 and 338; Japikse, 1st series, i, 81; Add. MS. 32,524, f. 2; Dalrymple, i, pt 2, 115; Foxcroft, *Halifax*, ii, 244 and 247.

CHAPTER 2

1   H. Horwitz, 'The General Election of 1690', *JBS*, xi (1971–2) 87; *Clarendon Corr.*, ii, 304; Add. MS. 33,589, f. 315; Ranke, iv, 583, n. 2; Japikse, 1st series, i, 13 and 40; lists in Browning, *Danby*, iii, 164–72; HMC, *Portland*, iii, 443–4; *Somers Tracts* (1748–52 edn), 1st coll., ii,

353–4; *The Whigs Address to His Majesty* (*c*. 1690), single sheet; Add. MS. 29,594, f. 196; Luttrell, ii, 19.

2   C. H. Firth (ed.), 'Memoirs of Lonsdale', *EHR*, xxx (1915) 94; Luttrell, ii, 25; Grey, x, 71; *Clarendon Corr.*, i, 304; *The Anatomy of a Jacobite Tory* (1690) 32; *Hatton Corr.*, ii, 149.

3   Foxcroft, *Halifax*, ii, 228; *Autobiography of Sir John Bramston*, Camden Society, xxxii (1845) 347; *LJ*, xiv, 433–44.

4   Grey, x, 10, 20, 86, 108–14 and 139–45; *Hatton Corr.*, ii, 149; *CJ*, x, 398.

5   Foxcroft, *Halifax*, ii, 250; Grey, x, 71 and 87.

6   Baxter, 277–8; Burnet, iv, 76; Japikse, 2nd series, iii, 211; Browning, *Danby*, i, 467, n. 1; HMC, *Finch*, iv, 425.

7   Ranke, vi, 148, 152 and 156; HMC, *Portland*, iii, 456; Browning, *Danby*, ii, 191–2; *CJ*, x, 550.

8   Musgrave, 1 Oct. 1691, Loan 29/312; Luttrell Diary, 9 Nov., 158a, 10–14; *CJ*, x, 552 and 583; HMC, *Portland*, iii, 481–2 and 485; Ranke, vi, 164 and 166–7.

9   Luttrell Diary, 18 Nov. and 11, 31 Dec., 158a, 40–1, 131–2 and 171–4; Grey, x, 171–5, 206–15 and 219–41.

10 Trumbull Diary (transcript), Add. MS. 52,279, *sub* 26 Feb. and 5 March.

11 HMC, *Finch*, iv, 425 and 537; Trumbull Diary (transcript) Add. MS. 52,279, 5 March; *State of the Parties*, in *State Tracts*, ii, 212.

12 Dalrymple, ii, app. 2, 242; Browning, *Danby*, ii, 209 and 213; HMC, *Finch*, iv, 422–3 and 428.

13 Foley, 17 Sept., Loan 29/135/7; Luttrell Diary, 11, 23, 30 Nov. and 11 Jan., 158b, 11–13, 110–16, 262–3 and 270–81; HMC, *Portland*, iii, 508; Ranke, vi, 183–5, 191 and 195; Add. MS. 29,594, f. 265; *CJ*, x, 698; HMC, *Finch*, iv, 512–13.

14 *CJ*, x, 730; Luttrell Diary, 1, 14 Dec., 28 Jan., and 2 Feb., 158b, 94–6, 122–3, 181–90, 307–13 and 318–20; Grey, x, 285–91 and 299–308; Ranke, vi, 197–8, 200, 206 and 212–13; HMC, *7th Report*, 212; Foxcroft, *Supplement*, 181; Burnet, iv, 192.

15 John Ehrman, *Navy in the War of William III* (Cambridge, 1953), 412; Add. MS. 29,594, f. 206.

16 Portland (Nottingham) MSS. PwA 1,171, 1,172 and 1,212; Japikse, 1st series, ii, 38; Kenyon, *Sunderland*, 250–1, 257–8 and 260–2; *Hatton Corr.*, ii, 198; Ranke, vi, 217; *Shrewsbury Corr.*, 21 and 25; Add. MS. 17,677 NN, f. 346.

17 Ranke, vi, 220, 223 and 229; Grey, x, 329–31 and 368–86; HMC, *7th Report*, 216; HMC, *Hastings*, ii, 233.

18 Ranke, vi, 240 and 245; HMC, *Kenyon*, 286; Burnet, iv, 221; R. Harley, 21 Dec. 1711, Loan 29/160/8.

19 *Shrewsbury Corr.*, 25; HMC, *7th Report*, 218; *Private Corr.*, ii, 7; *Dialogue Between Whig and Tory* (1693), in *State Tracts*, ii, 381 (for date of publication see *Letters of Humphrey Prideaux*, 160).

20 Portland (Nottingham) MSS. PwA 471, 472a, 1,233, 1,234 and 1,238a; Kenyon, *Sunderland*, 265.

21 Ranke, vi, 269; Add. MS. 29,595, ff. 72 and 74.
22 *Lexington Paper*s, 69; Add. MS. 17,677 PP, f. 194; Cobbett, v, 895–908 and 930–41; Ranke, v, 91; *Shrewsbury Corr.*, 399; Kenyon, *Sunderland*, 272; Browning, *Danby*, i, 517–24.
23 Portland (Nottingham) MSS. PwA 503, 504, 508 and 1,248; *Shrewsbury Corr.*, 96, 103–4; and 106–7; Add. MS. 28,879, ff. 231 and 242.

CHAPTER 3

1 Add. MS. 17,677 PP, ff. 406 and 430; Add. MS. 28,879, f. 219; Jacobsen, 291; Burnet, iv, 288.
2 Burton, Riley and Rowlands, 30–1.
3 *Letters of Locke*, 146; *Hatton Corr.*, ii, 232; *Vernon Corr.*, ii, 444.
4 Seymour, 13 Nov. 1695, Loan 29/156/6.
5 *Lexington Papers*, 148; Guy, 5/15, 13/23 July 1695. Portland (Nottingham) MSS.; Japikse, 1st series, ii, 59–61 (the first fuller in Portland (Nottingham) MSS.); Feiling, *Tory Party*, 317–18.
6 HMC, *Hastings*, ii, 253; L'Hermitage, in R. M. Lees, *EHR*, liv (1939) 49–52; Burton, Riley and Rowlands, 6–7 and 31–3; Burnet, iv, 295; Add. MS. 17,677 QQ, ff. 285–6.
7 Cobbett, v, 987–93; Add. MS. 17,677 QQ, f. 296; *Hatton Corr.*, ii, 221; Ranke, v, 121; HMC, *Portland*, iii, 575.
8 HMC, *Portland*, iii, 577; *Shrewsbury Corr.*, 122–3; *CSP Dom., William III, 1696*, 177; *Vernon Corr.*, i, 34–5; HMC *Kenyon*, 411.
9 Cholmondeley (Houghton) MS. 647, enclosure; cf. Dickson, 347–8; Horsefield, 197–205; Add. MS. 34,355, ff. 2 and 21; *Shrewsbury Corr.*, 122, 130–1 and 133–5.
10 *Shrewsbury Corr.*, 388, 411–15 and 417–20; Portland (Nottingham) MS. PwA 1,255.
11 *Vernon Corr.*, i, 46–50, 52–3, 73 and 82; Add. MS. 17,677 QQ, f. 596; *Shrewsbury Corr.*, 429; Cobbett, v, 998–1,149.
12 E. A. Reitan, 'From Revenue to Civil List', *HJ*, xiii (1970) 583; Clapham, i, 46–50.
13 Robert J. Allen, *Clubs of Augustan London* (Harvard, 1933) 40–2; *Vernon Corr.*, ii, 2, 15 and 217; Burnet, iv, 342, Onslow's note.
14 *Shrewsbury Corr.*, 499–500, 502 and 505–7; HMC, *Buccleuch*, ii, 587; *Vernon Corr.*, i, 359, 379–80, 391, 399, 411 and 432–3.
15 Lois G. Schwoerer, *JBS*, v (1966) 80; [Somers], *A Letter, Balancing . . .* (1697); Add. MS. 30,000 B, f. 8; HMC, *Portland*, iii, 593 and 595; *Vernon Corr.*, i, 439–42 and 445–6.
16 *Shrewsbury Corr.*, 521–2, 526–7, 528–31 and 560; *Vernon Corr.*, i, 77, 455, 461, 463–6, 468–70 and 477–8 and ii, 18–19; Add. MS. 30,000 B, ff. 41 and 71; Add. MS. 21,551, f. 7; *CJ*, xii, 116; *CSP Dom., 1698*, 102–3 and 105.
17 *Shrewsbury Corr.*, 532–3, 536, 540–1 and 560; Add. MS. 15,895, f. 19; Japikse, 1st series, i, 226 and 297; Grimblot, ii, 61–2; *Vernon Corr.*, ii, 106 and 111.

CHAPTER 4

1 *Vernon Corr.*, ii, 139, 141–3, 147–8, 152 and 165–7; HMC, *Portland*, iii, 599; *Shrewsbury Corr.*, 550–1 and 560; Grimblot, ii, 144; *Miscellaneous State Papers*, ii, 535–6.

2 Oldmixon, 170; HMC, *Portland*, iii, 595; Grimblot, i, 355.

3 *State Tracts*, ii, 631–7; 'The Fate of Favourites', Rawlinson MS. D37, 7; HMC, *Bath*, i, 73.

4 *Shrewsbury Corr.*, 553, 560 and 569–70.

5 HMC, *Bath*, iii, 302; Cobbett, v, cols cli–cliv; *Vernon Corr.*, ii, 223 and 235–6; Krämer, ii, 246; HMC, *Portland*, iii, 600; *CJ*, xii, 359 and 368.

6 *Shrewsbury Corr.*, 572–4; *CSP Dom., 1699–1700*, 5; Gaedeke, i, app., 150; *Hatton Corr.*, ii, 238; *Vernon Corr.*, ii, 238–9, 241, 245–6, 253, 263, 269–71 and 277; *CJ*, xii, 440 and 618; Burnet, iv, 400; Dalrymple, ii (*recte* iii), 130; Krämer, ii, 275; *Evelyn Diary*, v, 309; Grimblot, ii, 224 and 230–1; HMC, *Portland*, iii, 603 and vii, 57–8; HMC, *Bath*, iii, 324.

7 *Vernon Corr.*, ii, 279; *Somers Tracts* (1750) 2nd coll., iv, 207.

8 *Shrewsbury Corr.*, 588–95; HMC, *Portland*, iii, 607–9; Kenyon, *Sunderland*, 312–13; *Court and Society*, ii, 52.

9 *Vernon Corr.*, ii, 267–8, 375–6, 378–81, 388, 393–4, 412–13, 439–40, 444 and 446, and iii, 3–4 and 17–25; *Court and Society*, ii, 54; Add. MS. 28,053, f. 402.

10 *Vernon Corr.*, iii, 39, 52–4, 67–8 and 94–5.

11 E. Harley, 3 May and 28 Sept., Loan 29/143/2; HMC, *Portland*, iii, 619 and 622; Add. MS. 34,515, ff. 7, 10–11 and 13–14; *Vernon Corr.*, iii, 104–5; Burnet, iv, 470.

12 HMC, *Portland*, iii, 634 and 636; Gaedeke, i, app., 124; Krämer, iii, 249.

13 HMC, *Portland*, iv, 14–15; *Evelyn Diary*, v, 446; Burnet, iv, 476; Add. MS. 30,000 E, ff. 3 and 34; Klopp, ix, 193.

14 Voltaire, *Siècle de Louis XIV* (Paris, 1823 edn), i, 262; C. Cole, *Historical and Political Memoirs* (1735) 319 and 323; Add. MS. 30,000 E, ff. 44, 48, 89, 120–1 and 144; Add. MS. 34,515, f. 20; Burnet, iv, 488, Dartmouth's note; Klopp, ix, 217; *Vernon Corr.*, iii, 144.

15 Add. MS. 30,000 E, ff. 67–8, 73 and 77.

16 Add. MS. 30,000 E, ff. 178–9, 193 and 235; *Somers Tracts*, 2nd coll., iv, 300; Cobbett, v, cols clxxiv–clxxxviii; Ranke, v, 263; *Vernon Corr.*, iii, 151–2, 14 (misdated 19) July; Add. MS. 7,074, f. 32; Add. MS. 30,000 E, f. 291.

17 Add. MS. 7,074, f. 15; Burnet, iv, 518–19, Dartmouth's note, and 527.

18 *A Short Defence of the Last Parliament . . .* (1701) 20.

19 *Miscellaneous State Papers*, ii, 443–4, 448–9 and 453–6; *Evelyn Diary*, v, 480–1 and 481, n. 1.

20 Add. MS. 30,000 E, ff. 395, 416 and 420; Add. MS. 7,074, f. 55; cf. Add. MS. 34,518, ff. 140–1; *Vernon Corr.*, iii, 158; Add. MS. 34,515, f. 26; Klopp, ix, 428.

21 *Somers Tracts*, 4th coll., iii, 34–7; Add. MS. 7,074, ff. 61 and 72; *Letters of Locke*, 118–20; Klopp, ix, 499; Add. MS. 30,000 E, f. 420; Add. MS. 29,595, f. 204; Holmes and Speck, 25.

22 HMC, *Portland*, iv, 28; Add. MS. 7,074, ff. 73, 75, 77, 79 and 89; *Letters of Locke*, 120–1.
23 Burnet, iv, 551–2; HMC, *Cowper*, iii, 2; HMC, *Egmont Diary*, i, 89.
24 Klopp, ix, 503; Ranke, v, 289–90; *Letters of Locke*, 125–8.

CHAPTER 5

 1 Klopp, x, 43; Rochester, Preface to Clarendon's *History of the Great Rebellion* (1702); Add. MS. 7,074, f. 212.
 2 Cobbett, vi, 25; Add. MS. 28,055, f. 3; Add. MS. 29,588, f. 129; *Evelyn Diary*, v, 511; Burnet, v, 45; Speck, 123; H. L. Snyder, 'Party Configurations', *BIHR*, xlv (1972) 44.
 3 Cobbett, vi, 47; HMC, *Portland*, iv, 47.
 4 Ballard MS. 38, f. 137; newsletter, Add. MS. 7,078, f. 165; Add. MS. 17, 677 YY, f. 262; Ranke, v, 313; *Norris Papers*, 108; *Somers Tracts*, 4th coll., iii, 89; Cobbett, vi, 97–135; *CJ*, xiv, 12, 14 and 27sqq.
 5 *Letters of Locke*, 132 and 146; Cunningham, i, 315–17; Add. MS. 7,074, f. 127.
 6 Holmes, *British Politics*, 354.
 7 *Norris Papers*, 106; Boyer, *Annals*, i, 155, 172–204, 210–12 and 216–22.
 8 Add. MS. 29,588, ff. 253 and 316; Churchill, ii, 274.
 9 Add. MS. 28,055, f. 3; Add. MS. 29,589, f. 400; HMC, *8th Report*, 43; HMC, *Portland*, iv, 68.
10 Add. MS. 28,055, f. 3; Harley, 20 Sept. 1703, Blenheim MSS. B2–33; Bromley, Loan 29/191/93 (fuller than in HMC, *Portland*, iv, 67); Churchill, ii, 272.
11 HMC, *Portland*, iv, 75; *Shrewsbury Corr.*, 643–4.
12 *Vernon Corr.*, iii, 241 and 244; Cobbett, vi, 153–68; Boyer, *Annals*, ii, 190–206.
13 Coxe, *Marlborough*, i, 299; Burnet, v, 134 and 141; H. L. Snyder, *HLQ*, xxx (1967), 253; Add. MS. 17,677 WWW, f. 579.
14 *Vernon Corr.*, iii, 270; HMC, *Portland*, iv, 119 and 147.
15 Add. MS. 17,677 ZZ, ff. 497 and 515; *Vernon Corr.*, iii, 271; Ballard MS. 10, f. 118; HMC, *Bath*, i, 64.
16 Boyer, *Annals* iii, 157; *CJ* xiv, 437; Oldmixon, 346; *Shrewsbury Corr.*, 646–7; HMC, *Portland*, iv, 151.
17 HMC, *Portland*, ix, 169; *Vernon Corr.*, iii, 275 and 279; Burnet, v, 182–3, Dartmouth's note; *Shrewsbury Corr.*, 647–8.
18 Cunningham, i, 345; HMC, *Portland*, ii, 186–7 and 189; Add. MS. 17,677 ZZ, f. 352; Add. MS. 17,677 AAA, f. 210; *Thirtieth Report of the Deputy Keeper of Public Records* (1869) 371–5; HMC, *Bath*, i, 67.
19 Harley, 27 April, Blenheim MSS. A1–25.

CHAPTER 6

 1 *Seafield Corr.*, 401; *Somers Tracts* (1751) 4th coll., iii, 151–4; [James Drake *et al.*], *The Memorial of the Church of England* (1705) 1, 21–3 and 45; Japikse, 1st series, ii, 564; Speck, 106–8 and 123; cf. H. L. Snyder, 'Party Configurations', *BIHR*, xlv (1972) 45 and 59.
 2 Add. MS. 7,059, f. 63; Plumb, *Walpole*, i, 118; Add. MS. 28,070, f. 12;

Harley, 29 June, Blenheim MSS. A1–25; Coxe, *Marlborough*, 1, 376 and 481.

3   Portland (Nottingham), MS. PwA 410; Harley, 14 Aug., Loan 29/192/256; Harley, 26 July, Blenheim MSS. A1–25; HMC, *Cowper*, iii, 64.

4   W. A. Speck, 'The Choice of a Speaker', *BIHR*, xxxvii (1964) 29–35; Add. MS. 17,677 AAA, ff. 510–11; HMC, *Portland*, ii, 191.

5   Coxe, *Marlborough*, i, 489; Add. MS. 17,677 AAA, f. 521; Harley, 16 Nov., PRO SP 104/48, unfoliated.

6   Add. MS. 17,677 AAA, f. 529; *Original Papers*, ii, 32–6 and 43–4; cf. *EHR*, xiii (1898) 55–70 and 533–49; Cobbett, vi, 473 (misdated 14 Dec., cf. *CJ*, xv, 51–2, 4 Dec.); *Private Corr.*, ii, 221–3; Coxe, *Marlborough*, i, 489 and 490; HMC, *Portland*, iv, 154 (Nov.–Dec. 1705, misdated [1704]); *CJ*, xv, 58; *Anon. Diary*, 44–9; HMC, *Bath*, i, 79; *Lockhart Papers*, i, 139.

7   Burnet, v, 240; *CJ*, v, 85; *Anon. Diary*, 61–6; Add. MS. 17,677 BBB, ff. 49–50; G. Holmes, 'The Attack on the Influence of the Crown', *BIHR*, xxxix (1966) esp. 53–9.

8   HMC, *Portland*, iv, 291.

9   HMC, *Portland*, iv, 313; Trevelyan, ii, 262–3; P. W. J. Riley, 'The Union of 1707'; *EHR*, lxxxiv (1969) esp. 513–15.

10 Geikie and Montgomery, 46, n. 2; HMC, *Portland*, ii, 193; Portland (Nottingham) MS. PwZ Hy 662; Coxe, *Marlborough*, ii, 136; HMC, *9th Report*, pt 2, 471.

11 Coxe, *Marlborough*, ii, 139–40, 144, 161 and 164; Harley, 21 Sept., Loan 29/153/5; HMC, *Bath*, i, 107, 110 and 121; Add. MS. 7,059, f. 116; Add. MS. 17,677 CCC, f. 38.

12 Add. MS. 7,059, f. 120; Cobbett, vi, 558; *Addison Letters*, 69.

13 Add. MS. 40,776, f. 85; Add. MS. 17,667 CCC, f. 92; Boyer, *Annals*, v, 478–9; *Norris Papers*, 159; HMC, *Bath*, i, 169; Cobbett, vi, 580; *Court and Society*, ii, 233; HMC, *8th Report*, app., pt 1, 395.

14 Clapham, i, 58–9.

15 Add. MS. 17,677 CCC, f. 93; Coxe, *Marlborough*, ii, 268–9.

16 Coxe, *Marlborough*, ii, 272 and 343–4; *Court and Society*, ii, 231; G. V. Bennett, 'Robert Harley and the bishoprics crisis of 1707', *EHR*, lxxxii (1967), esp. 735–40.

17 HMC, *Portland*, iv, 442; Burnet, v, 341; HMC, *Bath*, i, 180.

18 Trevelyan, ii, 294–5 and 298; HMC, *Bath*, i, 186.

19 Ballard MS. 20, ff. 63–4; *Court and Society*, ii, 265; *CSP Colonial, 1706–8*, item 1,214; G. Davies, *HLQ*, xv (1951–2), 229 and 234; HMC, *Bath*, i, 188; Harley, qu. by H. L. Snyder, *HLQ*, xxx (1967), 265; Bennett, *EHR*, op. cit., 743–4.

20 *Addison Letters*, 83; Burnet, v, 340 and 343; Davies, *HLQ*, op. cit., 38–9; *Life of Sharp*, i, 323; Cobbett, vi, 605–9.

21 *Private Corr.*, ii, 16; *State Trials*, xiv, esp. 1,383–4; Blenheim MSS. C1–16 and D31.

22 *Norris Papers*, 161–4; Harley, 14 Jan., Loan 29/64/1; G. Holmes and W. A. Speck, 'The Fall of Harley', *EHR*, lxxx (1965) 673–98.

23   *Vernon Corr.*, iii, 328–30, 335, 343 and 345; *Court and Society*, ii, 272, 276 and 295; HMC, *Bath*, i, 189–90; De Beyries, 17/28 Feb., CBA 24 (England), 92 (part pr. in Holmes and Speck, *EHR*, op. cit., 694); *Addison Letters*, 89; Harley, 6 Feb., Loan 29/12/6; *Marlborough*, 7 Feb., Loan 29/12/5; Burnet, v, 353–4; *Swift Corr.*, i, 75.

CHAPTER 7

1   Burnet, vi, 224; Swift, '. . . Letter to a Whig Lord', in *Prose Works*, 131.
2   Lansdowne MS. 885, ff. 62–3; Japikse, 1st series, ii, 566; Portland (Nottingham) MS. PwA 1,188.
3   Holmes, *Sacheverell*, 33; James, 166–9; Nicholson Diary, *TCWAAS*, iv (1904) 24 and 27; *Addison Letters*, 93.
4   Klopp, xiii, 26, n. 2; Coxe, *Marlborough*, ii, 421, 434 and 517.
5   Trevelyan, ii, 413; Plumb, *Walpole*, i, 138; *Original Papers*, ii, 112; Burnet, v, 396; *Lockhart Papers*, i, 297; H. L. Snyder, 'Party Configurations', *BIHR*, xlv (1972) 50; Riley, 118.
6   John Arbuthnot, *The Law is a Bottomless Pit* (1712); Coxe, *Marlborough*, ii, 516; Harley, 20 Aug., and Bromley, 12 Oct., Loan 29/128/3; HMC, *Portland*, iv, 504; Bromley, 11 Nov., and Nottingham, 15 Nov., Finch (Leicestershire) Corr. Bundle 23; HMC, *Bath*, i, 193.
7   Add. MS. 34,521, f. 53; Trevelyan, ii, 414–16; Holmes, *British Politics*, 234 and 241.
8   Holmes, *British Politics*, 43 and 305–6; Walpole, 14, 21 Jan. 1709, Cholmondeley (Houghton) MS. 6; Add. MS. 17,677 DDD, f. 31; Plumb, *Walpole*, i, 143; Cobbett, vi, 788; H. T. Dickinson, 'The Poor Palatines', *EHR*, lxxxii (1967) 464–85; Bromley, 7 Dec., and Nottingham, 20 Dec., Finch (Leicestershire) MSS., Corr. Bundle 23; HMC, *Portland*, iv, 523; Riley, 119–20.
9   Geikie and Montgomery, 101–2, 131–2 and 142–7; Add. MS. 9,107, ff. 60 and 91 (part pr. in Trevelyan, iii, 21 and 28); St John, 9 July, English MS. Misc. E 180, ff. 4–5.
10   *Miscellaneous State Papers*, ii, 479; *Private Corr.*, i, 250; H. L. Snyder, 'Anne Versus the Junto', *HLQ*, xxv (1972) 323–42.
11   HMC, *Portland*, iv, 507; Sacheverell, *The Perils of False Brethren* (1709).
12   *State Trials*, xv, cols 61–2, 115, 127 and *passim*; Edmund Burke, *Appeal from the New to the Old Whigs* (1791); Holmes, *Sacheverell*, esp. 182–4; *Original Papers*, ii, 202.
13   HMC, *Portland*, iv, 537; Add. MS. 9,108, ff. 98 and 138; *Private Corr.*, ii, 420.
14   Add. MS. 40,776, f. 49; HMC, *Bath*, i, 191; HMC, *Portland*, iv, 519; Coxe, *Marlborough*, iii, 8; HMC, *13th Report*, pt 6, 250; Holmes, *British Politics*, 134.
15   HMC, *Portland*, iv, 524; Add. MS. 34,515, f. 106; Add. MS. 34,518, f. 11; *Private Corr.*, i, 295; Kinnoul, 26 April, Loan 29/146/4.
16   Coxe, *Marlborough*, iii, 230–2 and 244–5; Plumb, *Walpole*, i, 156; Harley, 'Memo 20 May, 1710' and 'July 3, 1710', Loan 29/10/19;

HMC, *Portland*, iv, 542; Burnet, vi, 9, Dartmouth's note; Lansdowne MS. 885, f. 24; B. W. Hill, 'Change of Government', *Econ. HR*, xxiv (1971), esp. 400–1; *Private Corr.*, ii, 444; Coxe, *Walpole*, ii, 29–30; [Walpole], *Four Letters to a Friend*, postscript dated 23 July, 1710.

17 HMC, *Bath*, i, 198; HMC, *House of Lords*, xi, 326; Add. MS. 9,110, f. 43; Buck and G. Davies, *HLQ*, iii (1940) 222–3 and 225; Hill, 'Change of Government', op. cit., 401–2.

18 Add. MS. 17,677 DDD, f. 573; Sloane MS. 4,223, f. 215; HMC, *Portland*, ii, 213; Ballard MS. 38, f. 150; *Wentworth Papers*, 135; HMC, *Dartmouth*, i, 297; Harley, 'Memorandum, Sept. 12, 1710', Loan 29/10/19.

19 HMC, *Portland*, ii, 218 and vii, 12 and 22; *Cowper Diary*, 42–3; *Lockhart Papers*, i, 319 and 323; Add. MS. 17,677 DDD, f. 618; *Wentworth Papers*, 149; Hanover list, Stowe MS. 223, ff. 453–6; Speck, 110 and 123; Plumb, *Walpole*, i, 164–5; Mary Ransome, *CHJ*, vi (1939) 209–21, and *EHR*, lvi (1941) 76–89.

20 Bennett, 112; HMC, *Portland*, ii, 219 and iv, 574; *Miscellaneous State Papers*, ii, 485–8.

CHAPTER 8

1 HMC, *Portland*, iv, 585; Swift, *Journal to Stella*, i, *passim*.

2 B. W. Hill, 'Change of Government', *Econ. HR*, xxiv (1971) 404–7; Add. MS. 17,677 EEE, f. 1; Add. MS. 22,231, f. 105; Boyer, *Quadriennium*, i, 42; H. T. Dickinson, 'The October Club', *HLQ*, xxxiii (1969–70) 155–73; *CJ*, xvi, 456.

3 Kreienberg, 28 Nov./9 Dec. and 19/30 Dec., *CBA* 24 (England), 99; *Wentworth Papers*, 132, 174 and 180; Cunningham, ii, 352; Harcourt, 15 Dec., Ballard MS. 10, f. 123; Plumb, *Walpole*, i, 165 and n. 2; Boyer, *Quadriennium*, i, 155; Swift, *Journal to Stella*, i, 195.

4 HMC, *Mar and Kellie*, i, 485–6; Kreienberg, 8/19 Dec., 30 Jan./9 Feb., 9/20 Feb., 20 Feb./3 March and 23 Feb./6 March, *CBA* 24 (England), 99; Rowney, 8 Feb., and Clarke, 1 March, Ballard MSS. 38, f. 191, and 20, f. 67; Add. MS. 22,231, f. 105.

5 *Swift Corr.*, i, 238–42; *Wentworth Papers*, 189; Kreienberg, 23 Feb./6 March, *CBA* 24 (England), 99.

6 HMC, *Portland*, iv, 656 and v, 655 and 675–6; HMC, *Bath*, i, 200; Dickinson, *Bolingbroke*, 81–6.

7 *CJ*, xvi, 456, 576, 611–13 and 619; Boyer, *Quadriennium*, i, 264–5 and 287; Kreienberg, 27 April/8 May, *CBA* 24 (England), 99; Swift, *Journal to Stella*, i, 252–3; *HLQ*, i (1938) 457; Add. MS. 17,677 EEE, f. 193; J. G. Sperling, 'The Division of 25 May 1711', *HJ*, iv (1961) 191–202.

8 Swift, *Journal to Stella*, i, 253; B. W. Hill, 'Oxford, Bolingbroke, and Utrecht', *HJ*, xvi (1973) 241–63; *Private Corr.*, ii, 70; Bromley, endorsed June 1711, Loan 29/128/3.

9 *The Whigs Appeal to the Tories* (1711) 10, 14; *Miscellaneous State Papers*, ii, 488; Salomon, 123; Klopp, xiv, 217 and 687sqq; HMC, *Portland*, v, 106.

10 Swift, *Journal to Stella*, ii, 378 and 394; Halifax, 14, 15 Nov., Loan 29/151/6; HMC, *Portland*, v, 120; Bromley, 3 Dec., Loan 29/128/3; Kreienberg, 4/15 Dec., *CBA* (England), 107a; Salomon, 126.

11 *Diary of Countess Cowper*, 18; Salomon, 128; Trevelyan, iii, 195; G. S. Holmes, 'The Commons Division . . . 7 December, 1711', *BIHR*, xxxiii (1966) 226–7; HMC, *Portland*, v, 119; Add. MS. 17,677 EEE, f. 389; Add. MS. 22,908, f. 87; *CJ*, xvii, 1–2; *LJ*, xix, 339.

12 HMC, *Polwarth*, i, 3; Coxe, *Marlborough*, iii, 404; Plumb, *Walpole*, i, 178–81; Cobbett, vi, 1,049–56; *CJ*, xvii, 28–30 and 37–8.

13 Kreienberg, 4/15 March and 28 March/8 April, *CBA* (England), 107a; *CJ*, xvii, 37–8; *Wentworth Papers*, 257 and 266; Holmes, *British Politics*, 134–5, 280 and 341–2; Dickinson, *HLQ*, op. cit., 167–9.

14 Cobbett, vi, 1,135–45 and vii, 175; Add. MS. 17,677 FFF, ff. 166 and 220; Hill, *HJ*, op. cit., 254–7; *Miscellaneous State Papers*, ii, 482.

15 HMC, *Portland*, v, 198; *Bolingbroke Corr.*, ii, 492; *Memoirs of the Marquis of Torcy* (1757) ii, 347–8; Add. MS. 37,272, ff. 155–6.

16 *Bolingbroke Corr.*, iii, 23 and 66–7; HMC, *Portland*, ix, 344 and vii, 93 and v, 234–5; Kreienberg, 26 Sept./7 Oct. and 3/14 and 7/18 Oct., *CBA* (England), 107a; Harcourt, 2 Oct., Loan 29/138/5; HMC, *Cowper*, iii, 174; HMC, *Bath*, i, 222.

17 Trevelyan, iii, 223–30; Dickinson, *Bolingbroke*, 106–7; Hill, *HJ*, op. cit., 253–62.

18 *Cowper Diary*, 54; Swift, *Journal to Stella*, ii, 643; HMC, *7th Report*, pt 1, 238; Bromley, 18 Feb., Loan 29/200; Cobbett, vi, 1,171–5; *Bolingbroke Corr.*, iv, 137; Trevelyan, iii, 255–8.

19 Edwards, 22 June, North MS. C9, f. 5; Bishop, 20 June, Ballard MS. 31, f. 104; *Bolingbroke Corr.*, iv, 166.

20 *Hanmer Corr.*, 143 and 148; *Swift Corr.*, ii, 55; *Lockhart Papers*, i, 412; HMC, *Bath*, i, 223; Add. MS. 22,233, f. 286; HMC, *Portland*, v, 311 and 467, and vii, 160–1 and 164; Cobbett, vi, app. IV, col. ccxlviii; HMC, *Dartmouth*, i, 318.

21 *Original Papers*, ii, 481–2, 499–500 and 505–6; Speck, 51–2; HMC, *Lonsdale*, 246; Add. MS. 17,677 GGG, f. 347; HMC, *Dartmouth*, i, 319; *Hanmer Corr.*, 153; *Lockhart Papers*, i, 438–9.

22 Add. MS. 25,495, pp. 197, 213, 234–46 and 267; HMC, *House of Lords*, x, 446; HMC, *Portland*, v, 661; *Bolingbroke Corr.*, iv, 452; McLachlan, 46; Burnet, vi, 162, Dartmouth's note; *Revue Nouvelle*, iii (1845) 48.

23 Lord Masham, rec. 26 Dec. 1713, Loan 29/45; *Bolingbroke Corr.*, iv, 417 and 444; HMC, *Seafield*, 226; Add. MS. 17,677 HHH, ff. 54–7.

24 Cobbett, vi, 1,252–4, 1,257–8 and 1,268–75; Add. MS. 47,087, ff. 61–2; *Acts of Parliament No Infallible Security* (1714); Holmes, *British Politics*, 34–5 nn., 135–6.

25 HMC, *Portland*, v, 400; Oxford, 19 March, Loan 29/138/5; *Revue Nouvelle*, iii (1845) 47; A. N. Newman (ed.), 'Proceedings . . . March–June 1714', *BIHR*, xxxiv (1961) 213–14; *Edinburgh Review*, lxii (1835) 24; Salomon, 335–7; Holmes, *Britain after the Glorious Revolution*, 227sqq; Dickinson, *Bolingbroke*, 118sqq.

26 Newman (ed.), 'Proceedings . . . March–June, 1714', op. cit., 214–15;

Holmes and Speck, 112–13; HMC, *Polwarth*, i, 19; HMC, *Portland*, v, 417; *Original Papers*, ii, 521 and 616; Holmes, *British Politics*, 283.

27 Add. MS. 17,677 HHH, f. 238; *Wentworth Papers*, 388; *Lockhart Papers*, i, 462; [Defoe], *Secret History of the White Staff* (1714) 33; Boyer, *Quadriennium*, iv, 550.

28 *CJ*, xvii, 673 and 689; *LJ*, xix, 741 and 749; notes, partly in Edward Harley's hand, subscribed '*To the Rt. Hon. the Lord Viscount Townshend*', Brampton Bryan MSS., Herefordshire (C. C. Harley Esq.); *Swift Corr.*, ii, 168.

29 Add. MS. 22,217, f. 58; Kreienberg, 6/17 July, *CBA* 24 (England), 113a; Salomon, 298; *CJ*, xvii, 722; *Swift Corr.*, ii, 174.

30 'July 4, 1714', Loan 29/10/6; Stowe MS. 277, f. 243; *Swift Corr.*, ii, 193; *Hanmer Corr.*, 169; Add. MS. 47,027, pp. 292–3; Trevelyan, iii, 302–4; H. L. Snyder, 'The Last Days of Queen Anne', *HLQ*, xxxiv (1971) 261–76.

CHAPTER 9

1 Add. MS. 47,027, p. 297; *Swift Corr.*, ii, 221 and 230–1; Add. MS. 4,326B, f. 8; Add. MS. 35,837, f. 509; HMC, *Mar and Kellie*, i, 506.

2 *Swift Corr.*, ii, 221 and 235–6; *Wentworth Papers*, 411 and 415; Michael, *Beginnings*, 69–70; *Political State*, viii, 154–5.

3 Add. MS. 47,027, pp. 328–31; Add. MS. 22,221, f. 37; HMC, *Dartmouth*, i, 321; John, Lord Campbell, *Lives of the Chancellors* (1846) iv, 427.

4 Michael, *Beginnings*, 90–3; Somerville, 339; *Political State*, viii, 277–8.

5 *HLB*, ix, 136; Smithers, 305–6; Add. MS. 47,027, pp. 345 and 349–51; Add. MS. 17,677 HHH, ff. 406–7 and 416; HMC, *Portland*, v, 497.

6 Add. MS. 47,027, pp. 352 and 354; Somerville, 340; Michael, *Quadruple Alliance*, ii; Plumb, *Walpole*, i, 205; *Political State*, viii, 280, 336–40, 345–7 and *passim*; *Hanmer Corr.*, 171–2; Ward, 64.

7 HMC, *Portland*, v, 501–5; *Political State*, ix, 50; *Diary of Countess Cowper*, 19–20 and 48; *Letters of Thomas Burnet*, 73; W. T. Morgan, 'Some Sidelights upon the Election of 1715', in *Essays . . . in Honor of Wilbur Cortez Abbott* (Harvard, 1941) 140.

8 *Annals of Stair*, i, 264–5 and 275; *HLB*, ix, 140; Add. MS. 34,737, f. 3; HMC, *Portland*, v, 506; HMC, *Dartmouth*, i, 321–2; Sedgwick, i, 165–85.

9 *Political State*, ix, 166–70; Add. MS. 47,028, pp. 31–2; Add. MS. 17,677 HHH, f. 503; Add. MS. 17,677 III, ff. 114 and 129; Cobbett, vii, 39–41 and 47–50; Sedgwick, i, 23.

10 Cobbett, vii, 51–7 and 64–72; *Addison Letters*, 321–2; Add. MS. 17,677 III, ff. 169, 175 and 262–3; Add. MS. 47,028, p. 55; *HLB*, ix, 141, 146 and 149–50; North MS. B2, ff. 99–100; HMC, *Portland*, v, 511–12 and 665; Salomon, 357; *Swift Corr.*, ii, 293; *Berkeley and Percival Corr.*, 139.

11 Cobbett, vii, 74–104, 105–6, 114–28 and 158–201; *State Trials*, xv, *passim*; Add. MS. 47,028, p. 110; *Berkeley and Percival Corr.*, 142–3; Roberts, 392sqq.

12   HMC, *Stuart*, i, 447 and 520; Coxe, *Walpole*, ii, 98.
13   Cobbett, vii, 111–13 and 216; Ranke, v, 371; Michael, *Beginnings*, 164.
14   *Political State*, xi, 218–19 and 229–30; Add. MS. 47,028, pp. 248 and
     264; Add. MS. 17,677 KKKI, ff. 132–3; Plumb, *Walpole*, i, 219.
15   Add. MS. 47,028, pp. 286, 287 and 297; Somerville, 349; Coxe, *Walpole*,
     i, 76–7 and ii, 63; Cobbett, vii, 310–67; HMC, *Stuart*, ii, 144–5; HMC,
     Portland, v, 522; *CJ*, viii, 429; Sedgwick, i, 25 and 81; *Second Letter
     to a Friend in Suffolk* (1716) 33.
16   Sedgwick, i, 80–1; Add. MS. 47,028, p. 297; Add. MS. 47,029, p. 179.
17   *Diary of Countess Cowper*, 65, 79 and 108; HMC, *Stuart*, ii, 303;
     Cobbett, vii, 58–60.
18   Coxe, *Walpole*, ii, 58, 61, 74–5, 86–90, 93, 95–7, 108–9, 110–12, 115–19,
     126–34 and 139–44; HMC, *Townshend*, 103; J. J. Murray (ed.), *An
     Honest Diplomat* (1955), 352–6.
19   Add. MS. 35,584, ff. 163–4; *Swift Corr.*, ii, 361.
20   Cobbett, vii, 395–429 and 437–40; Add. MS. 47,028, pp. 365–6 and 369;
     Add. MS. 17,677 KKK, f. 136; HMC, *Polwarth*, i, 211–12.
21   HMC, *Stuart*, iv, 291–2; Add. MS. 47,028, pp. 369 and 376–9; Michael,
     Quadruple Alliance, 18–19 and 272–3; *Political State*, xii, 478–89
     (488–9 considerably more informative than Cobbett's condensed
     account).
22   Add. MS. 47,028, pp. 381–2; Cobbett, vii, 452–3; *Annals of Stair*, ii,
     20–2; *Political State*, xiii, 702–5; Sedgwick, 1, 81–3; HMC, *Stuart*,
     v, 557.
23   Cobbett, vii, 454–66, 468–98; Dickson, 84–5; Plumb, *Walpole*, 1, 247–8;
     HMC, *Portland*, v, 527; Roberts, 416–19; Add. MS. 47,028, p. 396.
24   Michael, *Quadruple Alliance*, 272–4; HMC, *Stuart*, iv, 453.

CHAPTER 10

1   *The Defection Considered* (1717) 10; *Some Reasons Vindicated* (1718)
    15; *The Resigners Vindicated* (1718); *History of the Rise and Fall of
    Count Hotspur* (1717); HMC, *14th Report*, ix, 509 and 516.
2   Beattie, *passim*; T. Foley, 26 Nov., Loan 29/136/7; Glover, i, 14.
3   HMC, *Portland*, vii, 228 and 231–2; HMC, *Bath*, i, 249; Oxford, 20
    Jan. 1720, Loan 29/136/2; Coxe, *Walpole*, ii, 308–9; Baratier 43–9;
    Michael, *Quadruple Alliance*, 51; Foley, 26 Nov. 1717, Loan 29/136/7.
4   HMC, *Bath*, iii, 450; *Political State*, xiv, 580 and 584–95, and xv, 187;
    HMC, *Portland*, v, 545 and 554; Add. MS. 17,677 KKK2, ff. 390 and
    401–2; Add. MS. 47,028, pp. 428, 438–9, 443 and 445; Glover, i, 13–14;
    HMC, *Stuart*, v, 301–2; Cobbett, viii, 534–7 and 556; *Letters of Thomas
    Burnet*, 142.
5   G. C. Gibbs, 'Parliament and the Quadruple Alliance', in Ragnhild
    Hatton and J. S. Bromley, *William III and Louis XIV*, (1968), esp.
    266–9; *Political State*, xvi, 469–78; HMC, *Portland*, v, 570; Add. MS.
    17,677 KKK3, ff. 1–2; *Annals of Stair*, ii, 86 and 376; *CJ*, xix, 4 and 42;
    Mahan, i, app. lvii.
6   Sedgwick, i, 27–8 and 81; Add. MS. 47,028, pp. 444 and 513sqq.; *The
    Whigs Vindicated . . . by John Withers* (2nd edn. 1715) title page and

1, 4 and 6; Plumb, *Growth of Political Stability*, 177; *Reasons for Enabling the Protestant Dissenters* (1717); Williams, 393–4; HMC, *Portland*, v, 575–6.

7 Add. MS. 47,028, p. 514, dated Dec. but *recte post*–7 Jan. 1719; *Letters of Thomas Burnet*, 169; *Joint and Humble Address of the Tories and Whigs* (1719) 11–12; *Annals of Stair*, ii, 341; Coxe, *Walpole*, ii, 171; Sedgwick, i, 84–5; *Thoughts of a Member of the Lower House* (1719) 10; HMC, *14th Report*, ix, 459; Naylor, *passim*.

8 Mahan, i, app. lxxvi–lxxvii; HMC, *Carlisle*, 23; Beattie, 235 and 237–9.

9 Add. MS. 32,686, f. 149; Williams, app. E, 459–63; Cobbett, vii, 602–4.

10 Oxford, 23 Nov., Dartmouth (Stafford) MS. D 1778 I, ii, 538; *Wentworth Papers*, 447; Cobbett, vii, 609–27; Sedgwick, i, 81; *CJ*, xix, 178 and 186.

11 Cobbett, vii, 628–42, 644–6 and 649; HMC, *Polwarth*, ii, 416; HMC, *Portland*, v, 594–6 and 600, and vii, 265–6 and 275; Michael, *Quadruple Alliance*, 302–5; Coxe, *Walpole*, i, 357 n.; Plumb, *Walpole*, i, 281–92; *Diary of Countess Cowper*, 128–53.

12 Add. MS. 47,029, p. 67; HMC, *Bath*, iii, 489–90; Realey, 1–15; Plumb, *Walpole*, i, 293–328; *Political State*, xix, 334–5; *CJ*, xix, 317.

13 Cobbett, vii, 680–7, 691–2, 693–6, 706–9 and 711–51; Coxe, *Walpole*, ii, 201–5 and 213–14; HMC, *Portland*, v, 608–9, 610, 612, 614 and 618–19; Add. MS. 47,029, pp. 86–7, 91–2 and 100; HMC, *Carlisle*, 26; Thomas Foley of Stoke, 31 Jan., Loan 29/136/8; Sedgwick, ii, *sub* Shippen; *CJ*, xix, 482.

14 HMC, *Carlisle*, 28–9; HMC, *Portland*, v, 615–17; Add. MS. 47,029, pp. 107 and 109.

15 Coxe, *Walpole*, ii, 217; Add. MS. 47,029, pp. 139 and 179; Add. MS. 32,686, ff. 185 and 193; Plumb, *Walpole*, i, 361–4; Cobbett, vii, 856–8; HMC, *Portland*, vii, 295 and v, 625; *Lockhart Papers*, ii, 70–1.

16 HMC, *Portland*, vii, 309; *Political State*, xxiii, 200–2, 218–23 and 255–61; Cobbett, vii, 948–52 and 961–6 (Boyer and Cobbett each contain material not in the other); Plumb, *Walpole*, i, 371–6; *CJ*, xix, 715 and 733.

17 HMC, *Portland*, vii, 315 and 317; Foley, 20 Feb., Loan 29/136/8; *Lockhart Papers*, ii, 82; Greenwood, 26sqq.; cf. R. J. Robson, *The Oxfordshire Election of 1754* (1949) 3; Add. MS. 17,677 KKK5, f. 187; Sedgwick, i, 33–4; Realey, 107–13.

18 Feiling, *Second Tory Party*, 22–3; HMC, *Carlisle*, 38; *Marchmont Papers*, i, 3; G. V. Bennett, 'Jacobitism and the Rise of Walpole', in Neil McKendrick (ed.), *Historical Perspectives . . . in Honour of J. H. Plumb* (1974) 70–92.

19 Plumb, *Walpole*, ii, 92sqq.; HMC, *14th Report*, ix, 462.

20 Add. MS. 47,029, pp. 270–2; Add. MS. 17,677 KKK5, f. 383; Cobbett, viii, 36–41 (in error in stating no division on third reading, following *Political State*, xxiv, 436–7) and 46–7; *Knatchbull Diary*, 3 and 115–16; *CJ*, xx, 14.

21 Add. MS. 47,029, pp. 279–80; *Knatchbull Diary*, 7; Cobbett, viii, 51–3; *Political State*, xxv, 524–5 (garbled in Cobbett); *CJ*, xx, 63 and 214.

22 Add. MS. 47,029, pp. 318 and 422; *Knatchbull Diary*, 15–16 and 18; HMC, *14th Report*, ix, 513; Cobbett, viii, 195–8 and 209; Realey, 145.

23 Coxe, *Walpole*, ii, 260, 261–2 and 264 (fuller versions, and dates, in Stowe MS. 251, ff. 4, 17 and 23); Add. MS. 32,686, f. 301; Stowe MS. 242, f. 213.

24 Add. MS. 32,686, ff. 268–70; Stowe MS. 251, f. 42 (partly printed in Coxe, *Walpole*, ii, 267–9, and misdated 24 *recte* 21 Sept., N.S.).

25 Coxe, *Walpole*, ii, 278; HMC, *Portland*, v, 637–8; Sedgwick, i, 66.

26 Add. MS. 17,677 KKK6, ff. 23 and 50; *Knatchbull Diary*, 25–6 and 30; Cobbett, viii, 377–8; Plumb, *Walpole*, ii, 62–75.

CHAPTER 11

1 Sedgwick, *sub* Walpole; Hervey, i, 177–8; *Walpole Corr.*, xviii, 540; Add. MS. 32,308, f. 172; Plumb, *Growth of Political Stability*, 110; Dickinson, *Bolingbroke*, 192; HMC, *Egmont Diary*, i, 85.

2 HMC, *Egmont Diary*, i, 262; Sykes, *Edmund Gibson* and *Church and State*, *passim*, for church patronage; *Lockhart Papers*, ii, 156–7; Plumb, *Walpole*, ii, 104–6; Riley, 284–7.

3 Foord, 144, n. 3; Sedgwick, i, 71, 81, 86 and 89; Hervey, i, 4; Mahan, ii, app. p. xxxv; *Lockhart Papers*, ii, 397–8; HMC, *14th Report*, ix, 465.

4 Add. MS. 17,677 KKK6, f. 421; *CJ*, xx, 364 and 462; Henderson, 91–111; Plumb, *Walpole*, ii, 109; *Knatchbull Diary*, 33, 36–7, 39–40 and 42–5; Cobbett, viii, 416–18 and 454–5.

5 Hervey, i, 9 and 83; G. C. Gibbs, 'Britain and the Alliance of Hanover', *EHR*, lxxiii (1958); Add. MS. 32,687, ff. 101 and 137.

6 HMC, *Portland*, vii, 407, 419–21 and 423; Add. MS. 47,031, pp. 152, 156, 172 and 225; *Wentworth Papers*, 457; Coxe, *Walpole*, ii, 495–6; *Knatchbull Diary*, 50–2 and 57–8; Cobbett, viii, 501–2, 503–7 and 517.

7 *Harcourt Papers*, ii, 109–110; Coxe, *Horatio Walpole*, i, 125–6, and *Walpole*, ii, 342–3; The *Craftsman*, nos 2, 3 and 40 (9, 12 Dec. 1726, and 24 April 1727); Kramnick, 119–20.

8 *Knatchbull Diary*, 59–61 and 71; Add. MS. 47,032, pp. 1–2 and 21; Coxe, *Walpole*, ii, 515; Cobbett, viii, 529–33 and 563–5.

9 Add. MS. 47,032, p. 35; Add. MS. 32,687, f. 212; King, ii, 46–7 and 47–50; Hervey, i, 34–5; Coxe, *Walpole*, ii, 519–20.

10 Add. MS. 47,032, p. 41; Knatchbull, 21 July, Cholmondeley (Houghton) MS. 2,282a (misdated 1734); HMC, *Egmont Diary*, i, 91; Stebelton H. Nulle, 'Newcastle and the Election of 1727', *JMH*, ix (1937) 21; HMC, *Portland*, vii, 451 and 453; Sedgwick, i, 37.

11 Hervey, i, 39 and 74–5; HMC, *14th Report*, ix, 517–18; J. Steven Watson, 'Arthur Onslow and Party Politics', in H. R. Trevor Roper (ed.), *Essays in British History Presented to Sir Keith Feiling* (1964) 139–71; Coxe, *Walpole*, ii, 546–7 and 549; *Knatchbull Diary*, 73–4.

12 Hervey, i, 98 and 100–1; HMC, *Egmont Diary*, iii, 330–1, 336–42 and 345–7; *Knatchbull Diary*, 80–2, 83–4, 86–7, 91–2, 96 and 131–6; HMC, *Carlisle*, 57; Cobbett, viii, 668–70, 672–5 and 677–80; Sedgwick, i, 86.

13 Add. MS. 27,981, f. 11; Coxe, *Walpole*, ii, 671–2; Sedgwick, i, 68;

Knatchbull Diary, 97–8 and 147–51; HMC, *Egmont Diary*, i, 2–6 and 24–31; HMC, *Carlisle*, 63–4.

14   HMC, *Egmont Diary*, i, 34–8, 41–4 and 71–5; *Knatchbull Diary*, 104–5 and 109–10; HMC, *Carlisle*, 68; Coxe, *Walpole*, ii, 669; Hervey, i, 117.

15   HMC, *Egmont Diary*, i, 50, 57, 78, 83, 85–6 and 93–4; *Knatchbull Diary*, 106; Hervey, i, 119–20.

16   Plumb, *Walpole*, ii, 223–9; Add. MS. 47,033, pp. 11 and 115–25; HMC, *Egmont Diary*, i, 125–6 and 141–8; HMC, *Carlisle*, 81; Cobbett, viii, 834–8.

17   Add. MS. 18,915, ff. 6–7; Add. MS. 27,732, f. 49; *Hanmer Corr.*, 215–16; *Wentworth Papers*, 466; Cobbett, viii, 869–80 and 882–911; HMC, *Egmont Diary*, i, 214–15; Sedgwick, i, 86.

18   Plumb, *Walpole*, ii, 239–44 and 250–4; Cobbett, viii, 943–87 and 1,014–25; HMC, *Egmont Diary*, i, 220, 231 and 311–12; HMC, *Carlisle*, 88–9; Laprade, 337–45; Add. MS. 27,732, ff. 95 and 138; Add. MS. 27,733, f. 35.

19   Cobbett, viii, 1,268–1,313 and ix, 1–7 and 10; HMC, *Egmont Diary*, i, 342–3, 347–54, 358–61, 365–7 and 371–2; HMC, *Carlisle*, 103–5 and 107–8; Coxe, *Walpole*, iii, 129–31; Sedgwick, i, 86; Plumb, *Walpole*, ii, 263–71; Hervey, i, 178–84.

20   Plumb, *Walpole*, ii, 275–9; HMC, *Carlisle*, 115; Hervey, i, 169–71; Add. MS. 27,732, f. 170; HMC, *Lonsdale*, 125; Turberville, *Reign of William III*, 203–6.

21   Add. MS. 27,733, f. 11; Coxe, *Walpole*, iii, 153–6; HMC, *Carlisle*, 129–30 and 132–3; Halsband, 166–7; Turberville, *Reign of William III*, 207–9.

22   HMC, *Stopford Sackville*, i, 155; Cobbett, ix, 367–92 and 396–482 (incorrect on Pulteney's speech on the Septennial Bill, following *Political State*, xlviii, 514–18—*see* HMC, *Mar and Kellie*, i, 535–6); HMC, *Carlisle*, 133; HMC, *Egmont Diary*, ii, 55–8; Sedgwick, i, 86.

23   HMC, *Mar and Kellie*, i, 534; Stevens, ch. VIII; Hanson, esp. 109–15; Cranfield, 21 and ch. 6, *passim*.

24   Add. MS. 32,689, f. 185 and 268; Add. MS. 32,688, ff. 141 and 190; Add. MS. 27,773, ff. 63 and 102; *Wentworth Papers*, 507; Plumb, *Walpole*, ii, 314–24; Sedgwick, i, 42–3.

25   Sedgwick, i, 87–8; Coxe, *Walpole*, iii, 168; Hervey, i, 292.

CHAPTER 12

1   Bolingbroke, ii, 168; *Marchmont Papers*, ii, 187–8; Plumb, *Growth of Political Stability*, 129.

2   Coxe, *Walpole*, iii, 524; Foord, 176, n. 3; HMC, *Egmont Diary*, ii, 14.

3   HMC, *Mar and Kellie*, i, 536–40; *Marchmont Papers*, ii, 28 and 34; Harley Diary, i, ff. 1, 15, 18–20 and 25; *Reasons for War* (1734) p. iv; Plumb, *Walpole*, ii, 323; Coxe, *Walpole*, i, 456; HMC, *Carlisle*, 147, 149–50 and 152; Cobbett, ix, 671–90, 691–720 and 800–24; HMC, *Egmont Diary*, ii, 167; Hervey, ii, 418.

4   HMC, *Carlisle*, 162, 165 and 168; Add. MS. 27,734, f. 210; Cobbett, ix, 969–71; 1,046–59 and 1,156–220; Harley Diary, i, ff. 29, 60v–61,

62–6 and 57–60; *Swift Corr.* (William edn) iv, 435; Hervey, ii, 529 and 530–8; Halsband, 195; T. F. J. Kendrick, 'Walpole . . . and the Bishops', *HJ*, xi (1968) 421–45.

5 Harley Diary, i, ff. 71 and 72v–81; *Political State*, liv, 318–24 and 409–27; HMC, *Egmont Diary*, ii, 350–3 and 354; HMC, *Carlisle*, 176–7 and 178; Hervey, iii, 671–84; *Dodington Diary*, 443–4 and 469.

6 Harley Diary, i, ff. 89–96; Hervey, iii, 734–5; Cobbett, x, 247–319; Tuberville, *House of Lords in the XVIIIth Century*, 216–19.

7 *Wentworth Papers*, 534; HMC, *14th Report*, ix, 10–11 and 237–8; Add. MS. 34,512, f. 13; HMC, *Egmont Diary*, ii, 462; HMC, *Carlisle*, 193; Cobbett, x, 375–467.

8 Harley Diary, i, ff. 101–2 and 107–8; Cobbett, x, 561–727; HMC, *14th Report*, ix, 13 and 239–40.

9 Dickinson, *Bolingbroke*, 259–60; HMC, *Denbigh*, v, 231; *Lyttelton Memoirs*, ii, 797; *Marchmont Papers*, ii, 107.

10 Cobbett, x, 874–5, 1,050–90 and 1,246–324; HMC, *14th Report*, ix, 25–6; Harley Diary, i, ff. 114–16; Coxe, *Walpole*, iii, 518–20 and 608; Sedgwick, i, 89; *CJ*, xxiii, 277.

11 Coxe, *Walpole*, iii, 523–4; *Marchmont Papers*, ii, 115–18 and 144–6; *Chesterfield Letters*, ii, 401–2.

12 HMC, *14th Report*, ix, 36, 38 and 39; Harley Diary, i, ff. 124–5 and ii, 1–3, 10–11 and 12; Cobbett, xi, 328–80; Add. MS. 32,693, ff. 51–2.

13 HMC, *Egmont Diary*, iii, 131 and 138; Add. MS. 32,639, f. 435; Add. MS. 32,695, f. 273; *Life of Hardwicke*, i, 229–33 and 240–1; Sedgwick, *sub* Bubb; Feiling, *Second Tory Party*, 36.

14 *Chesterfield Letters*, ii, 433–5; Coxe, *Walpole*, iii, 557, 559–61 and 562–4; HMC, *14th Report*, ix, 62, 65 and 67; Harley Diary, ii, ff. 29; Cobbett, xi, 1,232; *Life of Hardwicke*, i, 252–3; HMC, *Egmont Diary*, iii, 191–3; *Annals of Stair*, ii, 269; *Marchmont Papers*, ii, 245–7; *The Sentiments of a Tory* (1741) 23–4.

15 *Marchmont Papers*, ii, 249–50; Harley Diary, ii, f. 34.

16 *Chesterfield Letters*, ii, 404; Sedgwick, i, 46 and 159; Coxe, *Walpole*, iii, 565–6 and 566–78; Add. MS. 9,200, f. 144.

17 Coxe, *Walpole*, iii, 569–77; *Annals of Stair*, ii, 275; *Chesterfield Letters*, ii, 467–70; *Life of Hardwicke*, i, 259, 264 and 268–71; Add. MS. 32,698, f. 115; Sedgwick, i, 50.

18 Add. MS. 47,137, p. 16; Coxe, *Walpole*, iii, 581–4; *Walpole Corr.*, xvii, 231–2, 242–6 and 250–3; Owen, 22–4; Sedgwick, i, 71 and 97–9.

19 Coxe, *Walpole*, iii, 587–8 and 590–1; *Walpole Corr.*, xvii, 295–300 and 318–19; Harley Diary, ii, ff. 37v–39; Cobbett, xii, 333–73.

20 Coxe, *Walpole*, iii, 592–3; Add. MS. 18,915, ff. 29–30; Harley Diary, ii, ff. 42–3 (the second occurrence of these f. nos); *Walpole Corr.*, xvii, 335–8; Sedgwick, i, 51–2; HMC, *Egmont Diary*, iii, 254–5 and 257–8.

21 HMC, *Egmont Diary*, iii, 249, 252, 254 and 260; Add. MS. 6,043, f. 110; *Walpole Corr.*, xvii, 363.

SELECT BIBLIOGRAPHY

The following list is intended principally to give the location or title of manuscript and printed sources mentioned in the Notes and footnotes by abbreviated descriptions. Other sources which are traceable directly from the Notes and footnotes, including all the contemporary tracts and modern articles cited, are not repeated here.

I. MANUSCRIPT COLLECTIONS

British Library
Loan 29. Lansdowne MS. 885. Stowe MSS. 222–3, 242, 251. Sloane MSS. 4,223–4. Additional (Add.) MSS. 4,326B, 6,043, 7,059, 7,074, 7,078, 9,107–8, 9,110, 9,200, 15,895, 17,677, 18,915, 21,551, 22,221, 22,231, 22,233, 27,732–4, 27,773, 27,981, 28,055, 28,879, 29,588–9, 29,594–5, 30,000, 32,308, 32,524, 32,686–9, 32,693, 32,698, 33,589, 33,923, 34,355, 34,512, 34,515, 34,518, 34,521, 34,737, 35,335, 35,584, 35,837, 37,272, 40,621, 40,776, 47,027–33, 47,137, 52,279.

Public Record Office
State Papers (SP).
Baschet transcripts (PRO 31).

Bodleian Library, Oxford
Rawlinson MSS.
Ballard MSS.
English MSS.
North MSS.

Cambridge University Library
Additional MS. 6,851 (Harley Diary).
Cholmondeley (Houghton) MSS.

Codrington Library, All Souls, Oxford
MSS. 158a–b (Luttrell Diary). Now published – *see under* Printed Sources. References in the Notes and footnotes are to the MS., but dates of entries are given to facilitate reference to the printed *Luttrell Diary*.

Nottingham University Library
Portland (Nottingham) MSS.

Niedersächsisches Staatsarchiv, Hanover
Calenberg Briefe Archiv (CBA).

Blenheim Palace (Duke of Marlborough)
Churchill Papers.
Spencer Papers.

William Salt Library, Stafford
Dartmouth (Stafford) MSS.

Leicestershire Record Office
Finch (Leicestershire) MSS.

II. PRINTED SOURCES

Addison Letters: Graham, Walter, *The Letters of Joseph Addison* (Oxford, 1941).

Annals of Stair: Graham, J. M., *Annals and Correspondence of . . . the First and Second Earls of Stair* (Edinburgh, 1875).

Anon. Diary: Speck, W. A., *An Anonymous Parliamentary Diary, 1705–6*, Camden Miscellany xxiii, Camden Society, 4th series, vii (Royal Hist. Soc., 1969).

Baratier, Paul (ed.), *Lettres Inédites de Bolingbroke à Lord Stair, 1716–1720* (Paris, 1939).

Berkeley and Percival Corr.: Benjamin Rand, *The Correspondence of George Berkeley and Sir John Percival* (Cambridge, 1914).

Bolingbroke Corr.: Parke, Gilbert, *The Letters and Correspondence of Henry St John, Lord Viscount Bolingbroke* (1798).

Bolingbroke, Viscount, *The Works of Lord Bolingbroke* (Philadelphia, 1841).

Boyer, Abel, *History of the Reign of Queen Anne, Digested into Annals* (1703–13).

Boyer, Abel, *Quadriennium Annae Postremum* (1718) – a revised edition of *The Political State* for the years 1710–14.

Boyer, Abel, *The Political State of Great Britain* (1711–37).

Browning, Andrew, *The Memoirs of Sir John Reresby* (Glasgow, 1936).

Burnet, Gilbert, *The History of My Own Time*, ed. M. J. Routh (1833).

Chesterfield Letters: Dobrée, Bonamy, *The Letters of Philip Dormer Stanhope, 4th Earl of Chesterfield* (1932).

Clarendon Corr.: Singer, S. W., *The Correspondence of Henry Hyde, Earl of Clarendon* (1828).

Cobbett, William, *Parliamentary History of England* (1806–20). [This work sometimes omits or garbles information in earlier compilations.]

Court and Society: Duke of Manchester, *Court and Society from Elizabeth to Anne* (1864).

Cowper Diary: Hawtrey, E. C., *The Private Diary of Lord Chancellor Cowper* (Roxburghe Club, 1833).

Coxe, William, *Memoirs of Horatio, Lord Walpole* (1820) [abbr. ref. *Horatio Walpole*].

Coxe, William, *Memoirs of John, Duke of Marlborough* (1818–19).

Coxe, William, *Memoirs of the Life and Administration of Sir Robert Walpole* (1798) [abbr. ref. Walpole].

CSP Dom.: *Calendar of State Papers: Domestic Series* (1860–).

Cunningham, Alexander, *The History of Great Britain from the Revolution in 1668 to the Accession of George I* (1787).

Dalrymple, John, *Memoirs of Great Britain and Ireland* (1771–3).

Diary of Countess Cowper: Cowper S., *The Diary of Mary, Countess Cowper* (1865).

Dodington Diary: Wyndham, H. P., *The Diary of . . . George Bubb Dodington, Baron of Melcombe Regis* (1784).

Evelyn Diary: Evelyn, John, *The Diary of John Evelyn*, ed. E. S. de Beer (Oxford, 1955).

Foxcroft, H. C., *A Supplement to Burnet's History of My Own Time* (Oxford, 1902).

Glover, J. H., *The Stuart Papers* (1847).

Grey, Anchitell, *The Debates of the House of Commons* (1763).

Grimblot, Paul, *Letters of William III and Louis XIV* (1848).

Hanmer Corr.: Bunbury, Sir Henry, *The Correspondence of Sir Thomas Hanmer, Bart.* (1838).

Harcourt Papers: Harcourt, E. W., *The Harcourt Papers* (Oxford, 1880).

Hatton Corr.: Thompson, E. M., *Correspondence of the Family of Hatton*, Camden Society, new series, xxiii (1878).

Hervey, John, *Some Materials Towards Memoirs of the Reign of George II*, ed. Romney Sedgwick (1931).

Historical Manuscript Commission, *7th Report, 8th Report, 9th Report, 13th Report, 14th Report, Portland, Finch, Hastings, Kenyon, Buccleuch, Stuart, Townshend, Carlisle, Stopford-Sackville, Bath, Cowper, Egmont Diary, Seafield, Mar and Kellie, Dartmouth, Denbigh, Polwarth, House of Lords, Lonsdale.*

Japikse, N., *Correspondentie van Willem III en Hans Willem Bentinck* (The Hague, 1927–35).

King, Peter, Lord, *The Life of John Locke* (1830).

Klopp, Onno, *Der Fall des Hauses Stuart, und die Succession des Hauses Hannover* (Vienna, 1875–8).

Knatchbull Diary: Newman, A. N., *The Parliamentary Diary of Sir Edward Knatchbull, 1722–1730*, Camden Society, 3rd series, xciv (1963).

Krämer, F. J. L., *Archives ou Correspondance Inédite de la Maison d'Orange-Nassau*, 3rd series (Leyden, 1907–9).

Letters of Humphrey Prideaux: Thompson, E. M., *The Letters of Humphrey Prideaux*, Camden Society, new series, xv (1875).

Letters of Locke: Forster, T., *Original Letters of Locke, Shaftesbury, Sidney . . .* (1847).

Letters of Thomas Burnet to George Ducket, 1712–1722 (Roxburghe Club, 1914).

Lexington Papers: Sutton, H. Manners, *The Lexington Papers* (1851).

Life of Hardwicke: Yorke, Philip C., *Life and Correspondence of . . . Hardwicke* (Cambridge, 1913).

Life of Sharp: Sharp, Thomas, *The Life of John Sharp, Archbishop of York* (1825).

Lockhart Papers: *The Lockhart Papers Containing Memoirs . . . by George Lockhart Esq. of Carnwath* (1817).

Luttrell Diary: Horwitz, Henry, *The Parliamentary Diary of Narcissus Luttrell, 1691–1693* (Oxford, 1972).

Luttrell Diary: Narcissus, *A Brief Historical Relation of State Affairs* (Oxford, 1857).

Lyttelton Memoirs: Phillimore, R., *Memoirs and Correspondence of George, Lord Lyttelton* (1845).

Mahan, Lord, *History of England from the Peace of Utrecht* (1836).

Marchmont Papers: Rose, G. H., *A Selection from the Papers of the Earls of Marchmont* (1861).

Miscellaneous State Papers: Yorke, Philip, 2nd Earl of Hardwicke, *Miscellaneous State Papers from the Collection of the Earl of Hardwicke* (1778).

Murrey, J. J., *An Honest Diplomat at the Hague: The Private Letters of Horatio Walpole, 1715–1716* (Indiana, 1955).

Norris Papers: Heywood T., *The Norris Papers* (1846).

Oldmixon, John, *The History of England During the Reigns of King William . . . George I* (1735).

Original Papers: Macpherson, James, *Original Papers Containing the Secret History of Great Britain* (1776).

Political State: see Boyer, Abel.

Private Corr.: *The Private Correspondence of Sarah, Duchess of Marlborough* (1838 edn).

Ranke, Leopold von, *A History of England, Principally in the Seventeenth Century* (Oxford, 1875).

Seafield Corr.: Grant, James, *The Seafield Correspondence* (Edinburgh, 1912).

Shrewsbury Corr.: Coxe, William, *Private and Original Correspondence of Charles Talbot, Duke of Shrewsbury* (1821).

State Trials: Howell, T. B., *A Complete Collection of State Trials* (1809–28).

Swift Corr.: Ball, F. Elrington, *The Correspondence of Jonathan Swift* (1910–14).

Swift Corr.: (Williams edition): Williams, H., *The Correspondence of Jonathan Swift* (Clarendon, 1965).

Swift, Jonathan, *Journal to Stella*, ed. H. Williams (Oxford, 1948).

Swift, Jonathan, *Prose Works . . . Political Tracts 1711–13*, ed. H. Davis (Oxford, 1951).

Vernon Corr.: James, G. P. R., *Letters Illustrative of the Reign of William III* (1841).

Walpole Corr.: Lewis, W. S., *The Yale Edition of Horace Walpole's Correspondence* (1937–   ).

Wentworth Papers: Cartwright, J. J., *The Wentworth Papers* (1833).

III. SECONDARY WORKS

Baxter, S. B., *William III* (1966).

Beattie, J. M., *The English Court in the Reign of George I* (Cambridge, 1967).

Bennett, G. V., *White Kennett, 1660–1728, Bishop of Peterborough* (1957).

Browning, Andrew, *Thomas Osborne, Earl of Danby . . . 1632–1712* (Glasgow, 1951).

Burton, I. F., Riley, P. W. J. and Rowlands, E., *Political Parties in the Reigns of William III and Anne: The Evidence of Division Lists*, *BIHR* Special Supplement no. 7 (1968).

Carswell, John, *The Old Cause: Three Biographical Studies in Whiggism* (1954).

Carswell, John, *The South Sea Bubble* (1960).

Churchill, W. S., *Marlborough: His Life and Times*, 4 vols (1933–8).

Clapham, Sir John, *The Bank of England, A History* (Cambridge, 1944).

Cranfield, G. A., *The Development of the Provincial Newspaper, 1700–1760* (Oxford, 1962).

Dickson, P. G. M., *The Financial Revolution in England* (1967).

Dickinson, H. T., *Bolingbroke* (1970).

Dickinson, H. T., *Walpole and the Whig Supremacy* (1973)

Ellis, E. L., 'The Whig Junto', D.Phil. Dissertation (Oxford, 1962).

Every, G., *The High Church Party, 1688–1718* (1956).

Feiling, Keith, *A History of the Tory Party, 1640–1714* (Oxford, 1924) [abbr. ref. *Tory Party*].

Feiling, Keith, *The Second Tory Party, 1714–1832* (1938) [abbr. ref. *Second Tory Party*].

Foord, Archibald M. S., *His Majesty's Opposition, 1714–1830* (Oxford, 1964).

Foxcroft, H. C., *Life and Letters of . . . Halifax* (1898).

Gaedeke, A., *Die Politik Oesterreichs . . .* (Leipzig, 1877).

Geikie, Roderick and Montgomery, I. A., *The Dutch Barrier, 1705–1719* (Cambridge, 1930).

Greenwood, David, *William King, Tory and Jacobite* (Oxford, 1969).

Gunn, J. A. W., *Factions No More* (1972).

Halsband, Robert, *Lord Hervey, Eighteenth-Century Courtier* (Oxford, 1973).

Hanson, Lawrence, *Government and the Press, 1695–1763* (Oxford, 1936).

Hart, Jeffrey, *Viscount Bolingbroke, Tory Humanist* (1965).

Henderson, C. J., *London and the National Government, 1721–1742* (North Carolina, 1945).

Holmes, Geoffrey (ed.), *Britain after the Glorious Revolution* (1969).

Holmes, Geoffrey, *British Politics in the Age of Anne* (1967).

Holmes, Geoffrey, *The Trial of Dr Sacheverell* (1973).

Holmes, Geoffrey, and Speck, W. A., *The Divided Society: Parties and Politics in England, 1694–1716* (1967).

Horsefield, J. K., *British Monetary Experiments* (1960).

Horwitz, Henry, *Revolution Politicks: The Career of Daniel Finch, Second Earl of Nottingham, 1647–1730* (Cambridge, 1968).

Jacobsen, G. A., *William Blathwayt* (New Haven, 1932).

Jäger, Wolfgang, *Politische Partei und Parlamentarische Opposition* (Berlin, 1971).

James, F. G., *North County Bishop* [William Nicolson] (New Haven, 1957).

Jones, J. R., *The First Whigs: The Politics of the Exclusion Crisis, 1678–1683* (Oxford, 1961).

Jones, J. R., *The Revolution of 1688 in England* (1972).

Kemp, Betty, *King and Commons, 1660–1832* (1959).

Kenyon, John P., *The Popish Plot* (1972).

Kenyon, John P., *Robert Spencer, Earl of Sunderland, 1641–1702* (1958).

Kluxen, Kurt, *Das Problem der Politischen Opposition* (Freiburg, 1956).

Kramnick, Isaac, *Bolingbroke and His Circle: The Politics of Nostalgia in the Age of Walpole* (Harvard, 1968).

Lacey, Douglas R., *Dissent and Parliamentary Politics* (New Brunswick, 1969).

Laprade, W. L., *Public Opinion and Politics in Eighteenth Century England* (New York, 1936).

McInnes, Angus, *Robert Harley, Puritan Politician* (1970).

McLachlan, J. O., *Trade and Peace with Old Spain, 1667–1750* (Cambridge, 1940).

Michael, Wolfgang, *The Beginnings of the Hanoverian Dynasty* (1936).

Michael, Wolfgang, *The Quadruple Alliance* (1939).

Namier, Lewis B., *The Structure of Politics at the Accession of George III* (1929).

Naylor, John F., *The British Aristocracy and the Peerage Bill of 1719* (1968).

Newman, Aubrey (ed.), *The Parliamentary Lists of the Early Eighteenth Century* (Leicester, 1973).

Newman, A. N., *The Stanhopes of Chevening* (1969).

Owen, John B., *The Rise of the Pelhams* (1957).

Plumb, J. H., *The Growth of Political Stability in England, 1675–1725* (1967).

Plumb, J. H., *Sir Robert Walpole*: i, *The Making of a Statesman* (1956) and ii, *The King's Minister* (1960).

Pocock, J. G. A., *Politics, Language and Time* (1971).

Pulzer, Peter, J. G., *Political Representation and Elections in Britain* (1967).

Realey, C. R., *The Early Opposition to Sir Robert Walpole, 1720–1727* (Kansas, 1931).

Richards, James O., *Party Propoganda Under Queen Anne* (Athens, Georgia, 1972).

Riley, P. W. J., *The English Ministers and Scotland, 1707–1727* (1964).

Roberts, Clayton, *The Growth of Responsible Government in Stuart England* (Cambridge, 1966).

Rubini, Dennis, *Court and Country, 1688–1702* (1967).

Salomon, Felix, *Geschichte des Lezten Ministeriums Annas von England* (Gotha, 1894).

Sedgwick, Romney (ed.), *The History of Parliament: The House of Commons, 1715–1754* (1970).

Smithers, P., *Life of Joseph Addison* (Oxford, 1954).

Somerville, Dorothy H., *The King of Hearts: Charles Talbot, Duke of Shrewsbury* (1962).

Speck, W. A., *Tory and Whig: The Struggle in the Constituencies, 1701–1715* (1970).

Sperling, John G., *The South Sea Company* (Boston, 1962).

Stevens, D. H., *Party Politics and English Journalism, 1702–1742* (New York, 1916).

Straka, G. M., *The Anglican Reaction to the Revolution of 1688* (Madison, 1962).

Sykes, Norman, *Church and State in England in the XVIIIth Century* (Cambridge, 1934).

Sykes, Norman, *Edmund Gibson, Bishop of London, 1669–1748* (Oxford, 1926).

Sykes, Norman, *William Wake, Archbishop of Canterbury* (Cambridge, 1957).

Thomas, P. D. G., *The House of Commons in the Eighteenth Century* (Oxford, 1971).

Trevelyan, G. M., *England Under Queen Anne* (1930–5).

Turberville, A. S., *The House of Lords in the Reign of William III* (Oxford, 1913).

Turberville, A. S., *The House of Lords in the XVIIIth Century* (Oxford, 1927).

Walcott, Robert, *English Politics in the Early Eighteenth Century* (Oxford, 1956).

Ward, W. R., *The English Land Tax in the Eighteenth Century* (Oxford, 1953).

Western, J. R., *The English Militia in the Eighteenth Century* (1965).

Western, J. R., *Monarchy and Revolution* (1972).

Wiggin, Lewis M., *The Faction of Cousins* (Yale, 1958).

Williams, Basil, *Stanhope: A Study of Eighteenth Century War and Politics* (Oxford, 1932).

Addenda

The following works, which were published or promised for publication after the present book was completed, will throw useful light on aspects of the history of the early parties:

Bennett, G. V., *The Tory Crisis in Church and State, 1688–1730: the Career of Francis Atterbury, Bishop of Rochester* (Oxford, 1975).

Browning, Reed, *The Duke of Newcastle* (Yale, 1975).

Holmes, Geoffrey, *Religion and Party in Late Stuart England*, Historical Association Pamphlet G.86 (1975).

Langford, Paul, *The Excise Crisis: Society and Politics in the Age of Walpole* (Oxford, 1975).

Sachse, W. L., *Lord Somers, a Political Portrait* (Manchester, 1975).

INDEX